ISBN 978-1-331-70918-3
PIBN 10224373

1 MONTH OF
FREE
READING

at

www.ForgottenBooks.com

By purchasing this book you are eligible for one month membership to ForgottenBooks.com, giving you unlimited access to our entire collection of over 700,000 titles via our web site and mobile apps.

To claim your free month visit:

www.forgottenbooks.com/free224373

English
Français
Deutsche
Italiano
Español
Português

www.forgottenbooks.com

Mythology Photography **Fiction**
Fishing Christianity **Art** Cooking
Essays Buddhism Freemasonry
Medicine **Biology** Music **Ancient**
Egypt Evolution Carpentry Physics
Dance Geology **Mathematics** Fitness
Shakespeare **Folklore** Yoga Marketing
Confidence Immortality Biographies
Poetry **Psychology** Witchcraft
Electronics Chemistry History **Law**
Accounting **Philosophy** Anthropology
Alchemy Drama Quantum Mechanics
Atheism Sexual Health **Ancient History**
Entrepreneurship Languages Sport
Paleontology Needlework Islam
Metaphysics Investment Archaeology
Parenting Statistics Criminology
Motivational

The Sea's Anthology

From the Earliest Times down to the Middle of the Nineteenth Century. Compiled and Edited with Notes, Introduction and an Appendix by

J. E. Patterson

Author of
"My Vagabondage," "The Lure of the Sea," etc.

> . . . *Make your chronicle as rich with praise,*
> *As is the ooze and bottom of the sea*
> *With sunken wreck and sunless treasures.*—SHAKESPEARE

London
William Heinemann
1913

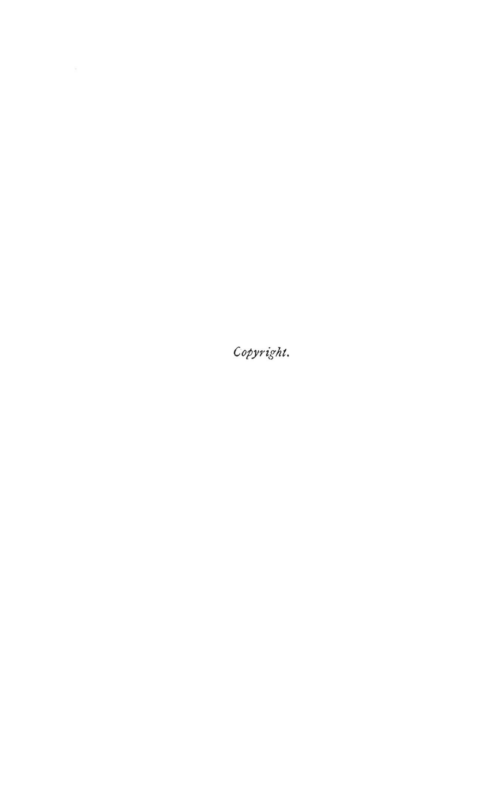

TO

DONALD MACLEAN, M.P.,

A FRIEND WHEN FRIENDS WERE WONDROUS FEW,

I DEDICATE THIS LONG-INTENDED LABOUR OF LOVE;

NOT THAT MY LATE RETURN CAN SO MUCH

HONOUR HIS QUALITIES, AS IT MAY

MARK MY RESPECT FOR HIM

AND THEM.

CONTENTS

[1] Where the piece is an extract from a longer poem the first fe' words are used as a title.

vii

Contents

Contents

Contents

Contents

CHANTIES :

NAVAL BATTLES AND SHIPS OF WAR

Contents

Contents

HUMOROUS PIECES

PREFACE

WE are told that the way of the transgressor is hard; but we are not assured, beyond our own minds, that he obtains periods of real enjoyment along the colourful course he follows—for, after all, the joy of one person is the sadness of another; there are sorts of pleasure, and no one of them is truly universal. So it is with the anthologist. Apart from the enthusiasm of hunting in half-forgotten coverts, the hot-and-cold feeling of tracing chance clues, and the thrill of delight at a "find," he is haunted now and then by the knowledge that, lurking along the wayside of publication, there are two literary footpads, each with a pistol—one bullet for the gold he brings, and the other for the jewels he has not brought. In other words, while a critical Scylla threatens to wreck him for omissions, a Charybdis of the pen is roaring to engulf him for what he has committed. Ah, well! the course of literature would run monotonously smooth if it were not disturbed from time to time by a critical gunshot across the honest voyager's bow, whether it comes from a pirate on the waters, or from a craft that has been properly authorised (first by Nature) to hold up all traders in *contrabándo*. And this is especially the case with those who have grown so blasé to adventure, or are so unconventional of temperament, as to be quick to accept any challenge that is not based on justice. Let be. Tritely, all things have their uses—pallid, still wines for the quiet of heart and mind; chamber music is excellent if well played in a chamber; the pomp and spirit of a martial air is not wanted at a mothers' gathering; it is not meet that the vegetarian should complain at the beefeater for that he loves it red and juicy.

It may be said—possibly it has been said—that to quarrel with an anthologist's tastes is about equal to finding fault with the subjects of a novelist or a painter. It is all a matter of taste, for which there is no more accounting than there appears to be reason in Nature's occasional breaking of her own set laws. Humanity may be divided roughly into three classes—those persons who tread this dull round of things from day to day, seeking not, and scarcely heeding, any change; those to whom it is a well-recognised bundle of sensations awkwardly arranged and ironically defying human amendment; and those who strive to make it a series of selections, rising stage by stage until the purpled hills of far-away perfection seem to peep above the horizon of effort and materialism, and to give the weary voyager new heart to clap on his last piece of canvas for that uncharted harbour of his high desires. So it is with anthologies : the only perfect one to every well-read person of individualistic tastes is the compilation that is made for oneself. For, after all, what is it but this? We (the anthologists generally) pass through the garden of poetry, taking a flowering plant here and another there (not blooms, because they would wither), then come forth and present our baskets in the market-place—to find, alas ! that all our gatherings have not their roots in the fine earth of human feeling, beautiful ideas and verbal music. Hoping to transplant our discoveries in the ever-sunny garden of popularity, we find that some of our examples have been taken from out-of-the-way nooks, where we ought to have let them remain. So, no doubt, it is with this basketful of sea peas, yellow poppies, starwort and other flowering plants (of the mind) that *have the breath of ocean and its salt spray about them;* every one of which has been included here because it seemed to me to have the other two paramount requirements : first, that it reflected or represented some actual or purely mythical phase of ocean life; and, second, that it was the best example of its own particular kind.

As to the making of the book—it is some twelve years since the work was begun—a labour of love taken up and dropped again and again, as occasion served, physicking effectually the pain of hard necessity. It has been wrought from such a number of books, manuscripts and collections of ballads—including several large volumes of broadsides which were accidentally discovered in the cellars of a certain great library—that to enumerate them here would be to make a rather dreary three-page catalogue. Enough, the list is ready for any person who comes after me and wishes to tread the same ground. The book itself contains sufficient evidence for the time being.

It was intended originally to have arranged the pieces, from first to last, chronologically, and to have brought the book up to date. But, on the first point, I found that this would have made a ragtime tune of what should be a dignified march; it would have meant an unpleasant higgledy-piggledy herding, with here and there a beautiful thing cheek-by-jowl with a loud, rum-flavoured laugh from the lower deck, or with the belching of cannon and black smoke and the groans of wounded men. Hence the present arrangement, with each section in chronological order, and the sections in what was apparently the sequence of creation. With regard to the second unfulfilled intention—to have kept this would have made the book one-half larger than it now is; because since about the middle of the past century there has been more *poetry* written of the sea than there was in any two previous centuries. Therefore it was decided to let this compilation go as it is, and to make another of more recent work to bear it company later on—should events appear to call for a second volume.

With a certain amount of dislike to change the face of old things, to say nothing of the censure that such vandalism may bring upon me, I have so far—yet only so far—altered some of the antique spelling that he who runs may read; at the same time care has been taken to retain every other possible scrap of the ancient qualities of the old pieces. How far a mere compiler may edit what he borrows must always be a delicate question, especially where the subject-matter may be better known to him than it was to the writers of what he edits. Think what enormities may come by a vandal stumbling amongst ancient things, for which he has no proper respect! A piece may contain gross errors of seafaring, or of some purely oceanic phase (as is often committed by painters, who have not seen what they try to depict and *think* is possible on the high seas), yet be worthy of preservation for some of its nautical qualities. Take Campbell's "delay the shattered bark ": if it were "shattered" there would be no bark. Or Stevens' deservedly popular (at least it was

b

popular enough thirty-five years ago for me to learn it
I know not where) "Cease, rude Boreas": how easy
it would be for an experienced sailor to apply destruc-
tive criticism until the "song" became no more than
a jumble of broken threads and patches!—which is
surely not the right conduct of a host towards his guest.
At the same time it is as surely within reason to point
out, here and there, a technical flaw of an unusually
gross kind, such as many that Dibdin perpetrated. And
what can be expected when the adventuring landsman
goes to sea in verse and deals with technicalities? If
the too-critical anthologist were to keep back every
piece of which he disapproved, because of such faults
as are meant here, or for other reasons, how small
would be his sheaf of gleanings! He must pay some
deference to popular opinion, and include what he
knows to be common favourites, even though they be
compounded of what he terms errors.

Again, how far may a compiler cut a piece to suit
his needs? This, too, is a matter that requires wisdom
for its proper settlement; and, goodness knows, wisdom
is rare amongst us—hence I expect to be condemned,
without trial, on my own written evidence. "Cutting"
is a habit with some persons, with others it is a dis-
cretion; and all I can say is that I have tried to be
discreet. As a cry of *peccavi* and an argument for the
defendant, take Shelley's thrice beautiful "Arethusa"—
I needed only what it contains relative to the sea and
enough of the previous lines to make the story intel-
ligible. Shall I be shrived for this cardinal offence?
The same applies to Coleridge's haunting fantasy,
deathless in spite of its impossible navigation. And
again to Gervase Markham's long-winded and moralis-
ing account of the defeat of the Armada.

This brings me to the notes, the plenitude of which
appears to make it necessary to remind the reader that
the author always writes for those who do not know.
Were it otherwise we should need no authors. At the
same time it was not intended to give thumb-nail
biographies of all the men and women whose work is
quoted here. But, on the supposition that clean gossip
of one's fellow-creatures is always welcome to all
inquiring minds, I have added a brief note wherever the
poet seemed to be of more interest than what is usually

found in "the daily round, the common task," or where he or she needed some little lift from the obscurity that has grown undeservedly around them.

One point more and I have done. It will be noted that the collection contains few 'longshore pieces. The reason is that my aim has been conservatively the sea, its creatures, attributes, ships, the lives of those who made it their calling, and that every piece should have had its origin in the English language. Your 'longshore poem is generally more of the land, or of the writer, than it is of the sea—as half of Whitman's so-called sea poems are. The only latitude allowed in this is "The Forging of the Anchor," "The Lighthouse," and "The High Tide on the Coast of Lincolnshire." As an instance of what is meant take these two stanzas from Emmanuel Gieble's beautiful lyric:

> " Behold the sea !
> The sun's swift beams unroll upon her track ;
> Yet in her deeps, where lies the perfect pearl,
> The night is black."

How altogether excellent! A true presentment, expressed in a masterly manner, clear-cut, finished, without a redundant word, yet emotional poetry. But :

> "I am the sea.
> In billows grand my senses boldly sweep,
> And all my songs stream like the sun's bright gold
> Across the deep !"

Again, how admirable !—especially the long-drawn-out image in the last two lines. Yet we see by it that the foregone exceptionally fine cameo of the sea is introduced only as a striking means of impressing its vast idea on the reader's mind, in order to draw a lasting parallel between it and the lyrist—a parallel that is almost grotesque in its immensity on the one side as against the finite humanity of the other. Yet the beauty of the whole hides this grotesqueness. In another stanza—which will not come back at memory's call— Gieble gives the other part of his simile : *i. e.* a heart that sorrow has made dark, cold and desolate as the floor of the deepest ocean. To have included such pieces as this one would have taken me outside the scope of the book and have almost doubled its length.

J. E. P.

Billericay: April, 1913.

b 2

INTRODUCTION

SOME seven years ago and again a year later (first for the *Book Monthly*, then for the *Daily Chronicle*) it fell to my lot to write of our dearth of poets of the sea, past and present, but especially in the further past. Since then other writers have dwelt on the subject; in spite of this, however, it seems—to me—to be imperative that I should return to it here. The nature of this book demands that much; for whatever others or I have said elsewhere, this collection of old and older things must carry with it its own credentials of all kinds—a lone traveller over unfamiliar lands it is necessary that it should have with it both its passports and the means of finding and paying its way.

"The sea, fire and women are three evils," was a proverb of the ancient Greeks, without even the qualifying "necessary." And, with such rare exceptions that they are hardly worth mentioning, our poets up to fifty years ago did, by their silence on the matter, fully admit their concurrence with the first in the triology. At the same time they produced a small library that shows how little they thought the last one to be an evil; ever drawn by the femininity of woman, they were yet too blind to notice the femininity of the sea. Or shall we say that the nearer and more kindred complexities and subtleties of woman kept them from trying to understand and depict the same greater though seemingly simpler characteristics of old ocean. It may be so. In any case it is astounding that little more than one hundred and fifty years have passed since our poets began to pay any particular attention to the sea as a subject for their inspiration. Even then it was only a beginning that went very little further till within the past three or four decades; and the laggardness of the movement was due to the fact that the oceanic beauty which our versemen then began to see was a beauty that lay beyond the pale of their *feeling*. To them the sea, and practically all that was seafaring, except sailors themselves, was a something afar, a something unknown, a something which they could no more grasp than they could size-up the forms of unrecorded ages' civilisations. In spite of the great, half-hidden truth in that *multum in parvo* old saw of ours, "Let him who knows not how to pray go to sea," it was with them as with Johnson, who said to Boswell, "When men come to like a sea-life they are not fit to live on land." How I would have liked to see Johnson afloat! What an experience to treasure up!

The charm of a fresh wind on a snappy sea and under a ragged sky, or that of a calm on the open seas, was entirely beyond our poets of the past. Where, then, could there be any touch of kin between them and the rhythm of fierce winds shrieking their wild anthems to the skies? On the one hand they were not seamen; on the other they had no love of the subject. And this is *par excellence* a case where some parts of both are needed; for without love or an intuitive knowledge of a fine degree there can be no understanding of the matter at issue, especially of such an aloof thing as the spirit of the great waters. And Scott, splendid storyman in verse that he was, fully realised this when Warren Hastings tried to incite him to an epic on the life of Nelson. Scott knew and said that whoever should do such a thing must be himself to some extent a sailor. And who but a seaman at heart and in fact could have that oneness with the ocean and the mere technical knowledge necessary for an epic of that kind? Surely no one, unless he were an absolute genius of such a cast as Nature has not yet given us. To write "The Waters of Lodore" Southey had to see them and hear them. How then shall one correctly picture high seas' situations unless he has been in them? And not even then if he has not a soul akin to them.

But it is most in the translation of that "spirit" into words, a sort of none-too-apparent atmosphere, a kind of *genius loci*, that English poets past and present are found wanting—because old ocean has not touched the vitals of their *feeling*, has not cast around them the magic of her charm and drawn them out from the land to learn what they could not know on shore. And it is on this same count that our makers of lesser verse have generally failed even when they have tried to achieve.

Yet all honour be to them that they have endeavoured.
For it is only by the path of Trialpain that we can reach
the City of Truegood. They, those more courageous
souls, are at least buoys along a course that is charted
only by imagination, and over which no Vasco de
Gama, no Columbus, no Humphrey Gilbert, no Cabot,
no Frobisher voyager of ours, in the service of the
Muses, has yet passed to the finding of new islands
and continents that lie awaiting discovery in the world
of oceanic poetry.

In this curiously suggestive shortage in our literature
there is one period that particularly draws attention,
both from the literary and from the historical points of
view, namely, that of Elizabeth. Looking at those times,
in the only light in which we now can see them, what
but a broadening, deepening, colouring effect could
they have had on the mind of the nation at large, and
the more so on that section which was the most sensi-
tive to outside influences? To expect aught else would
be to look for a break in the regular recurrence of
human affairs as would amount to a suspension in the
laws of Nature as they apply to man.

Yet greatly though the doings of the times—which
were mostly things of great venture in the new realm
of far-away ocean-scenes—did act on the national
imagination, mark how little they affected the nation's
sea poetry. It was our very Homeric period afloat,
for which, as yet, we have no Homer. It was the
breaking of a spacious, gloriously golden day after a
night of coldness, narrowness and general bigotry; a
night in the time of men and history over which the
Inquisition had exercised its all-too-baneful and dwarf-
ing influence. Spain and Portugal had led the way;
and England, which ever went one better than her
rivals when once she entered the arena of competition,
sprang into the running with all the ardent verve of
youth, and with the grip of that northern blood which
happily flowed in her veins. In fact, it could be pretty
safely said that Raleigh, the man and his life up to just
before its tragic end, was so essentially typical as to
be largely an allegory of those years and the hundred
or so that immediately followed. Greatness, expansion,
enthusiasm were in the air; and men of thought and
reading, of learning and imagination were smitten by

the fire. Above all things it was the dawn, the rose-
flush breaking of our greatness at sea; more, the time
of poetic expression was flowing at high-water mark;
but despite the set of these two powerful currents to-
wards one point, the formation of a great poet of the
sea, they were strangely deflected. The wonderful
happenings, a resetting and resettling in the stream
of men's affairs, did not produce from acknowledged
bards even good minor poetry of the sea. This truth
comes so hardly upon us that we can barely grasp it,
or give it belief.

Mind-voyagers and venturers before those times had
dreamt their dreams of the far-off lands and seas which
were then being discovered, and now came a wider
recurrence of the same thing, but in actual fact, in the
people's mind. Given a mountain-top in the foreground
of our perspective, and it is easy enough to imagine
higher peaks beyond. In the realm of thought it was
also a breaking away from the shackles of rigid formal-
ism which had been riveted on Catholic Europe, by the
domination of a priesthood that aimed at possessing
as much temporal power behind the curtain as it owned
spiritual authority in the open. In real affairs daring
spirits, giants of action and conquest, were repeatedly
going forth into the practically unknown and returning
with wondrous, almost hair-raising tales of the marvel-
lous things which they had seen and done; yet the
only poetic reflection which the times gave us of
those voyages and wonders is Shakespeare's *Tempest*.
More to the point, those who went brought back with
them spoils to prove their tales. So why should they
not be believed by those who were fain to believe them?
Hence the greatness did what an ordered Nature had
said it must do—it burst in on the minds of our drama-
tists in particular; it gave a new vigour to poetry and a
wider breadth to thought in general; but, and this is
the marvel of it all, it brought with it no real sense of
that sea whereon all this greatness was occurring. It
flung the imagination of the thinker and the gifted
versemaker as far away as even now lies our boasted
"far-flung battle line"; it made our poets Empire-
builders centuries before that term, as such, entered the
minds of Englishmen. But it failed to give us that
natural heritage which should have been ours under the

circumstances, a true and a great poet of the sea. Why was it that no true poet of those times chanced in at one of the waterside taverns of London or Plymouth, when the salt-crusted seamen of that day were there, freshly back from some daring things on the Spanish Main and overflowing with breathless yarns of their doings; some poet to catch and become imbued with the real spirit of it all, and with the instincts of a sailor in him, to put it all into verse of such a stamp that it would have borne on its face the everlasting youthfulness of the sea? Why did Fate deal so niggardly with us?

To us, this was the very *El Dorado* of romance in our maritime history, the beginning of the Empire that we know. What the discovery of northern Europe was to those trading Phœnicians, the marauding exploits of the Vikings to the Norsemen, the adventurous discoveries of the Portuguese east of the Cape of Good Hope to Portugal, so was the sixteenth century to us—with the significant difference that the towering structure of Empire has been built on the foundations then laid by a handful of seamen, who were dreamers and strenuous doers alike, as all the best of the world's great men have ever been. Yet with another difference, except in the case of the first of the above historical parallels. The Phœnicians had no poet to chronicle their seamen's doings in deathless verse; the Norsemen had their saga singers; Portugal had her Camoens, who gave her his "Lusiad," then died of neglect and want in a hospital of •his native city, Lisbon, to her everlasting shame. Yet, oh! for a Camoens—even though he, too, should die a similar death (for it is only in some atmosphere of tragedy that the greatest of verse is written)—to write us a "Lusiad" on the voyages of Drake, that fiery, fiddling, lovable, composite Devonian; the Hawkinses, father, sons and grandsons, Drake's fellow-countrymen, quieter than he, yet seamen-fighters and seamen-traders too; Frobisher, the only prominent sea-king of the time who did not spring from a more or less Devon stock, the quietly persistent Yorkshireman who married a daughter of the great house of Wentworth, and thus gained the ear of Queen Bess and her help in his efforts to find a north-west passage to the Indies, and who became a landed proprietor by the Spanish gold he took on the high seas, to die at last in the Channel; Gilbert, who sailed beam-to-beam with the Hawkinses, in whose very name there is a sense of blue waters and salt winds; and who was half-brother to Raleigh, the gallant of the velvet cloak, the puddle, Queen Bess, Virginia (which he named in her honour), and the block in Old Palace Yard—the man whose great projects would have made him an historical landmark even in a day of giants. These, with Lancaster and Cavendish—giants, too, in their way—were the men who worked and dreamt, dreamt and worked of and for an English Empire; who broke the proud heart of bigoted and tyrannous Spain, pricked the grandiloquent bubble of her self-appointed dictatorship to the world, and went far towards the emptying of her bursting coffers. And out of it all what have we reaped poetically, then or since? A mess of pottage and some brackish water, in place of the venison and the rich Burgundy that should have been ours.

Again, in the reign of Anne—one might say since somewhat prior to Dryden's time and down to the middle of the eighteenth century—there were different forces at work; a greatly dissimilar atmosphere was on and about life generally than what was the case in Elizabeth's time. The short age of large ventures and all the enthusiasm occasioned by them, of a romance that was new enough to be romance even to those who experienced it, and of the derring do of conquest had been replaced by the inset and the growth of plodding commercialism. In those years of slow reaping there was nothing to stir the nation's heart like the discoveries of the earlier years. That which the golden time had failed to produce could not be expected of the merely silver one.

Looking at the matter again there are other and equally strong points in the indictment. One would think, from our geographical conditions and our oft-cited inherent salt-water tendencies (if we really have them still) that a seafaring element would bulk largely in our whole literature. But such is not the case. There are nations with far less seaboard than we have, and with practically none of our maritime record, yet with a greater percentage of nautical material in their books. Why is it so? Is it because a long-drawn-out

familiarity has fostered a powerful indifference in us,
whilst distance and imagination have given them riches
which we fling away wantonly? Whether this be the
truth or only a personal view of the matter is a moot
point, possibly. But the fact stands. We are woefully
deficient in that branch of literature, especially the truly
poetic, wherein we should excel the whole world. The
quantity, as a percentage of the entirety, is but a
widow's mite; while the commendable part of that mite
is hardly a beggar's pittance. We are an insular race.
We boast a flag that "for a thousand years has borne
the battle and the breeze." During the latter half of
that time we have prided ourselves on ruling the waves,
real and imaginary. By descent and occupation we are
practically a sea-going nation, despite Napoleon's
stigma as to our being a shopkeeping one.[1] Our island
is so small comparatively that, with one sea at the back
door and another at the front one, it is almost envel-
oped by the breath of the ocean. We own, and for the
most part man, half the world's shipping. In our veins
there are reminiscences of many of creation's greatest
ocean ventures. We have inherited the blood and the
annals of such an array of great sea-captains as no other
nation, ancient or modern, can put against us. Yet
with all this, and our marked bent for literature to boot,
we have missed the fullness of our heritage.

Outside of Falconer's "Shipwreck" where is the
poem, even to-day, and more still the poem of any con-
siderable length, that has the real breath of the sea in
it; that is saturated with a true deep-water atmosphere;
that smacks of the brine as a seaman knows it; that
carries with it an unmistakable and inseparable sense
of heaving water, flying sprays, bellying canvas, creak-
ing spars, "shellbacks" coming and going—life at sea,
with all the concomitant colours and effects that go to
make that life? Such a thing is not to be found in the
language; though, of course, there are many little
"thumb-nail" sketches in verse—each one being a more
or less unfinished bit of the great picture. In fact, fine
or good prose books of this kind are so rare that when
one comes it is hailed as a wonder; or—and here is the

---

[1] Dean Tucker (1766), Adam Smith (1775), and Samuel Adams
(U.S.A., 1776) all used this phrase, though not quite as Napoleon is
said to have done.

tragic pathos of the matter—it is a phenomenon which so few persons understand that it very much runs the chance of having to be "discovered" later in life, ere it can take its place in the rank of its kind. Why is this? Have we grown so commercialised as to have no scrap of real poetic imagination, intuition or penetration left in us?—particularly where these three mind-features affect the nautical side of the national life. Not to say there is no immortal music being made, to echo down the corridors of time to come. How could one say there is not?—when those particular corridors are still to be built. The reality of one age is ever the romance of the next; and nothing short of the long perspective of Time's avenue can show really which of its pictures are to hang for all time. But in matters of the poetic maritime we do ape along the large course of destiny, shrunk dwarfs in the giants' robes which we have unworthily inherited; and we should turn to the immortal glory and beauty of that by which, as a nation and a power, we live and have our being. So wondrously small is the nation's knowledge of the sea's real individuality, and of the different atmospheres of its various localities, that any wrongly imagining writer who has never been out of sight of land—unless it be on a Channel steamer in a fog—can gull the reading public with literary nostrums, his false representations of things and conditions whereof he himself has no intuition and is divinely ignorant in practice. To such writers and their readers the sea is, as a certain versifier says it is to him, "the simple sea!"—that subtle, fawning, savage, gentle, insatiable, ever-changing (in certain matters primevally and everlastingly the same) phase of Nature over which we, as a people, erroneously boast a dominating Empire.

Why are the moods, the atmospheres of the sea so wondrously illusive? To express them in print appears to be as difficult as it would be to bring home a sample of the fog on Newfoundland's banks, or to bottle up summer sunshine for use in winter. Phrases that are, or were, in common use aboard ship do not make such songs of the sea as we should have, seeing that during five centuries we have lorded it over the boundless wave. Many have tried; but few indeed have been chosen as brief, true interpreters of that by which

we, as a nation in the war of commerce and ocean
supremacy, live and have our being. Why is it so?
Why is it that in all our long line of honoured verse-
makers not a single one has yet caught and conveyed
to us—beyond a few lines here and there—an absolute
sense of the sea's spirit, its message and its meaning?
The question is tantalising. It is a half-recognised fact
that the inspired poets of one age, or century, suggest
the history of the next. (Throughout this Introduction
"poets" and "poetry" are used in their large sense.)
Thus we see underlying the Elizabethan poets, espe-
cially those who wrote in the form of drama, so much
suggestion of these days of Empire that they can
almost be said to have inspired history. Nor do we
stand alone in this. But why, in the name of all that
is oceanic, poetic, racial, geographical and historical,
why have these forces not combined to give us an out-
standing delineator of the poetic phases of the sea, its
spirit and its mystery? We have many who have
sung their little sea songs, surface-items in a complexity
the utter truth of which lies so deep that the most of
those who go to study the tablets cannot decipher a
word of them. Others have more or less accurately
made poetic illustrations of sea phases, or have thrown
momentary figures of some of those phases on to their
line-wrought canvases; while a few—a very few indeed
—have succeeded in snatching a bare peep into some
presentment of old ocean's mystery or personality.
That we have a grand array of poets all the world of
intellect concedes. This proves that in the national
grain there is a poetic stratum, which not even the
adulteration of a greedy commerce can destroy. Add
to this that by breeding, geographical situation, com-
mercial and defensive necessity we are a race of sea-
farers, if not—to-day, at any rate—of real sea-lovers,
and one is stunned by the fact that we have no poet of
this side of the national character and activities.

Turning to what has been done for us in this branch
of literature, one's attention is first drawn to the higher
of the two portions into which it naturally falls—that is,
the poetry of the deep seas, of the sea itself, which
must perforce be given the first place; being the more
difficult of attainment, it is the more rare of the two.
And he who led the way in this division, albeit he gave

plenty of action with it all, was Falconer,[1] a Scots merchant seaman, who, in 1762, won a share of what we term immortality by his " Shipwreck," from which poem all the following quotations over his name, save only "the Midshipman," have been extracted. If there is any need to repeat here some of the praise that he won in his own day, and for a hundred years or so afterwards, take this from a posthumous edition[2] of the poem : "This admirable poem, which has fixed his fame on the solid basis of universal approbation, partakes more of the effusions of fancy than the labours of art, which he displays in new and original scenes, taken from nature and his own observations, and enriched with all the variety of description that can charm, interest and impress the mind of the reader. He displays an ample combination of nautical ability, in language conformable to marine technical terms, embellished with all the spontaneous flow and smooth harmony of verse." But this eulogy, fairly true though it be on the whole, must be read with an eye on the poetical conventions and artificialities of that day. For Falconer was not original enough to cast any of them aside. His is not the realism of some contemporary bards, who prefer to shout " Dunghill ! " rather than to whisper "A heap of dirt "; who paint their pictures with streaks of raw, primeval colours, and arrest attention by crude violence : neither has his work the vagueness of the poet of *suggestion,* who never makes a definite statement and never learns to like one. On the contrary, as descriptive matter, excellently reflecting Wordsworth's essence of the truth—by the way of rather stiff pentameter similies, we must admit —it is poetry of a kind which we have unhappily forgotten how to write. And one cannot but regret that

---

[1] *See* Appendix, p. 367.   [2] This is a copy for which I, many years ago, gave four annas to a Parsee pedlar near the market-place in Bombay ; and the interesting point is that on the inside of the front cover, in long-faded ink and evidently by an elderly hand that was not much accustomed to a pen, here are these two lines, as printed here :

> " Woes, which myself beheld ;
> Of which myself was one great part."

As though the writer had been one of the three survivors from the wreck of the *Britannia,* which was said to have been the actual disaster out of which Falconer also escaped and made his poem.

some of the nautical balladists of his, of later and of earlier times, did not ride his particular Pegasus, a true thoroughbred though it was not. Had they done so, we should not have to fall back on such accounts of naval engagements as have come down to us from the seventeenth and eighteenth centuries. It almost seems as if it was the acknowledged custom all along for poets to leave those glorious naval victories to be chronicled by cheap balladists and song writers, and so comes our beggarly state to-day.

It is a relief to turn to the songs, for here there is much to gladden us; yet even in this division we could echo Oliver Twist. Many sea songs have I heard, but never saw in print, songs that certainly belonged to an earlier day than my youth. In one of them there was this stanza :

> " She boundeth like a thing of life,
>   With strength and beauty crowned :
> Nor heeds, though tempests wildly blow,
>   For she is homeward bound."

Curiously enough Byron has in "The Corsair " :

> " She walks the waters like a thing of life,
>   And seems to dare the elements of strife."

Another, called "The Sailor's Grave," one that has older marks upon its face and was sung to the most doleful, weird air that I ever heard, was, so far as I remember it :

> " Our bark was far, far from land,
> When the fairest of our gallant band
> Grew deadly pale and weaned away,
> Like the twilight of an autumn day.
>
> We watched him through long hours of pain ;
> Our hopes were great, our task in vain.
>
> .   .   .   .   .   .
>
> We had no costly winding-sheet ;
> We placed two round-shot at his feet,
> And we rolled him up in his hammock sound,
> Like a king in his long shroud velvet-bound.
>
> We lowered him down the ship's dark side,
>
> .   .   .   .   .   .
> .   .   .   .   .   .
>
> With a splash and a plunge, and our task was o'er,
> And the billows rolled as they rolled before ;
> And many a wild prayer hallowed the wave,
> As we lowered him down to a sailor's grave."

Much to my disappointment all my searching amongst collections of broadsides has not resulted in finding a copy of the above song; nor of the original from which Henley seems to have adapted his "O, Falmouth is a fine town," with the refrain:

> " For it's home, dearie, home—it's home I want to be,
> Our topsails are hoisted, and we'll away to sea;
> O, the oak and the ash and the bonnie birken tree,
> They're all growing green in the old countrie."

The old version of which is a northern song called "It's Hame, and it's Hame," the chorus being:

> " It's hame, and it's hame, hame fain wad I be—
> Ay, it's hame, hame, hame in my ain countree!
> When the flower is i' the bud, and the leaf is on the tree,
> The lark sall sing me hame in my ain countree."

Yet another that I learnt amongst the men of the east coast, or from my grandmother's broadsides—kept in an old oak chest—I cannot remember which, began:

> " I'm afloat, I'm afloat on the deep rolling tide;
> The ocean's my home, and my bark is my pride.
> Then up, up with my flag, let it float o'er the sea,
> I'm afloat, I'm afloat, and the rover is free!
>
> I care not for monarch, I heed not the law;
> I've a compass to steer by, a dagger to draw;
> And ne'er as a slave or a coward will I kneel,
> While my gun carries shot or my belt wears a steel.
>   Then up, up, with my flag," etc.

Not to quote here all that I half-recollect of old sea-songs, one was:

> " As I was out walking one evening by the strand,
> I spied a gallant young sailor, on sentry he did stand;
> He kindly saluted me and, bidding me pass a joke,
> He enticed me into his sentry-box, in a bright tarpaulin coat.
>
> O we kissed and we fondled till the dawning of the day,
> When the boatswain piped to quarters, and the drums did merrily play,
> And he said—' My pretty young country lass, it's time to be going away;
> For you've passed the night in sentry-box and a bright tarpaulin coat.
>
> ' O master gentleman sailor, is it true that I must go!
> When I'd follow you and your gallant ship . . . .
>
> . . . .
>
> To spend my whole life with you in a bright tarpaulin coat.'

' O, no, my pretty young country lass, such things there never can
 be,—
It may be in civilian life, but not in the king's navy ;
For married I am already, and children I have three ;
How can I keep two wives in the navy, when one's too many for
 me ? '

' O master gentleman sailor, why didn't you tell me so?
For it will be my overthrow if you should make me go ;
For I love you, oh ! so dearly ; and as dearly must I rue
The night I spent in a sentry-box in your bright tarpaulin coat.' "

After the songs—some persons may think "before
them," but music gives to the song a function which the
narrative-ballad cannot fill—it is in the matter of ballads
proper that we have the most reason to be thankful,
poor enough though they be as poetry. The naval
ballads are good substitute for that epic verse which
should have been ours and is not, particularly in the
almost barren cases of the Armada and Trafalgar—our
greatest national deeds left most unsung ! The more
homely stories of love, faithful to the last or "weaned
away," are truly valuable as vignettes of their particular
stratum of life in those days; as, again in their own
way, are such ballads as " Sir Andrewe Barton," "Cap-
tain Ward," and other buccaneering pieces which were
written—in the most cases by half-illiterate hands—
somewhat near to the days of their happening. As to
the mermaid variety of this section, it is a curious fact
that in the past none of these mythical tales sprang
from an English source. Not to go further from home,
the Teutonic, Scandinavian and Celtic literatures and
folk-lore have their own developments of the Greek
nereid; but the English has none; neither have the
Welsh Celts, although in their oldest traditions there
are certain well-recognised water fairies of an elfin
nature, yet only in connection with pools and lakes. It
is to the Scots and the Irish Celts that we have to go
for old mermaid stories in these islands; and it is
interesting to note that the characteristics of those
supposed beings, as seen by these peoples, are quite
different from the traits of their southern progenitors,
imaginatively. The neken of the Baltic and the Ger-
man shores generally, like the siren of the Greeks and
the Latin races, was a wrecker of vessels and little
else; but the British Celtic mermaid, like some features
in the old Norse temperament, was of a personal rather

than of a general nature. Just as the average saga is
narrow in its vision, as against the epic of the south,
leaving side issues and many characters in order to
concentrate all its powers, and to fix all attention, on
the doings of a few selected persons; so the Celtic
mind, in adopting the mermaid as a part of Nature's
wonders and an all-sufficient point around which to
weave new tales of love's undoing, stripped her of her
general attributes and narrowed her down to a being
with merely a personal purpose. And in this we see
key-notes to certain broad traits in the respective races.
The more civilised and cultured a people are, the more
general—i. e. broad, far-reaching and complex—are its
thoughts, its tendencies, its philosophy, and all things
that come of these features; so is the converse true,
even down to the bottom of the scale. The savage is
the most personal of all, and that, too, in all he does and
says. Even his goods have only a few attributes each,
and often only one to two. So it was in the past with
the Celt, the Norseman and the Teuton, as against
the Greek, the Roman and the Egyptian. Thus when
he first heard of the mermaid—and no doubt believed
in her from that moment—he at once gave her a home
in the caves of his rocky coast and there imbued her
with those personal graces, blandishments, and the in-
evitably tragic ill-fate that sprang from her twofold
nature and her kind of double position in life. In fact,
just as the later Greek or Roman would have given a
somewhat impersonal character to such an importation,
the Scots and the Irish coastmen made her a Celt. So
it is that wherever we find her (never more than one to a
gulf, sound, or bay) she always has the comb and the
yellow hair, is singing to draw away a particular lover,
is endowed with a kind of perpetual youth and—greatest
wonder of all—can take her lovers or victims, whichever
they be, down to submarine caves without any discom-
fort or watery danger to them. Nearly every writer of
mermaid ballads in Northern Europe, from the earliest
down to Matthew Arnold, have left it as a matter of
course that the love of a sea-maid or a sea-man instantly
gave the human object of affection the magic to live
under water. (To ask where the story would be with-
out this feature would only beg the question.) It is
also to be noted that in all cases they were the love-

makers, and in most instances passionate, especially
when thwarted; all of which means merely that their
human imaginators gave them their own earthy
characteristics. A point of more interest is the fact that
only in the cases of John Leyden and Matthew Arnold
is the fishy nature admitted in one way or another.
Leyden, retelling what he had learnt from hearsay—
and no doubt garbled in its descent from generation to
generation—makes young Macphail say to the mermaid
in her cave, "Thy life-blood is the water cold," which
we may certainly look on as being from Leyden's own
mind; for there is nothing of its kind in any other old
narrative of this sort, and we know tolerably well that
none of the persons who gave life to such ballads knew
of the modern belief that the less and the colder the
blood, the less is the animal heat; and so of all kinds of
passion. In a very different way—and as it should be,
if done at all—Arnold contrives, with the subtlety of a
more complex and finished art, to keep before our
eyes, all through the piece, the pathetic story of a white-
blooded creature; this is the very texture, the weft and
the woof, of his ballad, that the narrator is *fishy,* being,
with one mournfully proud note at the end—a forsaken
king of the sea, with seven-tenths of the emphasis on
the first condition.

Of the ships' chanties and the humorous pieces there
is but little to say. The latter are put in just as all the
other sections are—to give the book that completeness
which it could not have if any one of them were missing.
As regards the work-songs, my object here has been to
include only what I have heard sung; but not all of
them, for while some would not bear repetition, others
are too utterly nonsensical. By drawing on printed
examples this section could have been enlarged, just as
the naval-battle and the piratical portions could. But
to what end? Merely that of bulk. For, after all, if
an anthology is not a case of judicious selection and
arrangement, it is then as a meal without savour and
had better not have been. In addition, nearly all the
chanties have been kept short of the length they often
attain to when sung aboard ship, especially the hauling
and capstan songs; for if the piece of work be long
enough and the chanty-man has any gift of invention
he frequently draws a ditty out to double its original

length. "Sánta Anna," "The Flash Packet," and "Rolling Home" none of which have I seen in any other collection—were taken down from the mouths of Bristolian seamen while on an East Indian voyage in a sailing-ship; one and two were from an elderly man in whose life there had been some dark nautical and South American patches; the third came from a young fellow who had learnt it during his previous voyage. The elder D'Israeli said that in his day work-songs were common to the Greek, Venetian and other sailors and boatmen. He might have added that our own North-country handloom-weavers used to sing to the rhythm of the shuttle; and, I believe, the same is done to-day in the Orient. We know that the Hebridean harvesters sang together to the swing of their sickles; and that the old-time dairymaids had milking songs, which were supposed to charm larger supplies of milk from the cows than the animals would give to milkers who did not sing. So far as my experience goes such songs are sung by seamen all the world over; and very often a negro is the best chanty-man in a ship's crew, which fact—it seems to me—is due to the whimsical, plaintive and rather wailing note that is common to the somewhat falsetto voice of the average black, and appears to be so fitting to the solo parts of the song; while the inspiriting nature of it, that which temporarily doubles the strength of every man in the pull or the heave, is got out of the chorus. The best chanty-man I ever heard was a native of the Seychelles, who went by the name of Allan Robin.

THE OCEAN'S SELF, MAN'S LOVE FOR IT, ITS MESSAGE AND ITS CALL

The moving waters at their priest-like task
Of pure ablution round earth's human shores.

KEATS.

I have loved thee, Ocean! and my joy
   Of youthful sports was on thy breast to be
Borne, like thy bubbles, onward: from a boy
   I wanton'd with thy breakers—they to me
   Were a delight; and if the freshening sea
Made them a terror—'twas a pleasing fear;
   For I was as it were a child of thee,
And trusted to thy billows far and near,
And laid my hand upon thy mane—as I do here.

BYRON.

A shepherd-lad, who, ere his sixteenth year,
Had· left that calling, tempted to entrust
His expectations to the fickle winds
And perilous waters—with the mariners
A fellow-mariner.

WORDSWORTH.

A HYMN IN PRAYSE OF NEPTUNE.[1]

Of Neptune's empire lett us sing,
  At whose commande the waves obey;
  To whome the rivers tribute pay,
Downe the high mountains sliding;
  To whome the scaly nation yeelds
  Homage for the crystal fields
Wherein they dwell;
  And every sea-god paies a gem
Yearly, out of hys watery cell,
  To decke great Neptune's diadem.

The Tritons, dancing in a ring,
  Before his palace-gates doe make
  The water with their echoes quake
Like the great thunder sounding.
  The sea-nymphs chante their accents shrill;
  And the sirens, taught to kill
With their sweete voyse,
  Make every echoing rock reply,
Unto their gentle murmuring noyse,
  The prayse of Neptune's empery.

Thomas Campion.

"EARTH HAS NOT A PLAIN."

Earth has not a plain
So boundless and so beautiful as thine,—
The eagle's vision cannot take it in;
The lightning's wing, too weak to sweep its space,
Sinks half-way o'er it, like a wearied bird:
It is the mirror of the stars, where all
Their hosts within the concave firmament,
Gay marching to the music of the spheres,
Can see themselves at once.

A. Campbell.

---

[1] This song was written for the Gray's Inn masque, 1594, eight years after Campion was admitted to the Inn, and seven years before the appearance of his first book in English. He held a doctor's degree in medicine, and wrote learnèdly on counterpoint. He was the "Sweet Master Campion" of his own day, and had a considerable following.

ON THE SEA.

It keeps eternal whisperings around
　　Desolate shores, and with its mighty swell
　　Gluts twice ten thousand caverns, till the spell
Of Hecate leaves them their old shadowy sound.
Often 'tis in such gentle temper found,
　　That scarcely will the very smallest shell
　　Be moved for days from whence it sometime fell,
When last the winds of Heaven were unbound.

Oh ye! who have your eye-balls vexed and tired,
　　Feast them upon the wideness of the Sea;
Oh ye! whose ears are dinn'd with uproar rude,
　　Or fed too much with cloying melody,—
Sit ye near some old cavern's mouth, and brood
Until ye start, as if the sea-nymphs quired!

KEATS.

"OLD OCEAN WAS."

Old ocean was
Infinity of ages ere we breathed
Existence; and he will be beautiful
When all the living world that sees him now
Shall roll unconscious dust around the sun.
Quelling from age to age the vital throb
In human hearts, Death shall not subjugate
The pulse that dwells in his tremendous breast,
Or interdict his minstrelsy to sound
In thundering concert with the quiring winds.
But long as man to parent Nature owns
Instinctive homage, and in times beyond
The power of thought to reach, bard after bard
Shall sing thy glory, beatific Sea!

A. CAMPBELL.

"MIGHTY SEA! CAMELEON-LIKE THOU CHANGEST."

Mighty Sea!
Cameleon-like thou changest; but there's love
In all thy change, and constant sympathy
With yonder sky—thy mistress. From her brow

Thou tak'st thy moods, and wear'st her colour on
Thy faithful bosom,—morning's milky white,
Noon's sapphire, or the saffron glow of eve;
And all thy balmier hours, fair Element,
Have such divine complexion, crispèd smiles,
Luxuriant heavings and sweet whisperings,
That little is the wonder Love's own Queen
Of old was fabled to have sprung from thee—
Creation's common!—which no human power
Can parcel or inclose. The lordliest floods
And cataracts, that the tiny hands of man
Can tame, conduct or bound, are drops of dew
To thee,—that could subdue the Earth itself,
And brook'st commandment from high Heaven alone
For marshalling thy waves.

A. CAMPBELL.

"ROLL ON, THOU DEEP AND DARK, BLUE OCEAN."

ROLL on, thou deep and dark, blue Ocean—roll!
   Then thousand fleets sweep over thee in vain;
Man marks the earth with ruin—his control
   Stops with the shore; upon the watery plain
   The wrecks are all thy deed, nor doth remain
A shadow of man's ravage, save his own,
   When, for a moment, like a drop of rain,
He sinks into thy depths with bubbling groan,
Without a grave, unknelled, uncoffined and unknown.

His steps are not upon thy paths,—thy fields
   Are not a spoil for him,—thou dost arise
And shake him from thee; the vile strength he wields
   For earth's destruction thou dost all despise,
   Spurning him from thy bosom to the skies,
And send'st him, shivering in thy playful spray,
   And howling to his gods, where haply lies
His petty hope in some near port or bay,
And dashest him again to earth; there let him lay.

The armaments which thunder-strike the walls
   Of rock-built cities, bidding nations quake,
And monarchs tremble in their capitals;
   The oak leviathans, whose huge ribs make
   Their clay creator the vain title take

Of lord of thee, and arbiter of war;
  These are thy toys; and, as the snowy flake,
They melt into the yeast of waves, which mar
Alike th' Armada's pride, or spoils of Trafalgar.

Thy shores are empires, changed in all save thee—
  Assyria, Greece, Rome, Carthage, what are they?
Thy waters wasted them while they were free,
  And many a tyrant since : their shores obey
  The stranger, slave or savage; their decay
Has dried up realms to deserts :—not so thou;—
  Unchangeable, save to thy wild waves' play :
Time writes no wrinkle on thine azure brow;
Such as creation's dawn beheld, thou rollest now.

Thou glorious mirror, where the Almighty's form
  Glasses itself in tempests; in all time,
Calm or convulsed—in breeze, or gale, or storm,
  Icing the pole, or in the torrid clime
  Dark-heaving; boundless, endless, and sublime—
The image of Eternity—the throne
  Of the invisible; even from out of thy slime
The monsters of the deep are made; each zone
Obeys thee; thou goest forth, dread, fathomless, alone.

BYRON.

"THOSE TRACKLESS DEEPS."

—THOSE trackless deeps, where many a weary sail
Has seen, above the illimitable plain,
Morning and night, and night on morning rise;
Whilst still no land to greet the wanderer spread
Its shadowy mountains on the sun-bright sea,
Where the loud roaring of the tempest-waves
So long have mingled with the gusty wind
In melancholy loneliness, and swept
The desert of those ocean solitudes;
But, vocal to the sea-bird's harrowing shriek,
The bellowing monster and the rushing storm,
Now to the sweet and many-mingling sounds
Of kindliest human impulses respond.

SHELLEY.

"OCEAN, UNEQUAL PRESSED."

OCEAN, unequal pressed, with broken tide
And blind commotion heaves; while from the shore—
Eat into caverns by the restless wave—
And forest-rustling mountain, comes a voice
That, solemn-sounding, bids the world prepare.
Then issues forth the storm with sudden burst,
And hurls the whole precipitated air
Down in a torrent! On the passive main
Descends the ethereal force, and with strong gust
Turns from its bottom the discoloured deep.
Through the black night that sits immense around,
Lashed into foam, the fierce conflicting brine
Seems o'er a thousand raging waves to burn.
Meantime the mountain-billows to the clouds,
In dreadful tumult swelled, surge above surge,
Burst into chaos with tremendous roar;
And anchored navies from their stations drive,
Wild as the winds across the howling waste
Of mighty waters : now the inflated wave
Straining thy scale, and now impetuous shoot
Into the secret chambers of the deep,—
The wintry Baltic thundering o'er their head.
Emerging thence again, before the breath
Of full-exerted heaven, they wing their course,
And dart on distant coasts,—if some sharp rock,
Or shoal insidious, break not their career,
And in loose fragments fling them floating round.

JAMES THOMSON.

A GENTLE SEA.

LOOK what immortal floods the sunset pours
    Upon us ! Mark how still—as though in dreams
    Round—the once wild and terrible ocean seems !
How silent are the winds ! No billow roars;
But all is tranquil as Elysian shores :
    The silver margin which aye runneth round
    The moon-enchanted sea hath here no sound;
Even echo speaks not on these radiant moors.

What !—Is the giant of the ocean dead?—
    Whose strength was all unmatched beneath the sun.

No, he reposes.   Now his toils are done;
   More quiet than the bubbling brook is he.
So mightiest powers by deepest calms are fed,
   And sleep—how oft!—in things that gentlest be.
                                    B. W. PROCTER.[1]

"O THOU VAST OCEAN."[2]

O THOU vast Ocean! Ever-sounding Sea!
Thou symbol of a drear immensity!
Thou thing that windest round the solid world
Like a huge animal; which, downward hurl'd
From the black clouds, lies weltering and alone,
Lashing and writhing till its strength be gone.
Thy voice is like the thunder, and thy sleep
Is a giant's slumber, loud and deep.
Thou speakest in the east and in the west
At once; and on thy heavily-laden breast
Fleets come and go, and shapes that have no life
Or motion, yet are moved and meet in strife.

     .   .   .   .   .

Thou only, terrible Ocean, hast a power,
A will, a voice; and in thy wrathful hour,
When thou dost lift thine anger to the clouds,
A fearful and magnificent beauty shrouds
Thy broad, green forehead. If thy waves be driven
Backwards and forwards by the shifting wind,
How quickly dost thou thy great strength unbind,
And stretch thine arms, and war at once with Heaven!

     .   .   .   .   .

[1] "Barry Cornwall"—a school-fellow with Byron, the younger Peel, a great and a true lover of the sea, as pieces in this volume prove—was a romantic poet with an inclination to be classic. Scant justice has been done to him since his death in 1874. The following is from Swinburne's poem to his memory:

> "Time takes them home that we loved, fair names and famous,
>   To the soft long sleep, to the broad sweet bosom of death;
> But the flower of their souls he shall not take away to shame us,
>   Nor the lips lack song for ever that now lack breath:
> For with us shall the music and perfume, that die not, dwell;
>   Though the dead to our dead bid welcome, and us farewell."

He served articles to a solicitor at Lamb's "sweet Colne" in Wiltshire, and had the peculiar power of making all men love him; nearly every noted man of his day was his *friend*.

[2] From "Marcian Colonna."

Thou trackless and immeasurable main,
On thee no record ever lived again,
To meet the hand that writ it; live nor dead
Hath ever fathomed thy profoundest deeps,
Where haply the huge monster swells and sleeps,
King of his watery limit.

.　　　.　　　.　　　.　　　.

Oh! wonderful thou art, great element,
And fearful in thy spleeny humours bent,
And lovely in repose: Thy summer form
Is beautiful; and when thy silvery waves
Make music in earth's dark and winding caves,
I love to wander on thy pebbled beach,
Marking the sunlight at the evening hour,
And hearken to the thoughts thy waters teach—
"Eternity, Eternity and Power."

B. W. Procter.

"IT IS THE MIDNIGHT HOUR." [1]

It is the midnight hour: The beauteous sea,
　Calm as the cloudless heaven, the heaven discloses;
While many a sparkling star, in quiet glee,
　Far down within the watery sky reposes.
As if the ocean's heart were stirred
With inward life, a sound is heard,
　Like that of dreamer murmuring in his sleep;
'Tis partly the billows, and partly the air
That lies like a garment floating fair
　Above the happy deep.
The sea, I ween, cannot be fann'd
By evening freshness from the land,
　For the land is far away;
But God hath will'd that the sky-borne breeze
In the centre of the loneliest seas
　Should ever sport and play.
　　The mighty Moon, she sits above,
　　Encircled by a zone [2] of love—

---

[1] These are the opening lines of the "Isle of Palms" (1812), a story in four cantos, wherein "Christopher North" showed that his love of the sea was as great as his fondness for lashing at English authors.

[2] This seems to have been that "ring round the moon," which is generally seen only in fine weather, and is put down by seamen, the world over, to mean the immediate coming of less happy conditions for them—and seldom, indeed, is the prognostication wrong. Wilson's

A zone of dim and tender light,
That makes her wakeful eye more bright:
She seems to shine with a sunny ray,
And the night looks like a mellow'd day.
The gracious mistress of the main
Hath now an undisturbèd reign;
And from her silent throne looks down,
As upon children of her own,
On the waves that lend their gentle breast
In gladness for her couch of rest.

JOHN WILSON.

SUNRISE AT SEA.

THE interminable ocean lay beneath,
At depth immense,—not quiet as before,
For a faint breath of air, e'en at the height
On which I stood scarce felt, play'd over it;
Waking innumerous dimples on its face,
As though 'twere conscious of the splendid guest
That e'en then touched the threshold of heaven's gates,
And smiled to bid him welcome.   Far away,
On either hand, the broad-curved beach stretched on;
And I could see the slow-paced waves advance
One after one, and spread upon the sands,
Making a slender edge of pearly foam
Just as they broke; then softly falling back,
Noiseless to me on that tall head of rock,
As it had been a picture, clear descried
Through optic tube, leagues off.
                                        A tender mist
Was round th' horizon and along the vales;
But the hill-tops stood in a crystal air.
The cope of heaven was clear and deeply blue,
And not a cloud was visible.   Toward the east
An atmosphere of golden light, that grew
Momently brighter, and intensely bright,
Proclaim'd th' approaching sun.   Now, now he comes:
A dazzling point emerges from the sea:
It spreads,—it rises,—now it seems a dome

---

use of the ring is but a single instance—dozens of which could be cited
in this volume—of how even the learnèd landsman is apt to err when
he goes "out of his depth" in nautical matters and phenomena.   Note
how well this ring is used in "The Wreck of the *Hesperus*," page 169.

Of burning gold !   Higher and rounder now
It mounts, it swells; now, like a huge balloon
Of light and fire, it rests upon the rim
Of waters,—lingers there a moment, then—
Soars up !

EDWIN ATHERSTONE.[1]

"BENEATH THEIR FEET A BURNISHED OCEAN LAY."

BENEATH their feet a burnished ocean lay,
Glittering in sunshine.   Far down, like snow
Shook from the bosom of a wintery cloud,
And drifting on the wind in feathery flakes,
The sea-gulls sailed betwixt the earth and sky,—
Or, floating on the bosom of the deep,
Pursued the herring-shoal with dexterous aim.
Far, far away on the horizon's edge,
The white sails of the homeward-scudding ships
Gleamed like the lilies in a garden plot,
Or like the scattered shreds of fleecy cloud
Left by the Evening at the gate of Night,
To shimmer in the leaden-coloured sky,
And drink the splendour of the harvest-moon,
Their glancing breasts reflected from afar
The noonday sunlight.

CHARLES MACKAY.[2]

"THE SEA IS MIGHTY."

THE sea is mighty; but a mightier sways
His restless billows.

          A hundred realms
Watch its broad shadow warping on the wind,
And in the drooping shower with gladness hear
The promise of the harvest.   I look forth
Over the boundless blue, where joyously
The bright crests of innumerable waves

---

[1] Atherstone attracted some attention in his time ; he did a considerable amount of work, but as a whole it is far too high-flown for a day that is harking back to the realities of things as mother Earth will persist in making them.   The above piece is from " A Midsummer Day's Dream " (1824).   [2] See note to " When the Wind Blows Fair," p. 211.

Glance to the sun at once, as when the hands
Of a great multitude are upward flung
In acclamation.   I behold the ships
Gliding from cape to cape, from isle to isle,
Or stemming towards far lands, or hastening home
From the Old World.   It is thy friendly breeze
That bears them, with the riches of the land
And treasure of dear lives; till, in the port,
The shouting seamen climb and furl the sails.

BRYANT.

THE SEA : IN-SHORE.

THERE comes to me a vision of the day
    When first I made acquaintance with the sea—
    Rolling and rushing up the beach to me,
Then tumbling back, a giant in his play :

So, with arched neck again, in foam and spray,
    Hoarse-voiced, he leaps !—recoils as speedily
    Leaving toy-shells, his shining legacy,—
Spars, pebbles, coral-weeds of brightest ray.

Anon the many-mooded thing would sleep,
    In lamb-like stillness, all a summer noon,
While sun-stars quivered on the hollow deep ;
    Then wake, refreshed from slumber ; and how soon,
With wet and windy manes, toss silver-bright
A wilderness of motion and of light.

E. H. BRODIE.

"WITH HUSKY—HAUGHTY LIPS, O SEA !"

WITH husky—haughty lips, O sea !
Where day and night I wend thy surf-beat shore,
Imaging to my sense thy varied strange suggestions,
(I see and plainly list thy talk and conference here,)
Thy troops of white-maned racers racing to the goal ;
Thy ample, smiling face, dash'd with the sparkling
    dimples of the sun ;
Thy brooding scowl and murk—thy unloos'd hurricanes ;
Thy unsubduedness, caprices, wilfulness ;
Great as thou art above the rest, thy many tears—a
    lack from all eternity in thy content,
(Naught but the greatest struggles, wrongs, defeats,
    could make thee greatest,—no less could make
    thee :) ;   •

Thy lonely state—something thou ever seek'st and
    seek'st yet never gain'st,
Surely some right withheld—some voice, in huge
    monotonous rage, of freedom-lover pent;
Some vast heart, like a planet's, chain'd and chafing
    in those breakers,
By lengthen'd swell and spasm and panting breath,
And rhythmic rasping of thy sands and waves,
And serpent hiss, and savage peals of laughter,
And undertones of distant lion-roar;
(Sounding, appealing to the sky's deaf ear—but now,
    rapport for once,
A phantom in the night thy confident for once :)
The first and last confession of the globe,
Outsurging, muttering from thy soul's abysms,
The tale of cosmic elemental passion,
Thou tellest to a kindred soul.

WHITMAN.

"A MIGHTY CHANGE IT IS."

A MIGHTY change it is—and ominous
Of mightier, sleeping in eternity.
The bare cliffs seem half-sinking in the sand,
Heaved high by winter seas; and their white crowns,
Struck by the whirlwinds, shed their hair-like snow
Upon the desolate air.   Sullen and black,
Their huge backs rearing far along the waves,
The rocks lie barrenly, which there have lain,
Revealed or hidden, from immemorial time;
And o'er them hangs a seaweed drapery,
Like some old Triton's hair, beneath which lurk
Myriads of crownèd shellfish, things whose life,
Like a celled hermit's, seemeth profitless.
Vast shiny masses hardened into stone
Rise smoothly from the surface of the deep;
Each with a hundred-thousand fairy cells,
Perforate, like a honeycomb, and cup-like,
Filled with the sea's salt crystal,—the soft beds,   '
Once of so many pebbles, thence divorced
By the continual waters, as they grew
Slowly to rock.   The bleak shore is o'erspread
With seaweeds green and sere, curled and dishevelled—

As they were mermaids' tresses, wildly torn
From some sea-sorrow.   The small mountain-stream,
Swol'n to a river, laves the quivering beach,
And flows in many channels to the sea,
Between high shingly banks that shake for ever.
The solitary sea-bird, like a spirit,
Balanced in air upon its crescent wings,
Hangs floating in the winds—as he were lord
Of the drear vastness round him, and alone
Natured for such dominion.   Spring and summer
And storèd autumn, of their liveries
Here is no vestige : Winter, tempest-robed,
In gloomy grandeur o'er the hills and seas
Reigneth omnipotent.

THOMAS WADE.

"WHERE IS THE SEA?"[1]

WHERE is the sea?—I languish here !
    Where is my own blue sea?—
With all its barks of fleet career,
    And flags and breezes free !

I miss the voice of waves—the first
    That woke my childish glee;
The measured chime, the thundering burst—
    Where is my own blue sea?

Oh, rich your myrtles' breath may rise !
    Soft, soft your winds may be :
Yet my sick heart within me dies !—
    Where is my own blue sea?

I hear the shepherd's mountain flute;
    I hear the whispering tree :
The echoes of my soul are mute—
    Where is my own blue sea?

FELICIA HEMANS.[2]

---

[1] Mrs. Hemans based this poem on the following :—A Greek Islander was taken to the Vale of Tempe and asked to admire its beauty. His only reply was—" The sea ! Where is my sea ?"
[2] See footnote on p. 71.

"ONCE MORE UPON THE WATERS."

ONCE more upon the waters!—yet once more!
  And the waves bound beneath me as a steed
That knows his rider.   Welcome to their roar!
  Swift be their guidance, wheresoe'er it lead:
  Though the strained mast should quiver as a reed,
And the rent canvas, fluttering, strew the gale,
  Still must I on; for I am as a weed,
Flung from the rock, on Ocean's foam, to sail
Where'er the surge may sweep, the tempest's breath
    prevail!

                                          BYRON.

"A SHIP IS FLOATING IN THE HARBOUR NOW."

A SHIP is floating in the harbour now;
A wind is hovering o'er the mountain's brow;
There is a path on the sea's azure floor,
No keel hath ever ploughed that path before;
The halcyons brood above the foamless isles;
The treacherous Ocean hath foresworn its wiles;
The merry mariners are bold and free.
Say, my heart's sister, wilt thou sail with me?
Our bark is as an albatross, whose nest
Is a far Eden of the purple East:
And we between her wings will sit, while Night
And Day and Storm and Calm pursue their flight,
Our ministers, along the boundless Sea,
Treading each other's heels unheededly.
It is an isle under Ionian skies,
Beautiful as a wreck of Paradise;
And—for the harbours are not safe and good—
This land would have remained a solitude,
But for some pastoral people native there;
Who from the Elysian clear and golden air
Draw the last spirit of the age of gold,
Simple and spirited, innocent and bold.
The blue Ægean girds this chosen home
With ever changing sound and light and foam,
Kissing the sifted sands and caverns hoar;
And all the winds wandering along the shore
Undulate with the undulating tide.

                                          SHELLEY.

THE SECRET OF THE SEA.

Ah ! what pleasant visions haunt me,
  As I gaze upon the sea;
All the old, romantic legends,
  All my dreams come back to me:

Sails of silk and ropes of sendel,
  Such as gleam in ancient lore;
And the singing of the sailors,
  And the answer from the shore.

Most of all the Spanish ballad
  Haunts me oft and tarries long,
Of the noble Count Arnaldos,
  And the sailor's mystic song.

Like the long waves on a sea-beach,
  Where the sand as silver shines,
With a soft, monotonous cadence
  Flow its unrhymed lyric lines;

Telling how the Count Arnaldos,
  With his hawk upon his hand,
Saw a fair and stately galley
  Steering onward to the land;

How he heard the ancient helmsman
  Chant a song so wild and clear,
That the sailing sea-bird slowly
  Poised upon the mast to hear,

Till his soul was full of longing,
  And he cried, with impulse strong—
"Helmsman, for the love of heaven,
  Teach me, too, that wondrous song ! "

"Wouldst thou," so the helmsman answered,
  "Learn the secrets of the sea?
Only those who brave its dangers
  Comprehend its mystery."

In each sail that skims the horizon,
  In each landward-blowing breeze,
I behold that stately galley,
  Hear those mournful melodies;

Till my soul is full of longing
  For the secret of the sea,
And the heart of the great ocean
  Sends a thrilling pulse through me.
LONGFELLOW.

"THE SEA IS CALM TO-NIGHT."

THE sea is calm to-night;
The tide is full; the moon lies fair
Upon the straits : on the French coast the light
Gleams and is gone; the cliffs of England stand,
Glimmering and vast, out in the tranquil bay.
Come to the window,—sweet is the night-air !
Listen,—you hear the grating roar
Of pebbles which the waves draw back, and fling,
At their return, up the high strand;
Begin and cease, and then again begin,
With tremulous cadence slow, and bring
The eternal note of sadness in.
MATTHEW ARNOLD.

"I SEE THE DEEP'S UNTRAMPLED FLOOR."

I SEE the Deep's untrampled floor
  With green and purple seaweeds strown :
I see the waves upon the shore,
  Like light dissolved in star-showers, thrown :
I sit upon the sands alone;
  The lightning of the noontide ocean
Is flashing round me, and a tone
  Arises from its measured motion.
How sweet !—did any heart now share in my emotion.
SHELLEY.

OLD OCEAN'S VOICE.

THE ocean, at the bidding of the moon,
  For ever changes with his restless tide :
Flung shoreward now, to be re-gathered soon,
  With kingly pauses of reluctant pride
And semblance of return.   Anon from home
  He issues forth again, high-ridged and free;
The gentlest murmurs of his seething foam,
  Like armies whispering where great echoes be.

Oh, leave me here upon this beach to rove,
  Mute listener to that sound so grand and lone !—
  A glorious sound, deep-drawn and strongly thrown,
And reaching those on mountain heights above :
  To British ears—as who shall scorn to own ?—
A tutelar fond voice, a saviour-tone of love !
                C. T. TURNER.

"METHINKS I FAIN WOULD LIE."

METHINKS I fain would lie by the lone sea,
  And hear the waters their white music weave.
  Methinks it were a pleasant thing to grieve,
So that our sorrows might companioned be
By that strange harmony
  Of winds and billows, and the living sound
    Sent down from heaven when the thunder speaks
    Unto the listening shores and torrent creeks,
  When the swol'n sea doth try to burst its bound !
                B. W. PROCTER.

"I HEARD, OR SEEMED TO HEAR."

I HEARD, or seemed to hear, the chiding Sea
Say : "Pilgrim, why so late and slow to come?
Am I not always here?—thy summer home.
Is not my voice thy music, morn and eve?—
My breath thy healthful climate in the heats,
My touch thy antidote, my bay thy bath?
Was ever building like my terraces?
Was ever couch magnificent as mine?
Lie on the warm rock-ledges, and there learn
A little hut suffices like a town.
I make your sculptured architecture vain—
Vain beside mine.   I drive my wedges home,
And carve the coastwise mountain into caves.
Lo ! here is Rome and Nineveh and Thebes,
Karnak and Pyramid and Giant's Stairs,
Half-piled or prostrate,—and my newest slab
Older than all thy race."
               Behold the Sea !—
The opaline, the plentiful and strong,
Yet beautiful as is the rose in June,

Fresh as the trickling rainbow of July;
Sea full of food; the nourisher of kinds,
Purger of earth, and medicine of men,
Creating a sweet climate by its breath,
Washing our arms and griefs from memory;
And, in its mathematic ebb and flow,
Giving a hint of that which changes not.
Rich are the sea-gods : Who gives gifts but they?
They grope the sea for pearls, but more than pearls.
They pluck Force thence, and give it to the wise :
For every wave is wealth to Dædalus—
Wealth to the cunning artist who can work
This matchless strength.   Where shall he find, O waves!
A load your Atlas shoulders cannot lift?

"I, with my hammer pounding evermore
The rocky coast, smite Andes into dust,
Strewing my bed; and, in another age,
Rebuild a continent of better men.
Then I unbar the doors : my paths lead out
The exodus of nations.   I disperse
Men to all shores that front the hoary main.
I, too, have arts and sorceries,—
Illusion dwells for ever with the wave.
I know what spells are laid,—leave me to deal
With credulous and imaginative man;
For, though he scoop my water in his palm,
A few rods off he deems it gems and clouds.
Planting strange fruits and sunshine on the shore,
I make some coast alluring, some lone isle,
To distant men, who must go there, or die."

EMERSON.

ITS WINDS, TIDES AND WATERS, ITS MYSTERY, MUSIC AND COLOURS

Methinks the wind has spoke aloud at land,—
A fuller blast ne'er shook our battlements.
If it hath ruffianed so upon the sea,
What ribs of oak, when mountains melt upon them,
Can hold the mortise?

SHAKESPEARE.

There the sea I found,
Calm as a cradled child in dreamless slumber bound.

SHELLEY.

Old Ocean is a mighty harmonist.

WORDSWORTH.

WINDS AND WAVES.

As ragyng seas are wonte to rore,
    When winterie storme hys wrathfulle wreck doth
        threate,
    The rollyng billowes beate the rugged shore,
As they the earthe wulde shulder from her seate;
    And greedie gulphe does gape, as hee wuld eate
    His naybor elemente in hys revenge :
Then 'gin the blusteryng bretherne boldlie threate
    To move the worlde from off hys stedfaste henge,
    And boisterous bataile make, eche other to avenge.

SPENCER.

For do but stand upon the foaming shore,—
The chidden billow seems to pelt the clouds ;
The wind-shaked surge, with high and monstrous mane,
Seems to cast water on the burning bear,
And quench the guards of th' ever-fixèd pole.
I never did such molestation view
On the enchafèd flood !

SHAKESPEARE.

Thou,
For whose path the Atlantic's level powers
Cleave themselves into chasms, while far below
The sea-blooms and the oozy woods, which wear
The sapless foliage of the ocean, know
Thy voice, and suddenly grow grey with fear,
And tremble and despoil themselves.

SHELLEY.

It curls the blue waves into foam ;
    It snaps the strongest mast ;
Then like a sorrowing thing it sighs,
    When the wild storm is past.

ELIZABETH HAWKSHAW.

THE STORM.

CEASE, rude Boreas, blustering railer!
　List, ye landsmen, all to me;
Messmates, hear a brother sailor
　Sing the dangers of the sea:
From bounding billows, fast in motion,
　When the distant whirlwinds rise,
To the tempest-troubled ocean,
　Where the seas contend with skies!

Hark! the boatswain hoarsely bawling [1]—
　"By topsail-sheets and halyards stand!
Down top-gallants quick be hauling!
　Down your stay-sails, hand, boys, hand!
Now it freshens; set the braces;
　The topsail-sheets now quick let go!
Luff, boys, luff!—Don't make wry faces,—
　Up your topsails nimbly clew!"

Now all you on down-beds sporting,
　Fondly locked in beauty's arms,
Fresh enjoyments wanton courting,
　Safe from all but love's alarms;
Round us roars the tempests louder—
　Think what fear our minds enthralls:
Harder yet—it yet blows harder!
　Now again the boatswain calls.

[1] This was grossly plagiarised by Dibden in a song, thus:

　"Hark! the boatswain hoarsely bawling—
　　By topsail sheets and haulyards stand, boys;
　Down top-gallants, down be hauling;
　　Down your stay-sails—hand, boys—hand, boys!
　　　Now set the braces—
　　　Don't make wry faces—
　　But the lee top-sail sheet let go.
　　　Starboard here, larboard there;
　　Turn your quid, take a swear—yo, yo, yo!"

　This is followed by two stanzas of Dibden's more than usually drivelling nonsense, where he pictures the eighteenth-century bluejacket as just a fighting, Poll-loving mixture of rum-bottle and punch-bowl! Another plagiarism of his, "Blow High, Blow Low," which he took, and beggared in the taking, from "Go High, Go Low," published in *Dairy-Maid*, at Edinburgh, in 1784, when he was thirteen years of age.

"The topsail-yards point to the wind, boys;
  See all clear to reef each course!
Let the foresheet go—don't mind, boys,
  Though the weather should be worse!
Fore and aft the spritsail-yard get;
  Reef the mizzen,—see all clear!
Hands up; each preventer-brace set;
  Man the foreyard,—cheer, lads, cheer!"

Now the dreadful thunder's roaring—
  Peal on peal contending clash!
On our heads fierce rain is pouring;
  In our eyes blue lightnings flash!
One wide water all around us;
  All above us one black sky;
Different deaths at once surround us—
  Hark! What means that dreadful cry?

"The fore-mast's gone!" cries ev'ry tongue out,
  "O'er the lee, twelve feet 'bove deck!
A leak beneath the chest-tree's sprung out!
  Call all hands to clear the wreck!
Quick the lanyards cut to pieces!
  Come, my hearts, be stout and bold!
Plumb the well—the leak increases,—
  Four feet of water in the hold!"

While o'er the ship wild waves are beating,
  We for wives or children mourn:
Alas, from hence there's no retreating!
  Alas, to them there's no return!
Still the leak is gaining on us!
  Both chain-pumps are choked below:
Heaven have mercy here upon us!—
  For only that can save us now.

O'er the lee-beam is the land, boys!
  Let the guns o'erboard be thrown!
To the pump come ev'ry hand, boys—
  See, our mizzen-mast is gone!
The leak we've found—it cannot pour fast;
  We've lightened her a foot or more:
Up and rig a jury-fore-mast—
  She rights! She rights, boys! We're off shore!

Now once more on joys we're thinking,
  Since kind Heaven has saved our lives!
Come, the can, boys!—Let's be drinking
  To our sweethearts and our wives.
Fill it up!—about ship wheel it;
  Close to our lips a brimmer join:
Where's the tempest now? Who feels it?
  None! The danger's drowned in wine.
                              G. A. STEVENS.

"NOW, BORNE IMPETUOUS O'ER."

Now, borne impetuous o'er the boiling deeps,
Her course to Attic shores the vessel keeps!
The pilots, as the waves behind her swell,
Still with the wheeling stern their force repel.
For this assault should either quarter feel,
Again to flank [1] the tempest she might reel:
The steersmen every bidden turn apply;
To right and left the spokes alternate fly.
Thus when some conquer'd host retreat in fear,
The bravest leaders guard the broken rear;

    .   .   .   .   .

So these direct the flying barque before
Th' impelling floods that lash her to the shore.

    .   .   .   .   .   .

High o'er the poop th' audacious seas aspire,
Uproll'd in hills of fluctuating fire.
As some fell conqueror, frantic with success,
Sheds o'er the nations ruin and distress;
So, while the watery wilderness he roams,
Incensed to sevenfold rage, the tempest foams;
And o'er the trembling pines, above, below,
Shrill through the cordage howls, with notes of woe.
Now, thunders driven from the burning zone,
Growl from afar a deafening, hollow groan!
The ship's high battlements, to either side
For ever rocking, drink the briny tide;

---

[1] When a vessel is running before a gale and in a heavy sea, as was
the case here, the greatest danger is when she swings nearly broadside-
on; which she sometimes does in consequence of a sea striking her
weather-quarter, and the helmsman not being smart enough to counter-
act the evil.

Her joints unhinged, in palsied languors play,
As ice dissolves beneath the noontide ray.
The skies, asunder torn, a deluge pour;
Th' impetuous hail descends in whirling show'r!
High up the masts, with pale and livid rays,
Amid the foam, portentous meteors blaze!
Th' ethereal dome, in mournful pomp array'd,
Now lurks behind impenetrable shade;
Now, flashing round intolerable light,
Redoubles all the terrors of the night!

   .   .   .   .   .   .

It seemed the wrathful angel of the wind
Had all the horrors of the skies combin'd;
And here, to one ill-fated ship opposed,
At once the dreadful magazine unclosed.
And lo! tremendous o'er the deep he springs,
Th' inflaming sulphur flashing from his wings!
Hark! his strong voice the dismal silence breaks!
Mad chaos from the chains of death awakes!
Loud and more loud the rolling peals enlarge,
And blue on deck their blazing sides discharge!
There, all aghast, the shivering wretches stood,
While chill suspense and fear congeal'd their blood.
Now in a deluge bursts the living flame,
And dread concussion rends th' ethereal frame!
Sick with convulsive groans from shore to shore,
And Nature, shuddering, feels the horrid roar!

FALCONER.[1]

THE COMING STORM.

THE day is low'ring: Stilly black
Sleeps the grim wave; while heaven's rack,
Dispers'd and wild 'twixt sea and sky,
Hangs like a shattered canopy!
There's not a cloud in that blue plain
But tells of storm to come or past:
Here flying loosely, as the mane
Of a young war-horse in the blast;
There roll'd in masses dark and swelling,
As proud to be the thunder's dwelling!
While some, already burst and riven,
Seem melting down the verge of heaven:

---

[1] See Appendix, p. 367.

As though the infant storm had rent
The mighty womb that gave him birth;
And, having swept the firmament,
Was now in fierce career for earth!

On earth 'twas yet all calm around—
A pulseless silence, dread, profound,
More awful than the tempest's sound.

The driver steer'd for Ormuz' bowers,
And moored his skiff till calmer hours;
The sea-birds, with portentous screech,
Flew fast to land: Upon the beach
The pilot oft had paus'd, with glance
Turn'd upward to that wild expanse.

MOORE.

PATROLLING BARNEGAT.

WILD, wild the storm, and the sea high running;
Steady the roar of the gale, with incessant undertone
    muttering;
Shouts of demoniac laughter fitfully piercing and
    pealing;
Waves, air, midnight, their savagest trinity lashing;
Out in the shadows there milk-white combs careering,
In beachy slush and sand spits of snow fierce slanting,
Where through the murk the easterly death-wind
    breasting,
Through cutting swirl and spray watchful and firm
    advancing.
(That in the distance!   Is that a wreck?   Is the red
    signal flaring?)
Slush and sand of the beach tireless till daylight wend-
    ing,
Steadily, slowly, through hoarse roar never remitting;
Along the midnight edge by those milk-white combs
    careering,
A group of dim, weird forms, struggling, the night
    confronting,
That savage trinity warily watching.

WHITMAN.

THE EQUINOX.

WHEN descends on the Atlantic
The gigantic
　　Storm-wind of the equinox,
Landward in his wrath he scourges
The toiling surges,
　　Laden with seaweed from the rocks.

From Bermuda's reefs; from the edges
Of sunken ledges
　　In some far-off, bright Azore;
From Bahama, and the dashing,
Silver-flashing
　　Surges of San Salvador;

From the tumbling surf, that buries
The Orkneyan skerries,
　　Answering the hoarse Hebrides;
And from wrecks of ships, and drifting
Spars, uplifting
　　On the desolate, rainy seas:

Ever drifting, drifting, drifting
On the shifting
　　Currents of the restless main;
Till in sheltered coves and reaches
Of sandy beaches
　　All have found repose again.
　　　　　　　　　　　LONGFELLOW.

SWEET AND LOW.

SWEET and low, sweet and low,
　　Wind of the western sea;
Low, low, breathe and blow,
　　Wind of the western sea.
Over the rolling waters go,
Come from the dying moon and blow,—
　　Blow him again to me;
While my little one, while my pretty one, sleeps.

Sleep and rest, sleep and rest,
   Father will come to thee soon;
Rest, rest on mother's breast,—
   Father will come to thee soon :

Father will come to his babe in the nest,—
Silver sails all out of the west,
   Under the silver moon :
Sleep, my little one; sleep, my pretty one,—sleep.

TENNYSON.

"YON' TIDES WITH CEASELESS SWELL."

YON' tides with ceaseless swell! yon' power that does
   this work!
Yon' unseen force, centripetal, centrifugal, through
   space's spread,
Rapport of sun, moon, earth, and all the constellations,
What are the messages by you from different stars to
   us?—what Sirius'?—what Capella's?
What central heart—and you the pulse—vivifies all?
   What boundless aggregate of all?
What subtle indirection and insignificance in you?
   What clue to all in you? What fluid, vast
   identity,
Holding the universe with all its parts as one—as sailing
   in a ship?
Last of ebb, and daylight waning,
Scented sea—cool landward; making, smells of sedge
   and salt incoming,
With many a half-caught voice sent up from the
   eddies,
Many a muffled confession, many a sob and whisper'd
   word,
As of speakers far or hid.
How they sweep down and out! How they mutter!
Poets unnamed—artists, greatest of any, with cherished
   last designs,
Love's unresponse, a chorus of age's complaints,
   hope's last words,
Some suicide's despairing cry, *Away to the boundless
   waste, and never again return.*
On to oblivion then!

On, on, and do your part, ye burying, ebbing tide!
On for your time, ye furious debauché!
And yet not you alone, twilight and burying ebb;
Nor you, ye lost designs alone—nor failures, aspira-
    tions;
I know, divine deceitful ones, your glamour's seeming;
Duly by you, from you, the tide and light again—duly
    the hinges turning,
Duly the needed discord—parts offsetting, blending,
Weaving from you, from Sleep, Light, Death itself,
The rhythmus of Birth Eternal.
Proudly the flood comes in, shouting, foaming,
    advancing;
Long it holds at the high, with bosom broad out-
    swelling,
All throbs, dilates—the farms, woods, streets of cities,
    workmen at work.
Mainsails, topsails, jibs, appear in the offing, steamers'
    pennants of smoke—and under the forenoon sun—
Freighted with human lives, gaily the outward-bound,
    gaily the inward-bound,
Flaunting from many a spar the flag I love.
By that long scan of waves, myself call'd back, resumed
    upon myself,
In ever crest some undulating light or shade, some
    retrospect.

.   .   .   .   .

Then last of all, caught from these shores, this hill,
Of you O tides, the mystic human meaning:
Only by law of you, your swell and ebb, enclosing me
    the same,
The brain that shapes, the voice that chants this song.
                         WHITMAN.

"TALL IDA'S SUMMIT.[1]"

TALL Ida's summit now more distant grew,
And Jove's high hill was rising to the view;
When on the larboard quarter they descry
A liquid column towering shoot on high.

[1] It appears to be pretty plain that in this description of a waterspout
at sea Falconer was drawing on his own experience.

The foaming base the angry whirlwinds sweep,
Where curling billows rouse the fearful deep.
Still round and round the fluid vortex flies,
Scattering dim night and horror through the skies!
This vast phenomenon, whose lofty head
In heaven immersed, embracing clouds o'erspread,
In spiral motion first, as seamen deem,
Swells when the raging whirlwind sweeps the stream.
(The swift volution and the enormous train
Let sages versed in Nature's lore explain.)
The horrid apparition still draws nigh,
And, white with foam, the whirling billows fly!
The guns are primed; the vessel northward veers,
Till her black battery on the column bears:
The nitre's fired; and, while the dreadful sound
Convulsive shakes the slumbering air around,
The watery volume, trembling to the sky,
Bursts down a dreadful deluge from on high!
Th' expanding ocean, trembling as it fell
Rolling in hills, disclosed th' abyss of hell.
But soon, this transient undulation o'er,
The sea subsided,—whirlwinds raged no more.

FALCONER.

"AFTER THE SEA-SHIP."

AFTER the sea-ship, after the whistling winds,
After the white-grey sails taut to their spars and
    ropes;
Below, a myriad-myriad waves hastening, lifting up
    their necks,
Tending in ceaseless flow toward the track of the
    ship;
Waves of the ocean bubbling and gurgling, blithely
    prying;
Waves, undulating waves, liquid, uneven, emulous
    waves,
Toward that whirling current—laughing and buoyant,
    with curves—
Where the great vessel, sailing and tacking, displaced
    the surface;
Larger and smaller waves in the spread of the ocean
    yearnfully flowing:

The wake of the sea-ship, after she passes, flashing and
    frolicsome under the sun;
A motley procession with many a fleck of foam and
    many fragments,
Following the stately and rapid ship—in the wake
    following.

WHITMAN.

SELF DEPENDENCE.[1]

WEARY of myself, and sick of asking
    What I am, and what I ought to be,
At the vessel's prow I stand, which bears me
    Forwards, forwards, o'er the starlit sea.

And a look of passionate desire
    O'er the sea and to the stars I send:
"Ye, who from my childhood up have calmed me,
    Calm me,—ah! compose me to the end.

"Ah, once more!" I cried, "Ye Stars, Ye Waters,
    On my heart your mighty charm renew;
Still, still let me, as I gaze upon you,
    Feel my soul becoming vast like you."

From the intense, clear, star-strewn vault of heaven,
    Over the lit sea's unquiet way,
In the rustling night air came the answer:
    "Wouldst thou *be* as these are?—*Live* as they.

"Unaffrighted by the silence around them,
    Undistracted by the sights they see,
These demand not that the things without them
    Yield them love, amusement, sympathy.

"And with joy the stars perform their shining,
    And the sea its long, moon-silvered roll;
For alone they live, nor pine with noting
    All the fever of some differing soul.

"Bounded by themselves and unobservant
    In what state God's other works may be,
In their own tasks all their powers pouring,
    These attain the mighty life you see."

[1] A good instance of the sea's mysterious influence over the human mind.

D

O airborne Voice! long since severely clear,
  A cry like thine in my own heart I hear:
"Resolve to be thyself; and know that he
  Who finds himself loses his misery."

MATTHEW ARNOLD.

"THE GENTLENESS OF HEAVEN."

THE gentleness of Heaven is on the sea:
  Listen—the mighty being is awake,
  And doth with his eternal motion make
A sound like thunder!—everlastingly.

WORDSWORTH.

"THE OCEAN WITH ITS VASTNESS."

THE Ocean with its vastness, its blue-green,
  Its ships, its rocks, its caves, its hopes, its fears—
  Its voice mysterious, which whoso hears
Must think on what will be and what has been.

KEATS.

"LINGER WHERE."

LINGER where the pebble-paven shore,
  Under the quiet, faint kisses of the sea,
  Trembles and sparkles as with ecstasy,
Possessing and possessed by all that is
Within that calm circumference of bliss.

SHELLEY.

"NOW LAY THINE EAR."

Now lay thine ear against this golden sand,
  And thou shalt hear the music of the sea,—
Those hollow tunes it plays against the land . . .
  Is't not a rich and wondrous melody?
I have lain hours, and fancied in its tone
I heard the languages of ages gone.

HOOD.

"THOU REMEMBER'ST."

THOU remember'st,
Since once I stood upon a promontory,
And heard a mermaid, on a dolphin's back,
Uttering such dulcet and harmonious breath,
That the rude sea grew civil at her song,
And certain stars shot madly from their spheres
To hear the sea-maid's music.

SHAKESPEARE.

THE FLOOR OF THE SEA.

THE floor is of sand, like the mountain-drift;
  And the pearl-shells spangle the flinty snow;
From coral-rocks the sea-plants lift
  Their bows, where tides nor billows flow:
The water is calm and still below,
  For the winds and waves are absent there:
And the sands are bright as the stars that glow
  In the motionless fields of upper air.
There, with its waving blade of green,
  The sea-flag streams through the silent water,
And the crimson leaf on the dulse is seen
  To blush like a banner bathed in slaughter;
There, with a light and easy motion,
  The fan-coral sweeps through the clear deep sea;
And the yellow and scarlet tufts of ocean
  Are bending, like corn on the upland lea.
And life, in rare and beautiful forms,
  Is sporting amidst those bowers of stone,
And is safe when the wrathful spirit of storms
  Has made the top of the wave his own.
And when the ship from his fury flies,
  Where the myriad voices of ocean roar,
When the wind-god frowns in the murky skies,
  And demons [1] are waiting the wreck on shore;

---

[1] Wreckers. Even in the latter part of the life of James Gates Percival, M.D.—an American geologist, scholar and poet, who was born in Berlin, Connecticut, 1795, and died at Hazelgrove, Illinois, 1856—there were professional wreckers on both sides of the Atlantic.

D 2

Then far below in the peaceful sea,
   The purple mullet and goldfish rove,
Where the waters murmur tranquilly
   Through the bending twigs of the coral-grove.

                              J. G. PERCIVAL.

"THE WORLD BELOW THE BRINE."

THE world below the brine—
Forests at the bottom of the sea, the branches and
   leaves,
Sea-lettuce, vast lichens, strange flowers and seeds, the
   thick tangle, openings, and pink turf;
Different colours, pale grey and green, purple, white,
   and gold, the play of light through the water;
Dumb swimmers there among the rocks, coral, gluten,
   grass, rushes and the ailment of the swimmers;
Sluggish existence grazing there suspended, or slowly
   crawling close to the bottom;
The sperm-whale at the surface, blowing air and spray,
   or disporting with his flukes;
The leaden-eyed shark, the walrus, the turtle, the hairy
   sea-leopard, and the string-ray;
Passions there, wars, pursuits, tribes, sight in those
   ocean-depths, breathing that thick-breathing air,
   as so many do.

                              WHITMAN.

ITS CREATURES, ITS MYTHS AND ITS TREASURES

O creatures marvellous, past the mind of man
  To compass, fathom or create;
Dumb, yet ye tell God's world-evolving plan
  From the embryo to a world beyond our date.
                                        ANONYMOUS.

And you, ye wondrous things of beauty and
    despair,
  With whom mankind once peopled Ocean's deeps,
Now gone your charms, pearl combs and golden
    hair—
  Your romance lost, where no tide ever sweeps.
                                        ANONYMOUS.

Full many a gem of purest ray serene
  The dark, unfathomed caves of ocean bear.
                                        GRAY.

THE STORMY PETREL.

A THOUSAND miles from land are we,
Tossing about on the roaring sea;
From billow to bounding billow cast,
Like fleecy snow on the stormy blast:
The sails are scattered about like weeds;
The strong masts shake like quiv'ring reeds;
The mighty cables and iron chains,
And the hull which all earthly strength disdains—
They strain and they crack; and, hearts of stone,
Their natural hard, proud strength disown.
Up and down, up and down!—
From the base of the wave to the billow's crown,
Amidst the flashing and feathery foam,
The stormy petrel finds a home;
A home—if such a place can be
For her who lives on the wide, wide sea,
On the craggy ice, in the frozen air,
And only seeking her rocky lair
To breed her young, and teach them to spring
At once o'er the waves on their stormy wing!
O'er the deep, o'er the deep!—
Where the whale and the shark and the swordfish sleep!
Outflying the blast and the driving rain,
The petrel telleth her tale in vain;
For the mariner curseth the warning bird,
That bringeth him news of the storm unheard.

B. W. PROCTER.

"HAST THOU HEARD OF A SHELL?"

HAST thou heard of a shell on the margin of ocean?—
　　Whose pearly recesses the echoes still keep,
Of the music it caught, when, with tremulous motion,
　　It joined in the concert pour'd forth by the deep.

Have fables not told us, when far inland carried
    To the waste sandy desert and dark ivied-cave,
In its musical chambers some murmurs have tarried,
    Which it learn'd long before of the wind and the wave?
                       BERNARD BARTON.[1]

"THE WHITE SEA-GULL."

THE white sea-gull, the wild sea-gull!—
    A joyful bird is he,
As he lies like a cradled thing at rest
    In the arms of a sunny sea!
The little waves rock to and fro,
    And the white gull lies asleep;
As the fisher's boat, with breeze and tide,
    Goes merrily over the deep.
The ship, with her fair sails set, goes by;
    And her people stand to note
How the sea-gull sits on the rocking waves,
    As still as an anchored boat.
The sea is fresh, and the sea is fair,
    And the sky calm overhead;
And the sea-gull lies on the deep, deep sea,
    Like a king in his royal bed!
                       MARY HOWITT.[2]

"BUT I HAVE SINUOUS SHELLS."

BUT I have sinuous shells of pearly hue
Within, and they that lustre have imbibed
In the sun's palace-porch, where, when unyoked,
His chariot wheels stand midway in the wave.
Shake one and it awakens; then apply
Its polished tips to your attentive ear,
And it remembers its august abodes,
And murmurs, as the ocean murmurs there.
                       LANDOR.

[1] "The Quaker Poet," born at Carlisle, Jan. 31, 1784, and died at Woodbridge, Suffolk, February 9, 1849. Nearly the whole of his working life was spent in Alexander's Bank, Woodbridge. Fitzgerald was a neighbour of his, and married his daughter Lucy. The main characteristics of his verse are fine feeling, beautiful fancy, and that didactic morality from which no minor poetry of his time was free.

[2] A contemporary of Bernard Barton, and, like him, a member of the Society of Friends—as was her husband, until he and she left it. They were known as William and Mary Howitt, and did some commendable literary work together.

"I HAVE SEEN A CURIOUS CHILD."

I HAVE seen
A curious child, who dwelt upon a tract
Of inland ground, applying to his ear
The convolution of a smooth-lipped shell;
To which, in silence hushed, his very soul
Listened intensely: And his countenance soon
Brightened with joy; for from within were heard
Murmurings, whereby the monitor expressed
Mysterious union with its native sea.

WORDSWORTH.

THE SEA-DIVER.

My way is on the bright blue sea,
  My sleep upon the rocking tide;
And many an eye has followed me
  Where billows clasp the worn seaside.

My plumage bears the crimson-blush,
  When ocean by the sun is kissed;
When fades the evening's purple flush,
  My dark wing cleaves the silver-mist.

Full many a fathom down beneath
  The bright arch of the splendid deep
My ear has heard the sea-shells breathe
  O'er living myriads in their sleep.

They rested by the coral throne,
  And by the pearly diadem,
Where the pale sea-grape had o'ergrown
  The glorious dwelling made for them.

At night, upon my storm-drenched wing,
  I poised above a helmless bark;
And soon I saw the shattered thing
  Had passed away and left no mark.

And when the wind and storm had done,
  A ship, that had rode out the gale,
Sunk down without a signal-gun,
  And none was left to tell the tale.

I saw the pomp of day depart,
    The cloud resign its golden crown,
When to the ocean's beating heart
    The sailor's wasted corse went down.

Peace be to those whose graves are made
    Beneath the bright and silver sea;
Peace that their relics there were laid
    With no vain pride and pageantry.

                                    LONGFELLOW.

TO A SEA-BIRD.

SAUNTERING hither on listless wings,
    Careless vagabond of the sea,
Little thou heedest the surf that sings,
The bar that thunders, the shale that rings,—
    Give me to keep thy company.

Little thou hast, old friend, that's new;
    Storms and wrecks are old things to thee;
Sick am I of these changes too;
Little to care for, little to rue,—
    I on the shore, and thou on the sea.

All of thy wanderings, far and near,
    Bring thee at last to shore and me;
All of my journeyings end them here,
This our tether must be our cheer,—
    I on the shore, and thou on the sea.

Lazily rocking on Ocean's breast,
    Something in common, old friend, have we;
Thou on the shingle seek'st thy nest,—
    I on the shore, and thou on the sea.

                                    BRET HARTE.

THE CHAMBERED NAUTILUS.

THIS is a ship of pearl, which, poets feign,
Sails the unshadowed main—
    The venturous bark that flings
    On the sweet summer wind its purpled wings
    In gulfs enchanted, where the siren sings,
        And coral reefs lie bare,—
        Where the cold sea-maids rise to sun their streaming
        hair.

Its webs of living gauze no more unfurl,—
Wrecked is the ship of pearl!
  And every chambered cell—
  Where its dim, dreaming life was wont to dwell,
  As the frail tenant shaped its growing shell—
    Before thee lies revealed,
    Its irised ceiling rent, its sunless crypt unsealed.

Year after year beheld the silent toil
That spread this lustrous coil;
  Still, as the spiral grew,
  He left the past year's dwelling for the new—
  Stole with soft step the shining archway through,
    Built up its idle door,
    Stretched in its last-found home and knew the old
      no more.

Thanks for the heavenly message brought by thee,
Child of the wandering sea,
  Cast from her lap, forlorn!
  From thy dead lips a clearer note is born
  Than ever Triton blew from wreathèd horn!
    While on mine ear it rings,
    Through the deep caves of thought I hear a voice
      that sings:

Build thee more stately mansions, O my soul!
As the swift seasons roll;
  Leave thy low-vaulted past;
  Let each new temple, nobler than the last,
  Shut thee from heaven with a dome more vast;
    Till thou at length art free,
    Leaving thine outgrown shell by life's unresting sea.
                O. W. HOLMES.

THE SEA-MEW.

How joyously the young sea-mew
Lay dreaming on the waters blue,
  Whereon our little bark had thrown
  A forward shadow,—the only one;
(But shadows ever man pursue.)

Familiar with the waves, and free
As if there own white foam were he;
   His heart, upon the heart of ocean,
   Lay learning all its mystic motion,
And throbbing to the throbbing sea:

And such a brightness in his eye,
As if the ocean and the sky
   Within him had lit up and nurst
   A soul, God gave him not at first,
To comprehend their majesty.
E. B. BROWNING.

TO THE MAN-OF-WAR BIRD.

THOU, who hast slept all night upon the storm,
Waking renew'd on thy prodigious pinions,
(Burst the wild storm! above it thou ascendest,
And rested on the sky, thy slave that cradled thee.);
Now a blue point, far, far in heaven floating,
As to the light emerging here on deck I watch thee,
(Myself a speck, a point on the world's floating vast.)

Far, far at sea,
After the night's fierce drifts have strewn the shore with
    wrecks,
With reappearing day, as now as happy and serene,
The rosy and elastic dawn, the flashing sun,
The limpid spread of air cerulean,
Thou also reappearest.

Thou born to match the gale (thou art all wings),
To cope with heaven and earth and sea and hurricane!
Thou ship of air that never furl'st thy sails,
Days, even weeks untired and onward, through spaces,
    realms gyrating,
At dusk that look'st on Senegal, at morn America;
That sport'st amid the lightning-flash and thunder-
    cloud:
In them, in thy experiences, had'st thou my soul,
What joys!—what joys were thine!
WHITMAN.

THE SILKIE[1] O' SULE SKERRIE.

An earthly nurrice[2] sits an' sings,
 An' aye she sings : "Bye, lilie-wean;
Little I ken my bairnis' fathèr,
 Far less the land whar maist he's seen."

Then up there rose at her bed-foot,
 And a grumlie guest was he:
"Here I am, thy bairnis' fathèr,
 Tho' I be not sae comelie.

"Upo' the land I am a man,
 A silkie i' yon' sounding sea;
An' when I'm far awa' frae land
 My dwelling is in Sule Skerriè."

"It was nae weel," quoth the young mothèr,
 "It was nae well, indeed," quoth she,
"That the Man-Silkie o' Sule Skerriè
 Should cum an' get a bairn ta me!"

Now he has taen a purse o' gowd
 An' he has put it on her knee,
Saying : "Gie thou ta me my little son,
 An' tak thee up thy nurrice-fee.

"An' it sall be on a summer's day,
 When the sun is hot on ev'ry stane,
That I will learn my little young son
 Ta swim in the saut sea faem.

"An' thou sall't marry a proud gunnèr,
 An' a proud gunnèr he's sure ta be;
An' the very first shot that he shoots out
 He'll shoot both my young son an' me."

ANONYMOUS.

[1] A seal. This old ballad is a short variant on the enchanting mermaid, with her usual yellow locks and comb of gold. But it goes further than merely to change the sex of the deceiver, for with the old idea of a siren-lover it blends that more strictly Teutonic conception, the man who, usually as the outcome of an unholy rite and pact, is doomed to be a beast or fish during a certain number of hours in every moon. [2] Nurse.

THE MERMAID.[1]

On Jura's heath how sweetly swell
    The murmurs of the mountain bee!
How softly mourns the wreathèd shell
    Of Jura's shore!—its parent sea.

But softer, floating o'er the deep,
    The mermaid's sweet, sea-soothing lay,
That charmed the dancing waves to sleep
    Before the bark of Colonsay.

Aloft the purple pennons wave,
    As parting gay from Crinan's shore;
From Morven's wars the seamen brave
    Their gallant chieftain homeward bore.

In youth's gay bloom, the brave Macphail
    Still blamed the lingering bark's delay;
For her he chid the flagging sail—
    The lovely Maid of Colonsay.

"And raise," he cried, "that song of love
    The maiden sung with tearful smile,
When first, o'er Jura's hills to rove,
    We left afar the lonely isle:

"'When on this ring of ruby-red
    Shall die,' she said, 'the crimson hue,
Know that thy favourite fair is dead,
    Or proves to thee and love untrue.'"

Now, lightly poised, the moving oar
    Disperses wide the foamy spray;
And, echoing far o'er Crinan's shore,
    Resounds the song of Colonsay:

    "Softly blow, thou western breeze,—
        Softly rustle past the sail;
    Soothe to rest the furrowy seas,
        Before my love, sweet western gale.

[1] The origin of this ballad was—Scott and others tell us—a traditional piece known as "Macphail of Colonsay and the Mermaid of Corrivrekin," the latter place being a dangerous passage between the islands of Scarba and Jura. It was written by Dr. John Leyden while working with Scott in gathering the material for the *Minstrelsy of the Scottish Border*, and was first published in that book. Leyden was the son of a Roxburghshire shepherd; he obtained an Edinburgh diploma in medicine, went to India, became a judge there and an Oriental scholar, and died there at the age of thirty-six.

Where the wave is tinged with red,
    And the russet sea-leaves grow,
Mariners, with prudent dread,
    Shun the shelving reefs below.

As you pass through Jura's sound,
    Bend your course by Scarba's shore,—
Shun—oh, shun the gulf profound
    Where Corrivrekin's surges roar !

If, from that unbottomed deep,
    With wrinkled form and wreathed train,
O'er the verge of Scarba's steep,
    The sea-smoke heaves his snowy mane ;

Oh, then, unwind his oozy coils,
    Sea-green sisters of the main !
And, in the gulf where ocean boils,
    Th' unwieldy, wallowing monster chain.

Softly blow, thou western breeze—
    Softly rustle past the sail ;
Soothe to rest the furrowed seas,
    Before my love, sweet western gale."

Thus, all to soothe the chieftain's woe,
    Far from the maid he loved so dear,
The song arose so soft and slow,
    He seemed her parting sigh to hear.

The lonely deck he paces o'er,
    Impatient for the rising day ;
And still, from Crinan's moonlit shore,
    He turns his eyes to Colonsay.

.   .   .   .

The moonbeams crisp the curling surge,
    That streaks with foam the ocean green ;
While forward still the rowers urge
    Their course, a female-form is seen.

The sea-maid's form, of pearly light,
    Is whiter than the downy spray ;
And round her bosom, heaving bright,
    Her glossy yellow [1] ringlets play.

[1] All over Northern Europe the mermaid was always given yellow hair—from the shores of the Baltic, where fair-haired people are the rule, to the western coasts of Ireland and France, where dark hair is the general thing ; and this seems to point to a common origin of all these legends.

Borne on a foamy crested wave,
    She reaches to the bending prow;
Then clasping fast the chieftain brave,
    She, plunging, seeks the deep below!

(Ah, long beside thy feignèd bier
    The monks their prayers of death shall say!
And long for thee the fruitless tear
    Shall weep the Maid of Colonsay!)

But downwards, like a powerless corse,
    The eddying waves the chieftain bear;
He only hears the mourning hoarse
    Of waters, murmuring in his ear.

The murmurs sink by slow degrees;
    No more the surges round him rave;
Lulled by the music of the seas,
    He lies within a coral cave.

In dreamy mood reclines he long,
    Nor dares his trancèd eyes unclose;
Till, warbling wild, the sea-maid's song
    Far in the crystal cavern goes—

Soft as that harp's unseen control,
    In morning dreams, which lovers hear;
Whose strains steal sweetly o'er the soul,
    But never reach the waking ear.

As sunbeams through the tepid air,
    When clouds dissolve the dews unseen,
Smile on the flowers that bloom more fair,
    And fields that glow with livelier green,—

So melting-soft the music fell,
    It seemed to soothe the fluttering spray—
"Say, heard'st thou not those wild notes swell!
    Ah, 'tis the song of Colonsay!"

Like one that from a fearful dream
    Awakes, the morning light to view,
And joys to see the purple beam,
    Yet fears to find the vision true,—

He heard that strain, so wildly sweet,
    Which bade his torpid languor fly;
He feared some spell had bound his feet,
    And hardly dared his limbs to try.

"This yellow sand, this sparry [1] cave,
  Shall bend thy soul to beauty's sway:
Canst thou the maiden of the wave
  Compare to her of Colonsay?"

Roused by that voice of silver sound,
  From the paved floor he lightly sprung;
And glancing wild his eyes around,
  Where the fair nymph her tresses wrung,

No form he saw of mortal mould—
  It shone like ocean's snowy foam;
Her ringlets waved in living gold,
  Her mirror crystal, pearl her comb.

Her pearly comb the siren took,
  And careless bound her tresses wild,—
Still o'er the mirror stole her look,
  As on the wondering youth she smiled.

Like music from the greenwood tree,
  Again she raised the melting lay:
"Fair warrior, wilt thou dwell with me,
  And leave the Maid of Colonsay?

"Fair is the crystal hall for me,
  With rubies and with emeralds set;
And sweet the music of the sea
  Shall sing, when we for love are met.

"How sweet to dance, with gliding feet,
  Along the level tide so green,
Responsive to the cadence sweet
  That breathes along the moonlit scene!

"And soft the music of the main
  Rings from the motley tortoise-shell;
While moonbeams, o'er the watery plain,
  Seem trembling in its fitful swell.

"How sweet, when billows heave their heads
  And shake their snowy crests on high,
Serene in ocean's sapphire-beds,
  Beneath the tumbling surge, to lie,—

"With tranquil step to trace the deep,
  Where pearly-drops of frozen dew
In concave shells unconscious sleep,
  Or shine with lustre, silver-blue!

[1] The crystalline mineral, spar.

E

"Then shall the summer sun, from far,
　　Pour through the wave a softer ray;
While diamonds, in a bower of spar,
　　At eve shall shed a brighter day.

"Nor stormy wind, nor wintry gale,
　　That o'er the angry ocean sweep,
Shall e'er our coral groves assail,
　　Calm in the bosom of the deep.

"Through the green meads beneath the sea,
　　Enamoured, we shall fondly stray,—
Then, gentle warrior, dwell with me,
　　And leave the Maid of Colonsay."

"Though bright thy locks of glistering gold,
　　Fair maiden of the foamy main,
Thy life-blood is the water cold,[1]
　　While mine beats high in every vein!

"If I, beneath thy sparry cave,
　　Should in thy snowy arms recline—
Inconstant as the restless wave—
　　My heart would grow as cold as thine."

As cygnet down, proud swelled her breast;
　　Her eye confessed the pearly tear;
His hand she to her bosom pressed—
　　"Is there no heart for rapture here?

"These limbs, sprung from the lucid sea—
　　Does no warm blood their currents fill?—
No heart-pulse riot, wild and free,
　　To joy and love's delirious thrill?"

"Though all the splendour of the sea
　　Around thy faultless beauty shine,
That heart that riots wild and free
　　Can hold no sympathy with mine.

"Those sparkling eyes, so wild and gay,
　　They swim not in the light of love;—
The beauteous Maid of Colonsay,
　　Her eyes are milder than the dove.

"Ev'n now, within the lonely isle,
　　Her eyes are dim with tears for me:
So canst thou think that siren-smile
　　Can lure my soul to dwell with thee?"

[1] *See* Introduction, p. xxxv.

An oozy film her limbs o'erspread;
  Uncoiled in length her scaly train;
She tossed, in proud disdain, her head,
  And lashed with webbèd fin the main.

"Dwell here alone!" the mermaid cried,
  "And view far-off the sea-nymphs play!
Thy prison-wall, the azure tide,
  Shall bar thy steps from Colonsay.

"Whene'er, like ocean's scaly brood,
  I cleave with rapid fin the wave,
Far from the daughters of the flood
  Conceal thee in this coral-cave.

"I feel my former soul return—
  It kindles at thy cold disdain.
Oh! has a mortal dared to spurn
  A daughter of the foamy main?"

She fled: Around the crystal cave
  The rolling waves rush on their road,
On the broad portal idly rave,
  But enter not the nymph's abode.

And many a weary night went by,
  As in the lonely cave he lay;
And many a sun rolled through the sky
  And poured its beams on Colonsay.

And oft, beneath the silvern moon,
  He heard afar the mermaid sing,
And oft, to many a melting tune,
  The shell-formed lyres of ocean ring.

And when the moon went down the sky,
  Still rose, in dreams, his native plain;
And oft he thought his love was by,
  And charmed him with some tender strain.

And, heart-sick, oft he waked to weep,
  When ceased that voice of silver-sound,
And thought to plunge into the deep
  That walled his crystal cavern round.

But still the ring of ruby-red
  Retained its vivid crimson hue;
And each despairing accent fled,
  To find his gentle love so true.

When seven long, lonely months were gone,
    The mermaid to his cavern came—
No more misshapen from the zone,
    But like a maid of mortal frame.[1]

"Oh, give to me that ruby ring,
    That on thy finger glances gay!
And thou shalt hear the mermaid sing
    The song thou lov'st of Colonsay."

"This ruby ring, of crimson grain,
    Shall on thy finger glitter gay,
If thou wilt bear me through the main,
    Again to visit Colonsay."

"Except thou quit thy former love,
    Content to dwell for.aye with me,
Thy scorn my finny frame might move
    To tear thy limbs amid the sea."

"Then bear me swift along the main,
    The lovely isle again to see;
And when I here return again,
    I plight my faith to dwell with thee."

An oozy film her limbs o'erspread,
    While slow uncoiled her scaly train;
With gluey fangs her hands were clad;
    She lashed with webbèd fin[2] the main.

He grasps the mermaid's scaly sides,
    As with broad fin she oars her way;
Beneath the silent moon she glides
    That sweetly sleeps on Colonsay.

Proud swelled her heart!   She deem'd at last
    To lure him with her silvern tongue;
And, as the shelving rocks they passed,
    She raised her voice and sweetly sung:

In softer, sweeter strains she sung,
    Slow-gliding o'er the moonlit bay!
When light to land the chieftain sprung,
    To hail the Maid of Colonsay.

---

[1] By these two lines, "I feel my former soul return," and her reassuming the mermaid-shape, Leyden points to a voluntary sort of werwolf ([2]) metamorphosis such as is seldom met with in legends of mermaids; and the unfinished nature of this, together with his repeated changes of tense—apparently for the sake of rhyme—form the main defects of his ballad.

Oh, sad the mermaid's gay notes fell,
   And sadly sank remote at sea!
So sadly mourned the writhèd shell
   Of Jura's shore, its parent sea.

.   .   .   .

And ever as the year returns,
   The charm-bound sailors know the day;
For sadly still the mermaid mourns
   The handsome Chief of Colonsay.

JOHN LEYDEN.

THE STORMY WINDS DID BLOW.[1]

ON a Friday morn, as we set sail,
   It was not far from land,
O there I spy'd a pretty fair maid,
   With a comb and a glass in her hand.

   And the stormy winds did blow,
      And the raging seas did roar,
   As we poor sailor-boys went to the top,
      And the land-lubbers laid them down below,
        below, below—
   And the land-lubbers laid them down below.

Then up spoke a boy of our gallant ship,
   And a well-speaking boy was he:
"My father and my mother they live in Portsmouth
     town,
   And to-night they will weep for me."

Then up spoke a man of our gallant ship,
   And a well-speaking man was he:
"I have a fair wife up in London town,
   And to-night she a widow will be."

Then up spoke the captain of our gallant ship,
   And a valiant man was he:
"For the want of a boat we all shall be drown'd,
   For she sunk to the bottom of the sea."

The moon shone bright, and the stars gave light,
   And my mother was looking for me;
She may look and weep with watery eyes,—
   She may look to the bottom of the sea.

[1] This song is almost word for word as I heard it sung by east coast fishermen some thirty years ago.

Three times round went our gallant ship,
    Full three times round went she;
Three times round and round she went,
    Then she sunk to the bottom of the sea.

ANONYMOUS.

THE DEMON LOVER.

"O WHAR hae ye been, my lang, lang love,
    These seven years past an' more?"
"O I am come to mind ye o' the vows
    Ye granted me before."

"Now hald your tongue o' former vows,
    For they wad cause sad strife;
O hald your tongue o' former vows,
    For I hae become a wife." [1]

He turn'd him right and roun' about,
    And tears blinded his e'e:
"I wad never hae trodden yon Irish groun'
    If it had not been for thee.

"I micht hae had a king's daughtèr,
    Far, far beyont the sea;
I micht hae had a king's daughtèr,
    Had I ne'er lovèd thee."

"An' if ye had nae king's daughtèr
    Your sel ye had to blame;
Ye micht hae taen the king's daughtèr,
    For ye ken'd that I was nane."

"O fause, fause vows o' womankind,
    An' fause is their fair bodiè!
I'd never hae trodden on Irish groun',
    But for the love o' thee."

"If I war to leave my husband dear
    And my twa babes also,
O whar hast thou to tak me to?—
    If with thee I shuld go."

"I hae seven ships upo' the sea;
    The eighth brought me to land,
Wi' four-an'-twenty brave marinèrs,
    An' music on ev'ry hand."

[1] Formerly supposed to have been the wife of an Aberdeen ship's carpenter, and here carried off by the spirit of her previous sailor-lover. In one form or another this ballad is common also to England and Ireland.

She has taken up her twa little babes,
 Kist them baith cheek an' chin :
"O fare ye weel, my ain twa babes,
 For I'll ne'er see ye agin."

She set her foot upo' the ship,—
 Nae mariners culd she behold;
But the sails they were o' the taffetil,
 And the masts o' the beaten gold.

They had nae sail'd a league, a league,
 A league but barely three,
Until she spy'd his cloven [1] foot,
 And she wept right bitterlie.

"O hald your tongue an' your din !" says he—
 "Of your weeping now let me be;
An' I'll show ye how the lilies grow
 On the banks o' Italie."

"O what hills are yon, yon pleasant hills,
 That the sun shines sweetly on?"
"O yon are the hills o' heaven," said he,
 "Whar ye will never win."

"O whaten a mountain is yon," said she.
 "All sae dreary wi' frost an' snow?"
"O yon is the mountain o' hell !" cried he,
 "Whar ye an' I will go."

And aye when she turn'd her roun' about,
 Aye taller he seem'd to be,
Till a' the tops o' the gallant ship
 Nae taller war than he.

He strack the topmast wi' his hand,
 The fore-mast wi' his knee;
An' he brak that gallant ship i' twain,
 An' sank her i' the sea.

ANONYMOUS.

[1] There are many seventeenth-century tales, both in verse and prose, of how a woman—a maid generally—was decoyed away by a seemingly gentleman-lover whose first indication of his true identity was a cloven foot: but this is the only instance I have found of the dual personality of Satan and a merman.

THE MERMAID.[1]

To yon fause stream that, by the sea,
  Hides mony an elf [2] and plum,[3]
And rives wi' fearful din the stanes,
  A witless knicht did come.

The day shines clear : Far in he's gane,
  Whar shells are silver bright;
Fishes war loupin' a' aroun'
  An' sparklin' to the light.

When, as he laved, sounds came sae sweet
  Frae ilka rock ajee [4] :
The brief [5] was out; 'twas him it doomed
  The mermaid's face to see.

Frae 'neath a rock sune, sune she rose,
  An' stately on she swam,
Stopped i' the midst, and becked and sang
  For him to stretch his han'.

Gowden glist the yellow links
  That roun' her neck she'd twine;
Her een war o' the skyie blue,
  Her lips did mock the wine.

The smile upon her bonnie cheek
  Was sweeter than the bee;
Her voice excell'd the birdie's sang
  Upon the birchen tree.

Sae couthie,[6] couthie did she look,
  And meikle had she fleeched [7];
Out shot his hand—alas ! alas !
  Fast in the swirl he screeched.

The mermaid leuched [8]; her brief was dane;
  The kelpie's blast was blawin' :
Fu' low she dived, ne'er cam' again;
  For deep, deep was the fawin' [9].

[1] This was first published by Finlay, in his *Scottish Ballads*, 1808. He said it "was recovered from the recitation of a lady, who heard it sung by the servants in her father's family above fifty years ago." Previous to that time, however, it appears to have been fairly well known along the Carrick coast of Ayrshire.   [2] Kelpies, *i. e.* water-spirits.   [3] A deep hole in a river.   [4] On one side.   [5] Doom, or sentence.   [6] Lovingly.   [7] Supplicated.   [8] Laughed.   [9] Flowing—meaning, probably, the ebb tide.

Aboon the stream his wraith was seen :
  Warlocks [1] tirl'd [2] lang at gloamin' :
That e'en was coarse ; the blast blew hoarse
  Ere lang the waves war foamin'.

ANONYMOUS.

THE RHYME OF THE ANCIENT MARINER.

AN ICE-BOUND SEA.

.   .   .   .   .

AND thus spake on that ancient man,
  The bright-eyed mariner.

"The ship was cheered, the harbour cleared ;
  Merrily did we drop
Below the kirk, below the hill,
  Below the lighthouse top.

"The sun came up upon the left,—
  Out of the sea came he ;
And he shone bright, and on the right
  Went down into the sea.

"Higher and higher every day,
  Till over the mast at noon——"
The Wedding-Guest here beat his breast,
  For he heard the loud bassoon.

.   .   .   .   .

And thus spake on that ancient man,
  The bright-eyed Mariner.

"And now the storm-blast came, and he
  Was tyrannous and strong :
He struck with his o'ertaking wings,
  And chased us south along.

"With sloping masts and dipping prow,—
As who pursued with yell and blow
Still treads the shadow of his foe,
  And forward bends his head—
The ship drove fast ; loud roared the blast,
  And southward aye we fled.

"And now there came both mist and snow ;
  And it grew wondrous cold ;
And ice, mast-high, came floating by,
  As green as emerald.

---

[1] Wizards   [2] Knocked.

"And through the drifts the snowy clifts
Did send a dismal sheen;
Nor shapes of men nor beasts we ken—
The ice was all between!

"The ice was here,—the ice was there,—
The ice was all around;
It cracked and growled and roared and howled,
Like noises in a swound!

"At length did come an albatross—
Through the fog it came:
As if it had been a Christian soul,
We hailed it in God's name.

"It ate the food it ne'er had eat,
And round and round it flew:
The ice did split, with a thunder-fit;
The helmsman steered us through!

"And a good south wind came up behind,—
The albatross did follow,
And every day, for food or play,
He came to the mariners' hollo.

"In mist or cloud, on mast or shroud,[1]
It perched for vespers nine;
Whiles all the night, through fog-smoke white,
Glimmered the white moonshine."

"God save thee, ancient Mariner,
From the fiends that plague thee thus!—
Why look'st thou so?"—"With my crossbow
I shot the Albatross."

.   .   .   .

"And I had done a hellish thing,
And it would work 'em woe;
For, all averred, I had killed the bird
That made the breeze to blow.
'Ah, wretch!' said they, 'the bird to slay,
That made the breeze to blow!'"

.   .   .   .   .

[1] It would be impossible for an albatross to perch on the mast or
shrouds fixed on a ship, and there are other such errors in this poem.
But it were a bootless, even an ungrateful, task to point out further
technical faults in a piece of nautical wonderment, so stark and weird
that it must go down the ages, an immortal, so long as man finds
interest in the sea.

A STAGNANT SEA.

"The fair breeze blew; the white foam flew;
The furrow fallowed free :
We were the first that ever burst
Into that silent sea !

"Down dropt the breeze; the sails dropt down,—
'Twas sad as sad could be;
And we did speak only to break
The silence of the sea.

"All in a hot and copper sky
The bloody sun, at noon,
Right above the mast did stand,
No bigger than the moon.

"Day after day, day after day
We stuck—nor breath nor motion—
As idle as a painted ship
Upon a painted ocean !

"Water, water everywhere—
And all the boards did shrink !
Water, water everywhere,
Nor any drop to drink !

"The very deep did rot.—O Christ,
That ever this should be !
Yea, slimy things did crawl with legs
Upon the slimy sea !

"About, about in reel and rout
The death fires danced at night,—
The water, like a witch's oils,
Burnt green and blue and white !

"And some in dreams assured were
Of the Spirit that plagued us so;
Nine fathom deep he had followed us
From the land of mist and snow.

"And every tongue, through utter drought,
Was withered at the root;
We could not speak, no more than if
We had been choked with soot.

"Ah, well-a-day, what evil looks
Had I from old and young !
Instead of the Cross, the albatross
About my neck was hung ! "

A GHOSTLY SAIL.

"There passed a weary time.   Each throat
Was parched, and glazed each eye.

.   .   .   .   .

"When, looking westward, I beheld
A something in the sky.

"At first it seemed a little speck,
And then it seemed a mist :
It moved and moved, and took at last
A certain shape, I wist.

.   .   .   .   .   .

"With throats unslaked, with black lips baked,
We could nor laugh nor wail;
Through utter drought all dumb we stood.
I bit my arm; I sucked the blood,
And cried—A sail, a sail !

"With throats unslaked, with black lips baked,
Agape they heard me call.
Gramercy ! they for joy did grin;
And all at once their breath drew in,
As they were drinking all.

"See, see, I cried, she tacks no more !
Hither to work us weal—
Without a breeze, without a tide,
She steadies with upright keel !

"The western wave was all aflame;
The day was well-nigh done :
Almost upon the western wave
Rested the broad, bright sun;
When that strange shape drove suddenly
Betwixt us and the sun.

"And straight the sun was flecked with bars,
(Heaven's Mother send us grace !)
As if through a dungeon-grate he peered
With broad and burning face.

"Alas! thought I—and my heart beat loud—
How fast she nears and nears!
Are those her sails that glance in the sun,
Like restless gossamers?

"Are those her ribs, through which the sun
Did peer, as through a grate?
And is that Woman all her crew?
Is that a Death?—And are there two?
Is Death that Woman's mate?

"Her lips were red; her looks were free;
Her locks were yellow as gold;
Her skin was as white as leprosy,—
The nightmare Life-in-Death was she,
Who thicks man's blood with cold.

"The naked hulk alongside came,
And the twain were casting dice.
'The game is done! I've won, I've won!'
Quoth she, and whistles thrice.

"The sun's rim dips; the stars rush out:
At one stride comes the dark;
With far-heard whisper, o'er the sea
Off shot the spectre-bark!

"We listened and looked sideways up,—
Fear at my heart, as at a cup,
My life-blood seemed to sip.
The stars were dim, and thick the night;
The steersman's face by his lamp gleamed white;
From the sails the dew did drip,—
Till cloam above the eastern bar
The hornèd moon, with one bright star
Within the nether tip.[1]

"One after one, by the star-dogged moon,
Too quick for groan or sigh,
Each turned his face, with a ghastly pang,
And cursed me with his eye.

"Four times fifty living men,
(And I heard nor sigh nor groan.)
With heavy thump, a lifeless lump,
They dropt down one by one."

[1] To make this possible the star would have to be this side of the moon, for we know that we cannot see through the moon.

.   .   .   .

"I fear thee, ancient Mariner!
I fear thy skinny hand!
And thou art long and lank, and brown
As is the ribbed sea-sand.

"I fear thee and thy glittering eye,
And thy skinny hand so brown."—
"Fear not, fear not, thou Wedding-Guest!
This body dropt not down.

"Alone, alone!—all, all alone!—
Alone on the wide, wide sea!
And never a saint took pity on
My soul in agony.

"The many men, so beautiful!
And they all dead did lie;
And a thousand-thousand slimy things
Lived on,—and so did I.

"I looked upon the rotting sea,
And drew my eyes away:
I looked upon the rotting deck,
And there the dead men lay."

.   .   .   .   .   .

"An orphan's curse would drag to hell
A spirit from on high;
But, oh, more horrible than that
Is the curse in a dead man's eye!
Seven days, seven nights I saw that curse,—
And yet I could not die."

COLERIDGE.

ARETHUSA.

ARETHUSA arose
From her couch of snows
In the Acrocerannian mountains,—
From cloud and from crag
With many a jag,
Shepherding her bright fountains.

The beard and the hair
Of the river-god were
Seen through the torrent's sweep,
As he followed the light
Of the fleet nymph's flight
To the brink of the Dorian deep.

"Oh, save me ! Oh, guide me !
And bid the deep hide me !
For he grasps me now by the hair ! "
The loud Ocean heard,
To its blue depths stirred,
And divided at her prayer :
And under the water
The Earth's white daughter
Fled like a sunny beam ;
Behind her descended
Her billows, unblended
With the brackish Dorian stream.
Like a gloomy stain
On the emerald main,
Alpheus rushed behind,—
As an eagle pursuing
A dove to its ruin
Down the streams of the cloudy wind.

Under the bowers
Where the Ocean Powers
Sit on their pearlèd thrones,
Through the coral woods
Of the weltering floods,
Over heaps of unvalued stones,
Through the dim beams—
Which amid the streams
Weave a network of coloured light—
And under the caves—
Where the shadowy waves
Are as green as the forest's night—
Outspeeding the shark
And the swordfish dark,
Under the ocean-foam,
And up through the rifts
And the mountain-clifts,
They passed to their Dorian home.

And now from their fountains
In Enna's mountains,
Down one vale—where the morning basks—
Like friends, once parted,
Grown single-hearted,
They ply their watery tasks.
At sunrise they leap
From their cradles steep
In the cave of the shelving hill;
At noontide they flow,
Through the woods below
And the meadows of asphodel;
And at night they sleep
In the rocking deep
Beneath the Ortygian shore,—
Like the spirits that lie
In the azure sky,
When they love but live no more.[1]

SHELLEY.

MERMAIDS AND MERMEN.

Mermaids.

FATHOMS deep beneath the wave,
  Stringing beads of glistening pearl;
Singing the achievements brave
  Of many an old Norwegian earl;
Dwelling where the tempest's raving
  Falls as light upon our ear
As the sigh of lover, craving
  Pity from his lady dear,—
Children of Thule, we,
From the deep caves of the sea,
As the lark springs from the lea,
Hither come to share your glee.

Mermen.

From reining of the water-horse,
  That bounded till the waves were foaming,
Watching the infant tempest's course,
  Chasing the sea-snake in its roaming;

[1] The Greek fable is that Alpheus, a river-god, fell in violent love with Arethusa, a nereid. She disdained him; he pursued her; and Diana, to save the nymph, turned her into a fountain and Alpheus into a river. Greek legends have many instances of such changes.

From winding charge-notes on the shell,
  When the huge whale and swordfish duel;
Or tolling shroudless seamen's knell,
  When the winds and waves are cruel,—
Children of wild Thule, we
Have ploughed such furrows on the sea,
As the steer draws on the lea,—
And hither we come to share your glee.

Mermaids and Mermen.

We heard you in our twilight caves,
  A hundred fathoms deep below;
For notes of joy can pierce the waves
  That drown each sound of war and woe.
Those who dwell beneath the sea
  Love the sons of Thule so well;
Thus, to aid your mirth, bring we
  Dance and song and sounding shell.
Children of dark Thule, know
Those who dwell by haaf and voe,
Where your daring shallops row,
Come to share the festal row.

                        SCOTT.

THE SEA FAIRIES.

SLOW sailed the weary mariners and saw,
Betwixt the green brink and the running foam,
Sweet faces, rounded arms, and bosoms prest
To little harps of gold: And while they mused,
Whispering to each other, half in fear,
Shrill music reached them on the middle sea.

Whither away, whither away, whither away? Fly no
    more!
Whither away from the high green field and the happy
    blossoming shore?
Day and night to the billows the fountain calls;
Down shower the gambolling waterfalls
From wandering o'er the lea;
Out of the live green heart of the dells
They freshen the silvery crimson shells;
And, thick with white bells, the clover-hill swells
High over the full-toned sea.
Oh, hither—come hither and furl your sails,—

F

Come hither to me, and to me;
Hither, come hither and frolic and play :
Here it is only the mew that wails.
We will sing to you all the day,—
Mariners, mariners, furl your sails;
For here are the blissful downs and dales;
And merrily, merrily carol the gales;
And the spangle dances in bight and bay;
And the rainbow forms and flies on the land,
Over the islands free :
And the rainbow lives in the curve of the sand—
Hither, come hither and see—
And the rainbow hangs on the poising wave;
And sweet is the colour of cove and cave,
And sweet shall your welcome be.
Oh, hither, come hither and be our lords,—
For merry brides are we.
We will kiss sweet kisses, and speak sweet words. ,
Oh, listen, listen, your eyes shall glisten
With pleasure and love and jubilee !
Oh, listen, listen, your eyes shall glisten,
When the sharp, clear twang of the golden chords
Runs up the ridged sea !
Who can light on as happy a shore,
All the world o'er—all the world o'er?
Whither away?   Listen and stay.—Mariner, mariner,
        fly no more !

                                        TENNYSON.

THE FORSAKEN MERMAN.

Come, dear children, let us away,—
    Down and away below !
Now my brothers call from the bay;
    Now the great winds shoreward blow;
    Now the salt tides seaward flow;
Now the wild, white horses play,
Champ and chafe and toss in the spray.
Children dear, let us away—
This way, this way !

Call her once, before you go—
    Call once yet !
In a voice that she will know,—
    "Margaret ! Margaret !"

Children's voices should be dear
(Call once more) to a mother's ear;
Children's voices wild with pain—
Surely, she will come again!
Call her once, and come away—
This way, this way. '
"Mother, dear, we cannot stay;
The wild, white horses foam and fret."
"Margaret! Margaret!"

Come, dear children,—come away down.
   Call no more!
One last look at the white-walled town,
   And the little, grey church on the windy hill,
Then come down.
   She will not come, though you call all day.—
   Come away! Come away!

  Children dear, was it yesterday
   We heard the sweet bells over the bay?—
   In the caverns where we lay,
Through the surf and through the swell,
The far-off sound of a silver bell?—
Sand-strewn caverns, cool and deep,
Where the winds are all asleep;
Where the spent lights quiver and gleam;
Where the salt weed sways in the stream;
Where the sea-beasts, ranged all round
Feed in the ooze of their pasture-ground;
Where the sea-snakes coil and twine,
Dry their mail and bask in the brine;
Where great whales come sailing by,
Sail and sail, with unshut eye,
   Round the world for ever and aye.
   When did music come this way,
   Children dear, was it yesterday?

   Children dear, was it yesterday
   (Call yet once) that she went away?
Once she sat with you and me
On a red-gold throne in the heart of the sea,
And the youngest sat on her knee.
She combed its bright hair, and she tended it well —
When down swung the sound of a far-off bell.

F 2

She sighed.   She looked up through the clear, green
    sea.
She said—"I must go; for my kinsfolk pray
In the little, grey church on the shore to-day.
'Twill be Easter-time in the world.   Ah, me!
And I lose my poor soul, Merman, here with thee."
I said—"Go up, dear heart, through the waves:
Say thy prayer, and come back to the kind sea-caves."
    She smiled.   She went up through the surf in the
        bay.
    Children dear, was it yesterday?

Children dear, were we long alone?—
"The sea grows stormy," the little ones moan.
Long prayers—I said—in the world they say.
"Come," I said; and we rose through the surf in the
    bay.
We went up the beach, by the sandy down
Where the sea-stocks bloom, to the white-walled
    town,—
Through the narrow, paved streets, where all was still,
To the little, grey church on the windy hill.
From the church came a murmur of folk at their
    prayers;
But we stood without, in the cold-blowing airs.
We climbed on the graves, on the stones worn with
    rains,
And we gazed up the aisle through the small, leaded
    panes.
    She sate by the pillar.   We saw her clear.
    "Margaret, hist!—Come quick!—We are here.
    Dear heart," I said, "we are long alone,—
    The sea grows stormy—the little ones moan."
But, ah, she gave me never a look!
For her eyes were sealed to the holy Book.
Loud prays the priest: shut stands the door.—
Come away, children,—call no more;
Come away—come down—call no more.

Down, down, down,
    Down to the depths of the sea!
She sits at her wheel in the humming town,
    Singing most joyfully.
Hark what she sings—"O joy! O joy!
For the humming street and the child with its toy;

For the priest and the bell and the holy well;
   For the wheel where I spun,
   And the blessèd light of the sun ! "
And so she sings her fill—
   Singing most joyfully ;
Till the shuttle falls from her hand,
  And the whizzing wheel stands still.
She steals to the window and looks at the sand,
   And over the sand at the sea ;
   And her eyes are set in a stare,
    And anon there breaks a sigh,
   And anon there drops a tear
    From a sorrow-clouded eye,
And a heart sorrow-laden,—
   A long, long sigh
For the cold, strange eyes of a little mermaiden
   And the gleam of her golden hair.

   Come away—away, children.
   Come, children—come down.
    The hoarse wind blows colder ;
   Lights shine in the town.
   She will start from her slumber,
    When gusts shake the door ;
   She will hear the winds howling,
    Will hear the waves roar.
   We shall see, while above us
    The waves roar and whirl,
   A ceiling of amber,
    A pavement of pearl ;
   Singing—" Here came a mortal,
    But faithless was she :
   And alone dwell for ever
    The Kings of the Sea."

   But, children, at midnight,
    When soft the winds blow,—
   When clear falls the moonlight,—
    When spring-tides are low,—
   When sweet airs come seaward,
    From heaths starred with broom,
   And high rocks throw mildly
    On the blanched sands a gloom—

Up the still glistening beaches,
  Up the creeks we will hie,
Over banks of bright seaweed,
  The ebb-tide leaves dry.
We will gaze, from the sand-hills,
  At the white, sleeping town,—
At the church on the hill-side,
  And then come back down :
Singing—"There dwells a loved one;
  But cruel is she.
She left lonely for ever
  The Kings of the Sea ! "
MATTHEW ARNOLD.

"METHOUGHT I SAW."

METHOUGHT I saw a thousand fearful wrecks,
A thousand men that fishes gnawed upon,
Wedges of gold, great anchors, heaps of pearl,
Inestimable stones, unvalued jewels,
All scattered in the bosom of the sea.
Some lay in dead men's skulls; and in those holes,
Where eyes did once inhabit, there were crept,
As 'twere in scorn of eyes, reflecting gems
That woo'd the slimy bottom of the deep,
And mocked the dead bones that lay scattered by.
SHAKESPEARE.

THE TREASURES OF THE DEEP.

WHAT hid'st thou in thy treasure caves and cells,
  Thou hollow sounding and mysterious Main?
Pale glistening pearls and rainbow-coloured shells,
  Bright things which gleam unrecked of and in vain !—
  Keep, keep thy riches, melancholy Sea !
  We ask not such from thee.

Yet more,—thy depths have more ! What wealth
    untold
Far down, and shining through their stillness, lies !
Thou hast the starry gems, the burning gold,
  Won from ten thousand argosies !
    Sweep o'er thy spoils, thou wild and wrathful
      Main !
    Earth claims not these again.

Yet more,—thy depths have more! Thy waves have
   rolled
Above the cities of a world gone by;
Sand hath filled up the palaces of old,
   Seaweed o'er grown the halls of revelry.
      Dash o'er them, Ocean, in thy scornful play!
      Man yields them to decay.

Yet more,—thy billows and thy depths have more!
   High hearts and brave are gathered to thy breast;
They hear not now the booming waters roar,—
   The battle-thunders will not break their rest.
      Keep thy red gold and gems, thou stormy wave!
      Give back the true and brave:

Give back the lost and lovely!—those for whom
   The place was kept at board and hearth so long,
The prayer went up, through midnight's breathless
      gloom,
   And the vain yearning woke 'midst festal song.
      Hold fast thy buried isles, thy towers o'erthrown:
      But all is not thine own.

To thee the love of women hath gone down;
   Dark flow thy tides o'er manhood's noble head,
O'er youth's bright locks and beauty's flowery crown.
   Yet must thou hear a voice: Restore the dead—
      Earth shall reclaim her precious things from thee—
      Restore the dead, thou Sea!
                FELICIA HEMANS.[1]

[1] The daughter of George Browne, a Liverpool merchant of Irish
extraction. Her mother was of Italio-German blood; so that Felicia
had three nationalities in her veins, the ways of a fourth in her bringing
up and education, and became a Nature worshipper in her childhood in
North Wales, where reverses of fortune compelled her father to retire.
At the age of fifteen she published her first book, at eighteen her second,
and at once married Capt. Hemans, an army man whose health had
been shattered in the Peninsular campaign. After six years of unhappy
married life, they parted for ever; she spent the remainder of her life
in bringing up and educating her children, and in writing poetry.
Amongst her friends were Scott, Wordsworth, Campbell, Archbishop
Whately, Heber and others. She was an enthusiast in music, and was
proficient in four foreign languages. She had the "fatal facility" of
the highly talented verse-makers whose work falls just short of the
divine touch of transmutation. Without any particular force or
originality she has left a few lyrics, the natural sweetness of which,
combined with their "reflected essence of truth," ensures them a long
life in English poetry.

ITS MEN, ITS SHIPS AND ITS WRECKS

Let him who knows not how to pray go to sea.
OLD PROVERB.

A surly boatman, rough as seas and winds.
PRIOR.

Some stately ship that from afar
Shone sudden, like a star,
With all her bravery on.
MILMAN.

Full fathom five my father lies:
Of his bones are coral made;
Those are pearls that were his eyes:
Nothing of him that doth fade,
But doth suffer a sea-change
Into something rich and strange.
Sea-nymphs hourly ring his knell:
Hark! now I hear them,—
Ding, dong, bell.
SHAKESPEARE.

CARRYING PYLGRYMS.[1]

Men maye leve all gamys
That sayle unto St. Jamys; [2]
For many a man itt gramys,[3]
 When they begin to sayle.
For when they have to take the sea
Att Sandwyche, or att Wynchylsea,
Att Bristowe, or where itt maye bee,
 Theyr herts begyn to fayle.

Anone the mastyr ordereth faste
To hys shippe-men in all the hast,[4]
To dresse hem sonne about the maste,
 Ther takelyng to make.[5]
With "Howe! hissa!" [6] then they cry:
"What, howe, mate, thou stondst to ny; [7]
Thy felowe maye nat hayle thee hye!"
 Thus they begyn to crake.[8]

A boy, or twaine, anone upsteyen [9]
And overthwart the sayleyerde lyen;
"Y howe! taylia!" [10] the remenaunt cryen,
 And pull with all thyre myght.
"Bestowe the bote,[11] boteswayne, anone,
That our pylgryms [12] maye pley theron;
For som ar lyke to coughe and grone,
 Ere itt bee full mydnyght.

"Hale the bowleyne! Nowe vere the sheete!
Cooke, make redy anone our mete,—
Our pylgryms have noe lust to etc;
 I pray God yeve hem rest!

[1] This is probably one of the oldest sea-songs in the language; it appears to date from about the middle of the fifteenth century, and, judging by phrases, it must have been written originally by a sailor. [2] During the fifteenth century there was much carrying of English pilgrims to the shrine of St. James of Compostella, whose great day was July 25th. [3] Grieves. [4] Speed. [5] Get tackling ready. [6] "Ho, hoist!" [7] He stands too near for the next man to be able to haul properly. [8] Cry out, as seamen always do when hauling. [9] Go up. [10] "Yo-ho, tally!" i. e. make fast. [11] and [12] Stow the boat; make things ship-shape for the pilgrims to lie down.

Goe to the helme! What, howe, no nere![1]
Steward, felowe, a pot of bere!"
"Ye shall have 't, sir, with goode chere,
    Anone all of the best."

"Y howe!—trussa![2] Hayle in the breyles!
Thou haylest nat! Bye God, thou fayles![3]
O see howe wel owre goode shippe sayles!"
    And thus they saie among.
"Hayle in the wartake!"[4] "Itt shall be done!"
"Steward! cover the borde[5] anone,
And sett bred and salt theron—
    And tary nat to long."

Then cometh onne and seyth "Bee mery,—
Ye shall have a storme or a pery."[6]
"Holde thou thy pese![7] Thou canst no whery![8]
    Thou medlyst wondyr sore!"
Thys menewhyle the pylgryms lye,
And have theyr bowlys faste them wye,
And cry aftyr hott malvesy—
    "Thou helpe for to restore."

And som wold have a saltyd tost,
For they myght ete neyther sode ne rost;[9]
A man myght sonne paie for theyr cost,
    As for onne daye or twaine.
Som laydes ther, bookys on theyr kne,
And rede soe long they myght nat see:
"Allas, myne hede woll cleve in thre!"[10]
    Thus seyth another certayne.

Then commeth owre owner, lyke a lorde,
And speketh manye a royall worde,
And dresseth hym to the hygh borde[11]
    To see all thyngs be wel.

---

[1] No closer to the wind. [2] Probably "Truss the yard"—*i. e.* square it, so that the truss bears its weight more. [3] Fails. [4] A large rope. [5] If tablecloths were then used aboard-ship, which is very doubtful, this must have meant put food on the table—a phrase with that meaning is sometimes met with in old chronicles. [6] A squall. [7] and [8] Telling the pilgrim to hold his peace, as he could not be wearied, and should not meddle so wondrously. [9] Boiled or roast. [10] A severe headache. [11] Goes on to the poop to look on the decks below.

Anone hee calleth a carpentere,
And biddyth hym bryng with hym hys gere [1]
To make the cabans here and ther,
    With manye a febyll [2] cell.

A sak of strawe wer ther ryght goode,
For som must lyg [3] them in theyr hood : [4]
I had as lefe bee in a woode
    Without mete or drynk.
For when that wee sall goe to bedde
The pumpe [5] was ny oure beddes hede—
A man wer as goode to bee dede,
    As smel therof the stynk. [6]

                    Anonymous.

IN PRAIS OF SEAFARYNGE MEN : IN HOPE OF GOODE FORTUNE. [7]

Whoe sekes the waye to win renowne,
    Or flyes with wynges of his hertes fyre;
Whoe sekes to weare the lawrel crowne,
    Or hath the mynd that wold aspire—
        Lett him hys native soylle eschew,
        Lett him goe raynge and seke a newe.

Eche hawtie herte is wel contente
    With everie chaunce that shall betyde;
Noe hap can hynder hys intente;
    Hys stedfoot standes, thogh fortune slyde.
        "The sunne," quoth hee, "doth shine as wel
        Abrode, as erst wher I did dwell."

In chaynge of streams eche fish can range,
    Eche fowle contente with everie ayre,
Eche hawtie herte knowe noght of change,
    Nor bee nat dround in depe despaire :
        Wherfor I judg al landes aleeke
        To hawtie hertes that fortune seke.

[1] Gear-tools, still used aboard-ship generally. [2] A hurriedly-built cabin, such as was still built for passengers, particularly pilgrims in the East, till the maritime laws of the past century put an end to such things. [3] and [4] Lie in their clothes ; in the north of England "lig" is still used in this sense. [5] and [6] The stench coming up the pump from the bilges ; the less a vessel leaks, the more her bilge-water stinks.

[7] By a note at the end of this song in the Sloane MS. in the British Museum, it would appear that the writer was either one of Sir Richard Grenville's party of discoverers in 1585, or the piece was written in reference to that voyage.

To passe the seaes som thinkes a toylle;
  Som thinkes itt strange abrode to rome;
Som thinkes itt grefe to leve theyr soille,
  Theyr parents, cynsfolke and theyr whome.
    Think soe whoe liste, I leke itt not;
    I must abrode to trie my lott.

Whoe liste att whome att carte to drudge,
  And carke and care for worldlie trishe; [1]
With buckld sheoes lett hym goe trudge,
  Instead of launce [2] a whipp to slishe.
    A mynd soe base hys kind wil showe—
    Of caronne sweete to feed a crowe. [3]

If Jasonne of that mynd had toylld,
  The Gresions, when they cam to Troye,
Had never soe the Trojians foylde,
  Nor never caused them suche anoye.
    Wherfor whoe wysh maye lyve att whome :
    To purches fame I wil goe rome.

ANONYMOUS.

SEA FARDINGERS : THEYR EVILL FORTUNE.

WHAT pen can well reporte the plighte
  Of those that travell on the seaes?
To pas the werie wynters nighte,
  With stormie clouds, wisshynge for ease;
    With waves that tosse them to and fro—
    Theyr pore estate is hard to showe.

When boisteryng wynds begin to roar
  On cruell coasts, from haven wee,
The foggie mysts soe dimes the shore,
  The rocks and sands wee maye not see;
    Nor have nae roome on seaes to trie, [4]
    But praie to God, and yeld to die.

When shauldes [5] and sandie bankes apeare,
  What pilott can direct his course?
When fomynge tides drift us soe nere,
  Allas ! what fortun can bee worse?

---

[1] Tiash. [2] Learn to crack a whip. [3] The only meaning that one can see in this line is : carrion sweet enough—good enough—for a crow, which is the least particular about its food amongst the birds of prey. It may also mean that to put high adventures before a grovelling mind would be as good—sweet—food to a crow, i.e. a pearl to a pig.
[4] No sea room in which to handle the vessel. [5] Shoals.

Then ankers' haald must bee our staye,
Or ellce wee falle into decaye.

Wee wander still from loffe to lie,[1]
And fynd noe stedfast wynd to blowe;
Wee still remaine in jeopardie—
Eche perilos poynt is hard to showe :
In tyme wee hope to fynd redresse,
That long have lived in hevines.

O pinchynge, werie, lothsom lyfe !—
Whoe travell still in far exsylle,
The dangers grete on seaes bee ryfe,
Whose recompence doth yeld but toylle.
O Fortun, graunte mee mie desyre !—
A hapie end I doe requyre.

When freats and states [2] have had theyr fill,
And gentill calm the cost wil clere,
Then hawtie hertes shall have theyr wil,
That long have wept with mournyng chere;
And leve the seaes, with theyr anoye,
Att home att ease to live in joy.

ANONYMOUS.

THE GREENLAND SAILOR'S ADVICE.[3]

You merchant men of Billingsgate,
I wonder you can thrive;
You get your men for six months,
And pay them for but five !
But long as water runs downhill,
And tides do ebb and flow,
I'll no more to Greenland sail—no, no, no !

Our drink it is fair water,
That floweth from the rocks;
And as for other dainties—
We eat both bear and fox.
They boil our biscuits in whale-oil,
All to increase our woe :
So I'll no more to Greenland go—no, no, no !

[1] From windward to leeward.   [2] Frets and bad weather conditions.
[3] Allowing for a little exaggeration this song appears to be a good
example of how matters were conducted in Greenland whalers a hundred
to a hundred and fifty years ago, and in that only lies its value.

Our captains and commanders
    Are valiant men and stout;
They've fought in France and Flanders,
    And never would give out:
They beat us men like stock-fish,
    All to increase our woe:
So I'll no more to Greenland go—no, no, no!

In storms we must stand to it,
    When thundering tempests rage,
When cables snap and the masts do split,
    And the briny seas ingage;
Whilst sable blackness spreads its veil,
    All to increase our woe:
Then I'll no more to Greenland go—no, no, no!

Testy Neptune's mounting waves
    Still o'er our hatches tower;
Each minute threatens silent graves,
    For fishes to devour,
Or be entomb'd by some vast whale,
    And there to end our woe:
So I'll no more to Greenland go—no, no, no!

To face the cold north-eastern winds,
    Whilst shrouds and tackle roar;
And man our racking pinnace,
    Which seas mountain-high bore:
To larboard, starboard, tack we trail,
    Our joints benumb'd with snow:
But I'll no more to Greenland go—no, no, no!

Abaft, before—helm a-lee!
    All hands aloft! they cry;
When straight there comes a rolling sea
    That mounts us to the sky.
Like drownèd rats, we cordage hail,
    Whilst serene we've strength to go:
Then I'll no more to Greenland sail—no, no, no!

For if we faint or falter
    To ply our cruel work,
The boatswain with a halter
    Doth beat us like a Turk:
Whilst we in vain our case bewail,
    He does increase our woe:
So I'll no more to Greenland go—no, no, no!

Then to take our lading in
  We moil like Angiers slaves;
And if we to complain begin,
  The capstan lash [1] we have,—
A cursèd cat with thrice three tails
  Doth much increase our woe:
So I'll no more to Greenland go—no, no, no!

And when we faint, to bring us back
  They give us broth so strong,
The which does not creepers [2] lack
  To usher it along;
With element which smells so stale,
  All to increase our woe:
But I'll no more to Greenland go—no, no, no!

Therefore young men I all advise,
  Before it is too late;
And then you'll say that you are wise
  By mending of your fate—
The which your rashness might entail
  For to assist your woe:
So I'll no more to Greenland go—no, no, no!

                       ANONYMOUS.

NEPTUNE'S RAGING FURY: OR THE GALLANT SEAMEN'S SUFFERINGS.

    YOU gentlemen of England,
      That live at home at ease,
    Ah! little do you think upon
      The dangers of the seas;
    Give ear unto the mariners,
      And they will plainly show,
    The cares and the fears
      When the stormy winds do blow.

    All you that will be seamen
      Must bear a valiant heart,
    For when you come upon the seas,
      You must not think to start;

[1] On merchant-craft, men were lashed to the capstan for the infliction of "the cat"; on men-o'-war a grating was used.   [2] Most likely cockroaches—very common in ships' galleys—and weevils from stale biscuits which had been put into the broth.

Nor once to be faint-hearted,
  In hail, rain, blow or snow;
Nor to think for to shrink,
  When the stormy winds do blow.

The bitter storms and tempests
  Poor seamen must endure
Both day and night, with many a fight,—
  We seldom rest secure:
Our sleep it is disturbèd
  With visions strange to know,
And with dreams, on the streams,
  When the stormy winds do blow.

In claps of roaring thunder,
  Which darkness doth enforce,
We often find our ship to stray
  Beyond our wonted course;
Which causeth great distractions,
  And sinks our hearts full low,—
'Tis in vain to complain
  When the stormy winds do blow.

Sometimes in Neptune's bosom
  Our ship is tost on waves,
And every man expecting
  The sea to be their graves:
Then up aloft she mounteth,
  And down again so low,—
'Tis with waves, O with waves!
  When the stormy winds do blow.

Then down again we fall to prayer,
  With all our might and thought;
When refuge all doth fail us,
  'Tis that must bear us out;
To God we call for succour,
  For He it is, we know,
That must aid us and save us,
  When the stormy winds do blow.

The lawyer and the usurer
  That sit in gowns of fur,.
In closets warm, can take no harm,—
  Abroad they need not stir;

When winter fierce with cold doth pierce,
  And beats with hail and snow,
We are sure to endure,
  When the stormy winds do blow.

We bring home costly merchandize
  And jewels of great price,
To serve our English gallantry
  With many a rare device:
To please our English gallantry
  Our pains we freely show;
For we toil, and we moil,
  When the stormy winds do blow.

We sometimes sail to th' Indies,
  To fetch home spices rare;
Sometimes again to France and Spain
  For wines beyond compare;
While gallants are carousing
  In taverns on a row,
Then we sweep o'er the deep,
  When the stormy winds do blow.

When tempests are blown over,
  And greatest fears are past,
In weather fair, and temperate air,
  We straight lie down to rest:
But when the billows tumble,
  And waves do furious grow;
Then we rouse—up we rouse,
  When the stormy winds do blow.

If enemies oppose us,
  When England is at war
With any foreign nations,
  We fear not wound nor scar;
Our roaring guns shall teach 'em
  Our valour for to know;
Whilst they reel, in the keel,
  When the stormy winds do blow.

We are no cowardly shrinkers,
  But true Englishmen bred;
We'll play our parts, like valiant hearts,
  And never fly for dread;

We'll play our business nimbly
  Where'er we come or go,
With our mates, to the Straits,
  When the stormy winds do blow.

Then courage, all brave mariners,
  And never be dismay'd;
Whilst we have bold adventurers
  We ne'er shall want a trade :
Our merchants will employ us
  To fetch them wealth, I know;
Then be bold, work for gold,
  When the stormy winds do blow.

When we return in safety,
  With wages for our pains,
The tapster and the vintner
  Will help to share our gains.
We'll call for liquor roundly,
  And pay before we go;
Then roar on the shore
  When the stormy winds do blow.

MARTIN PARKER.[1]

"YE MARINERS OF ENGLAND."

YE mariners of England,
  That guard our native seas,
Whose flag has braved a thousand years
  The battle and the breeze !
Your glorious standard launch again
  To match another foe !
And sweep through the deep
  While the stormy winds do blow—
While the battle rages loud and long,
  And the stormy winds do blow.

The spirits of your fathers
  Shall start from every wave !—
For the deck it was their field of fame;
  The Ocean was their grave.

---

[1] The balladist of his day—*i. e.* second quarter of the XVIIth cent. He is supposed to have been a tavern-keeper. The first version of this piece was printed by him under the title "Saylers for my Money."

Where Blake and mighty Nelson fell
  Your manly hearts shall glow,
As ye sweep through the deep,
  While the stormy winds do blow—
While the battle rages loud and long,
  And the stormy winds do blow.

Britannia needs no bulwarks,
  No towers along the steep;
Her march is o'er the mountain-waves,—
  Her home is on the deep.
With thunders from her native oaks
  She quells the floods below,—
As they roar on the shore,
  When the stormy winds do blow—
When the battle rages loud and long,
  And the stormy winds do blow.

The meteor-flag of England
  Shall yet terrific burn,—
Till danger's troubled night depart,
  And the star of peace return.
Then, then, ye ocean-warriors!
  Our song and feast shall flow
To the fame of your name,
  When the storm has ceased to blow—
When the fiery fight is heard no more,
  And the storm has ceased to blow.

                    CAMPBELL.

"THE STATELY SHIP."

(*A Master-Mariner.*)

THE stately ship with all her daring band
To skilful Albert own'd the chief command:
Though trained in boisterous elements, his mind
Was yet by soft humanity refin'd;
Each joy of wedded love at home he knew,
Abroad, confess'd the father of his crew!
Brave, liberal, just! the calm domestic scene
Had o'er his temper breathed a gay serene;
Him science taught by mystic lore to brace
The planets wheeling in eternal race;
To mark the ship in floating balance held,
By earth attracted, and by seas repell'd;

Or point her devious tracks thro' climes unknown
That leads to every shore and every zone.
He saw the moon thro' heaven's blue concave glide,
And into motion charm th' expanding tide,
While earth impetuous round her axle rolls,
Exalts her watery zone, and sinks the poles;
Light and attraction, from their genial source,
He saw still wandering with diminished force;
While on the margin of declining day
Night's shadowy cone reluctant melts away.
Inured to peril, with unconquer'd soul,
The chief beheld tempestuous ocean's roll:
O'er the wild surge, when dismal shades preside,
His equal skill the lonely bark could guide;
His genius, ever for th' event prepar'd,
Rose with the storm, and all its dangers shared.

FALCONER.

"RODMOND THE NEXT DEGREE."

(A Chief Mate.)

RODMOND the next degree to Albert bore,
A hardy son of England's furthest shore!
Where bleak Northumbria pours her savage train
In sable squadrons o'er the northern main;
That, with her pitchy entrails stor'd, resort,
A sooty tribe! to fair Augusta's port.
Where'er in ambush lurk the fatal sands,
They claim the danger; proud of skilful bands;
For while with darkling course their vessels sweep
The winding shore, or plough the faithless deep,
O'er bar and shelf the wat'ry patch they sound,
With dext'rous arm; sagacious of the ground!
Fearless they combat every hostile wind,
Wheeling in mazy tracks, with course inclin'd.
Expert to moor where terrors line the road,
Or win the anchor from its dark abode;
But drooping and relax'd in climes afar,
Tumultuous and undisciplin'd in war.
Such Rodmond was; by learning unrefin'd,
That oft enlightens to corrupt the mind.
Boisterous of manners; train'd in early youth,
To scenes that shame the conscious cheek of Truth;

To scenes that Nature's struggling voice control,
And freeze compassion rising in the soul!
Where the grim hell-hounds,[1] prowling round the shore,
With foul intent the stranded bark explore—
Deaf to the voice of war, her decks they board,
While tardy Justice slumbers o'er her sword—
Thus Rodmond, train'd by this unhallow'd crew,
The sacred social passions never knew;
Unskill'd to argue; in dispute yet loud;
Bold without caution; without honours proud;
In art unschool'd; each veteran rule he priz'd,
And all improvement haughtily despis'd;
Yet tho' full oft to future perils blind,
With skill superior glow'd his daring mind,
Thro' snares of death the reeling barque to guide,
When midnight shades involve the raging tide.

FALCONER.

"POOR CHILD OF DANGER."

Poor child of danger, nursling of the storm!
Sad are the woes that wreck thy manly form:
Rocks, waves and winds the shattered bark delay;
Thy heart is sad, thy home is far away.
But Hope can here her moonlight vigils keep,
And sing to charm the spirit of the deep;
Swift as yon streamer lights the starry pole,
Her visions warm the helmsman's pensive soul:
His native hills that rise in happier climes,—
The grot that heard his song of other times,—
His cottage-home,—his boat, of slender sail,—
His glassy lake, and broomwood-blossomed vale,
Rush on his thought: He sweeps before the wind,
Treads the loved shore he sighed to leave behind;
Meets at each step a friend's familiar face,
And flies at last to Helen's long embrace;
Wipes from her cheek the rapture-speaking tear;
And clasps, with many a sigh, his children dear!
While long-neglected, but at length caressed,
His faithful dog salutes the smiling guest,
Points to the master's eyes, where'er they roam,
His wistful face, and whines a welcome home.

CAMPBELL.

[1] From this it would appear that Falconer knew something of the Northumberland wreckers of his day.

"WHILE ALOFT THE ORDER SOME ATTEND."

. . . WHILE aloft the order some attend,
To furl the main-sail, then on deck descend,
A sea, uprising with stupendous roll,
To instant ruin seems to doom the whole.
"Oh, mates, secure your hold!" Arion cries.—
It comes all dreadful! Down the vessel lies,
Half-buried sideways! While, beneath it tossed,
Four seamen off the lee-yardarm are lost!
Torn with resistless fury from their hold,
In vain their struggling arms the yard enfold.
In vain to grapple flying ropes they try—
The ropes, alas, a solid grip deny!
Prone on the midnight surge, with panting breath,
They cry for aid, and long contend with death;
High o'er their heads the rolling billows sweep,
And down they sink in everlasting sleep.
Bereft of power to help, their comrades see
The wretched victims die beneath the lee;
With fruitless sorrow their lost state bemoan,—
Perhaps a fatal prelude to their own.

FALCONER.

POOR JACK.[1]

Go patter to lubbers and swabs, d'ye see,
  'Bout danger and fear and the like;
A tight-water boat and good sea-room give me,
  And t'ent to a little I'll strike.
Though the tempest top-gallant-masts smack smooth
    should smite,
  And shiver each splinter of wood;
Clear the wreck, stow the yards,[2] and bouse everything
    tight,
  And under reefed foresail we'll scud.

[1] This is, no doubt, a fairly correct representation of one type of blue-jacket in Dibdin's time, and before then and after; but we must not forget that other type, the men who created the mutiny at the Nore, the mutiny of the *Bounty*, etc. There are at least two kinds in every class, and the naval seaman of the past was not always a loving, lovable, dancing and romping retriever of a man with a penchant for fighting, such as some writers have regularly pictured him. [2] *See* [1] and [2] p. 89.

Avast! And don't think me a milksop so soft
  To be taken for trifles aback;
For they say there's a Providence sits up aloft
  To keep watch for the life of Poor Jack.

Why, I heard the good chaplain palaver one day
  About souls, Heaven, mercy and such;
And, my timbers, what lingo he'd coil and belay![1]
  Why, 'twas just all as one as High Dutch.
But he said how a sparrow can't founder, d'ye see,
  Without orders that come down below;
And many fine things that proved clearly to me
  That Providence takes us in tow.
"For," says he, "do you mind me, let storms[2] e'er
    so oft
  Take the topsails of sailors aback;
There's a sweet little cherub that sits up aloft
  To keep watch for the life of Poor Jack."

I said to our Poll—for, you see, she would cry,
  When last we weighed anchor for sea—
"What argufies sniv'ling and piping your eye?
  Why, what a great fool you must be!
Can't you see the world's wide, and there's room for
    us all
  Both for seamen and lubbers ashore?
And if to old Davy I should go, friend Poll,—
  Why, you never would hear of me more.
What, then, all's a hazard: Come, don't be so soft;
  Perhaps I may laughing come back:
For, d'ye see, there's a cherub that sits up aloft
  To keep watch for the life of Poor Jack."

D'ye mind me, a sailor should be every inch
  All as one as a piece of the ship;
And with her brave the world without offering to flinch,
  From the moment the anchor's a-trip.
As for me, in all weathers, all times, tides and ends,
  Nought's a trouble from duty that springs;

[1] and [2] As for Dibdin's seamanship: sails, cargo, etc. are " stowed,"
but "yards" only when they are sent down; a rope or line is coiled
after it is belayed; and squalls, not "storms," strike sails aback. .This
feature, as well as the mere jingle, prevents one from quoting much of
Dibdin's work.

For my heart is my Poll's, and my rhino's my friend's—
    And as for my life, 'tis the King's.
Even when my time comes, ne'er believe me so soft
    As for grief to be taken aback:
That same little cherub that sits up aloft
    Will look out a good berth for Poor Jack.

DIBDIN.

THE SAILOR'S JOURNAL.

'TWAS post meridian half-past four,
    By signal I from Nancy parted;
At six she lingered on the shore,
    With uplift hands and broken-hearted;
At seven, while taughtening the forestay,
    I saw her faint—or else 'twas fancy;
At eight we all got under weigh,
    And bid a long adieu to Nancy.

Night came : And now eight bells had rung;
    While careless sailors, ever cheery,
On the mid-watch so jovial sung,[1]
    With tempers labour cannot weary.
I—little to their mirth inclined,
    While tender thoughts rushed on my fancy,
And my warm sighs increased the wind—
    Looked on the moon, and thought of Nancy.

And now arrived that jovial night,
    When every true-bred tar carouses,—
When, o'er the grog, all hands delight
    To toast their sweethearts and their spouses:
Round went the can, the jest, the glee,
    While tender wishes filled each fancy;
And when, in turn, it came to me,
    I heaved a sigh—and toasted Nancy!

[1] Here Dibdin (Garrick's godson, therefore less at home aboard ship than at Drury Lane, where he considerably improved the scene-painting of his day), lost both his longitude and his latitude ; for if there is, and always was, a quiet time aboard ship, that time is, above all others, the middle watch—*i. e.* from midnight to four o'clock in the morning. Otherwise, the song is worthy of being preserved as the supposed journal of a bluejacket of those days.

Next morn a storm came on at four :
　　At six the elements, in motion,
Plunged me and three poor sailors more
　　Headlong within the foaming ocean.
Poor wretches !—they soon found their graves :
　　For me—it may be only fancy—
But love seemed to forbid the waves
　　To snatch me from the arms of Nancy.

Scarce the foul hurricane had cleared,
　　Scarce winds and waves had ceased to rattle,
When a bold enemy appeared
　　And, dauntless, we prepared for battle.
And now, while some loved friend or wife
　　Like lightning rushed on every fancy,
To Providence I trusted life,—
　　Put up a prayer, and thought of Nancy.

And last ('twas in the month of May)
　　The crew, it being lovely weather,
At three A.M. discovered day
　　And England's chalky cliffs together :
At seven up Channel—how we bore !
　　While hopes and fears rushed on my fancy ;
At twelve I gaily jumped ashore,
　　And to my throbbing heart pressed Nancy !

DIBDIN.

"AS ONE THAT IN A SILVER VISION FLOATS."

As one that in a silver vision floats,
Obedient to the sweep of odorous winds,
Upon resplendent clouds, so rapidly
Along the dark and ruffled waters fled
The straining boat.　A whirlwind swept it on,
With fierce gusts and precipitating force,
Through the white ridges of the chafèd sea !
The waves arose,—higher and higher still
Their fierce necks writhed beneath the tempest's
　　scourge,
Like serpents struggling in a vulture's grasp.

Calm and rejoicing in the fearful war
Of wave running on wave, and blast on blast

Descending, and black flood on whirlpool driven
With dark obliterating course, he sate,—
As if their genii were the ministers
Appointed to conduct him to the light
Of those beloved eyes, the Poet sate,
Holding the steady helm.
                  Evening came on;
The beams of sunset hung their rainbow hues
High 'mid the shifting domes of sheeted spray
That canopied his path o'er the waste deep.
Twilight, ascending slowly from the east,
Entwined in duskier wreaths her braided locks
O'er the fair front and radiant eyes of day.
Night followed, clad with stars.   On every side
More horribly the multitudinous streams
Of ocean's mountainous waste to mutual war
Rushed in dark tumult thundering, as to mock
The calm and spangled sky.   The little boat
Still fled before the storm,—still fled, like foam
Down the steep cataract of a wintery river;
Now passing on the edge of the river wave;
Now leaving far behind the bursting mass
That fell, convulsing ocean,—safely fled,
As if that frail and wasted human form
Had been an elemental god.
                At midnight
The moon arose; and, lo! the æthereal cliffs
Of Caucasus, whose icy summits shone
Among the stars like sunlight, and around
Whose caverned base the whirlpools and the waves,
Bursting and eddying irresistibly,
Rage and resound for ever.—Who shall save?
The boat fled on!   The boiling torrent drove;
The crags closed round with black and jaggèd arms;
The shattered mountain overhung the sea;
And faster still, beyond all human speed,
The little boat was driven.   A cavern there
Yawned, and amid its slant and winding depths
Ingulphed the sea!   The boat fled on,
With unrelaxing speed.   "Vision and Love,"
The Poet cried aloud, "I have beheld
The path of thy departure!   Sleep and death
Shall not divide us long!"

                        SHELLEY.

"THE HELM, TO HIS STRONG ARM." [1]

THE helm, to his strong arm consigned,
Gave the reefed sail to meet the wind;
   And on her altered way,
Fierce bounding, sprung the ship,
Like greyhound starting from the slip
   To seize his flying prey.

Awaked before the rushing prow,
The mimic fires of ocean glow—
   The lightnings of the wave;
Wild sparkles crest the broken tides,
And, flashing round, the vessel's sides
   With elvish lustre lave:
While, far behind, their livid light
To the dark billows of the night
   A gloomy splendour gave. [2]
It seems as if old Ocean shakes
From his dark brow the lucid flakes
   In envious pageantry,
To match the meteor-light that streaks
   Grim Heela's midnight sky.

Nor lacked they steadier light to keep
Their course upon the darkened deep:
   Atornish, on her frowning steep,
   'Twixt cloud and ocean hung,
Glanced with a thousand lights of glee,
And landward far, and far to sea,
   Her festal radiance flung.
By the blithe beacon-light they steered,
   Whose lustre mingled well
With the pale beam that now appeared,
As the cold moon her head upreared
   Above the eastern fell.

                        SCOTT.

[1] We know that Scott was no poet of the sea, and his refusal to try
his hand on an epic of Trafalgar—on the ground that whoever essayed
the task should be in feeling and experience as much a sailor as a poet
—is proof of his own opinion in this direction. All the same, however,
when he turned his rare descriptive powers to things nautical the natural
magic of the man seldom failed to touch the right note and, withal, to
be as accurate as a landsman may be at sea.   [2] Still one cannot keep
away a feeling of disappointment when a writer of Scott's ability changes
his tense, yet not his time or scene, in this manner for the paltry sake
of a rhyme.

GOD HELP OUR MEN AT SEA.

THE wild night comes like an owl to its lair;
  The black clouds follow fast;
And the sun-gleams die, and the lightnings glare,
    And the ships go heaving past, past, past—
    And the ships go heaving past!
  Bar the doors, and higher, higher
  Pile the faggots on the fire!
  Now abroad by many a light
  Empty seats there are to-night,—
  Empty seats that none may fill,
  For the storm grows louder still!
How it surges and swells through the gorges and dells,
    Under the ledges and over the lea,
Where a watery sound goeth moaning around—-
    God help our men at sea!

Oh, never a tempest blew to shore,
    But that some heart did groan
For a darling voice it would hear no more,
    And a face that had left it lone, lone, lone—
    A face that had left it lone.
  I am watching by a pane,
  Darkened with the gusty rain,—
  Watching through a mist of tears,
  Sad with thoughts of other years,
  For a brother I did miss
  In a stormy time like this.
Ha, the torrent howls past, like a fiend on the blast,
    Under the ledges and over the lea!
And the pent waters gleam, and the wild surges scream!
    God help our men at sea!

Ah, Lord, they may grope through the dark to find
    Thy hand within the gale!
And cries may rise on the wings of the wind
    From mariners weary and pale, pale, pale—
    From mariners weary and pale.
  'Tis a fearful thing to know,
  When the storm-winds loudly blow,
  That a man can sometimes come
  Too near to his father's home;
  So that he shall kneel and say:
  "Lord, I would be far away!"

Ho, the hurricanes roar round a dangerous shore!—
    Under the ledges and over the lea.
And there twinkles a light on the billows so white—
    God help our men at sea!

                HENRY KENDAL.

THE DIVER.

THOU hast been where the rocks of coral grow,
    Thou hast fought with eddying waves;—
Thy cheek is pale, and thy heart beats low,
    Thou searcher of ocean's caves!

Thou hast looked on the gleaming wealth of old,
    And wrecks where the brave have striven;
The deep is a strong and a fearful hold,
    But thou its bar hast riven!

A wild and weary life is thine;
    A wasting task and lone,
Though treasure-grots for thee may shine,
    To all besides unknown!

A weary life!—But a swift decay
    Soon, soon shall set thee free;
Thou'rt passing fast from thy toils away,
    Thou wrestler with the sea!

In thy dim eye, on thy hollow cheek,
    Well are the death-signs read—
Go! for the pearl in its cavern seek,
    Ere hope and power be fled!

And bright in beauty's caronal
    That glistening gem shall be;
A star to all in the festive hall—
    But who will think on thee?

None! As it gleams from the queen-like head,
    Not one 'midst throngs will say,
"A life hath been like a rain-drop shed,
    For that pale quivering ray."

'Twas for the wealth thus dearly bought!—
    And are not those like thee
Who win for earth the gems of thought?
    O wrestler with the Sea!

                FELICIA HEMANS.

THE SAILOR-BOY.

HE rose at dawn, and, fired with hope,
　Shot o'er the seething harbour-bar,
And reached the ship, and caught the rope,
　And whistled to the morning star.

And, while he whistled long and loud,
　He heard a fierce mermaiden cry—
"O boy, though thou art young and proud,
　I see the place where thou wilt lie.

"The sands and yeasty surges mix
　In caves about the dreary bay;
And on thy ribs the limpet sticks,
　And in thy heart the scrawl shall play."

"Fool!" he answered, "death is sure
· To those that stay and those that roam;
But I will nevermore endure
　To sit with empty hands at home.

"My mother clings about my neck;
　My sisters crying—'Stay for shame'!
My father raves of death and wreck,—
　They are all to blame! They are all to blame!

"God help me! Save I take my part
　Of danger on the roaring sea,
A devil rises in my heart
　Far worse than death to me!"

TENNYSON.

THE CAPTAIN.

(*A Legend of the Navy.*)

HE that only rules by terror
　Doeth grievous wrong.
Deep as Hell I count his error:
　Let him hear my song.

Brave the captain was: the seamen
　Made a gallant crew,—
Gallant sons of English freemen,
　Sailors bold and true;

But they hated his oppression :
  Stern he was and rash,
So for every light transgression
  Doomed them to the lash.
Day by day more harsh and cruel
  Seemed the captain's mood :
Secret wrath, like smothered fuel,
  Burnt in each man's blood.
Yet he hoped to purchase glory—
  Hoped to make the name
Of his vessel great in story,
  Wheresoe'er he came.

So they passed by capes and islands,
  Many a harbour-mouth,
Sailing under palmy highlands
  Far within the south.
On a day, when they were going
  O'er the lone expanse,
In the north, her canvas flowing
  Rose a ship of France.
Then the captain's colour heightened,
  Joyful came his speech ;
But a cloudy gladness lightened
  In the eyes of each.
"Chase ! " he said.   The ship flew forward,
  And the wind did blow ;
Stately, lightly went she nor'ward,
  Till she neared the foe.

Then they looked at him they hated—
  Had what they desired :
Mute, with folded arms, they waited,—
  Not a gun was fired.
But they heard the foeman's thunder
  Roaring out their doom ;
All the air was torn in sunder—
  Crashing went the boom !
Spars were splintered ; decks were shattered ;
  Bullets fell like rain ;
Over mast and deck were scattered
  Blood and brains of men !
Spars were splintered ; decks were broken ;
  Every mother's son,
Down they dropt—no word was spoken—
  Each beside his gun.

H

On the decks, as they were lying,
  Were their faces grim;
In their blood, as they lay dying,
  Did they smile on him.
Those, in whom he had reliance
  For his noble name,
With one smile of still defiance
  Sold him unto shame.
Shame and wrath his heart confounded;
  Pale he turned, and red,
Till himself was deadly wounded—
  Falling on the dead.

Dismal error! Fearful slaughter!
  Years have wandered by:
Side by side beneath the water
  Crew and captain lie.
There the sunlit ocean tosses
  O'er them, mouldering;
And the lonely sea-bird crosses
  With one waft of wing.

                     TENNYSON.

"A SHIP THOU MUST NEEDS DIGHT." [1]

A SHIP thou must needs dight;
Myself shall be the Master-wright.
I shall tell thee how broad and long,
Of what measure and how strong.
When the timber is fastened well,
Bend the sides over each end beam;
Bind it well with balk and band,
And wind it then with good wand.
With pitch—look it be not thin—
Plaster it well without and in.

Make it of boards, and wands between, [2]
Thus thriftily, and not over thin;
Look that thy seams be subtly [3] seen,
And nailèd well, that they not twin. [4]

---

[1] This curious excerpt is from *Cursor Mundi*, a verse history of most things down to that day—early part of the thirteenth century. The other four lines are from the earlier miracle-play known as the York *Deluge*; they are both put into the mouth of the Almighty when directing Noah how to build the ark, and are interesting as evidence of shipbuilding in those times.   [2] Laths over the seams.   [3] Closed up, not easily seen.   [4] Twist, or warp out of place.

SPANISH GALLEONS.

(As first seen by an Aztec.)

Guiom. As far as I could cast my eyes
Upon the sea, something, methought, did rise
Like bluish mists; which, still appearing more,
Took dreadful shapes, and thus mov'd towards the
    shore.
The objects I could first distinctly view
Were tall, straight trees, which on the water flew;
Wings on their sides instead of leaves did grow,
Which gathered all the breath the winds did blow;
And at their roots grew floating palaces,
Whose outblown bellies cut the yielding seas.

Montezuma. What divine monsters, O ye gods! are
    these,
That float in air, and fly upon the seas?
Came they alive, or dead, upon the shore?

Guiom. Alas, they lived too sure! I heard them
    roar!
All turned their sides and to each other spoke,—
I saw their words break out in fire and smoke.
(Sure 'tis their voices thundering from on high,
And these the younger brothers from the sky.)
Deaf with the noise, I took my hasty flight;
No mortal courage could support the fright.

DRYDEN.

"HE THAT HAS SAILED UPON."[1]

HE that has sailed upon the dark-blue sea
    Has viewed at times, I ween, a full fair sight;
When the fresh breeze is fair as breeze may be,
    The white sails set, the gallant frigate tight:
    Masts, spires and strand retiring to the right;

---

[1] This extract, from "Childe Harold," is one of the very few pieces extant that describe a man-o'-war convoying a fleet of merchantmen, a condition of things that was made needful by our long wars with Spain, France and Holland.

H 2

The glorious main expanding o'er the bow;
  The convoy spread, like wild swans in their flight;
The dullest sailer wearing bravely now,
So gaily curl the waves before each dashing prow.

And, oh, the little warlike world within!
  The well-reev'd guns; the netted canopy;
The hoarse command; the busy, humming din,
    When, at a word, the tops are manned on high:
    Hark to the Boatswain's call, the cheering cry!
While through the seaman's hand the tackle glides;
  Or schoolboy Midshipman that, standing by,
Strains his shrill pipe, as good or ill betides—
And well the docile crew that skilful urchin guides.

White is the glassy deck, without a stain,
  Whereon the watch the staid Lieutenant walks:
Look on that part which sacred doth remain
  For the lone chieftain, who majestic stalks,
  Silent and fear'd by all—not oft he talks
With aught beneath him, if he would preserve
  That strict restraint, which, broken, ever balks
Conquest and Fame: but Britons rarely swerve
From Law, however stern, which tends their strength
    to nerve.

Blow! swiftly blow, thou keel-compelling gale!
  Till the broad sun withdraws his lessening ray;
Then must the pennant-bearer slacken sail,
  That lagging barks may make their lazy way.
  Ah, grievance sore! and listless dull delay,
To waste on sluggish hulks the sweetest breeze!
  What leagues are lost before the dawn of day,
Thus loitering pensive on the willing seas,
The flapping sail hauled down to halt for logs like
    these![1]

[1] Here one sees at once that Byron, that "noble imp," as Scott termed him on one occasion, who refused John Murray's guineas for his poems. To him there is nothing fine or beautiful except Nature and the frigate that bears him—nothing else is worthy of his lordly description. The "sluggish hulks" of merchantmen, without which the upkeep of his man-o'-war would be impossible, are only objects of contempt; while his rage boils up at the usual evening custom of waiting till the sternmost "logs" have come up within the protecting fire of the frigate.

The moon is up,—by Heaven a lovely eve!
  Long streams of light o'er dancing waves expand;
Now lads on shore may sigh and maids believe:
  Such be our fate when we return to land!
  Meantime some rude Arion's restless hand
Wakes the brisk harmony that sailors love;
  A circle there of merry listeners stand,
Or to some well-known measure featly move,
Thoughtless, as if on shore they still were free to rove.
                             BYRON.

THE CONVICT SHIP.

MORN on the waters! And purple and bright
Bursts on the billows the flashing of light:
O'er the glad waves, like a child of the sun,
See, the tall vessel goes gallantly on;
Full to the breeze she unbosoms her sail,
And her pennon streams onward, like hope, in the gale.

The winds came around her with murmur and song,
And the surges rejoice as they bear her along:
See! she looks up to the golden-edged clouds;
And the sailor sings gaily aloft in the shrouds:
Onward she glides amidst ripple and spray—
Over the waters, away and away!

Bright as the visions of youth ere they part,—
Passing away, like a dream of the heart!
Who, as the beautiful pageant sweeps by—
Music around her, and sunshine on high—
Pauses to think, amid glitter and glow,
Oh, there be hearts that are breaking below!

    · ·   "   ,   ·   ·

Night on the waves! And the moon is on high,
Hung like a gem on the brow of the sky,
Treading its depths in the power of her might,
And turning the clouds, as they pass her, to light:
Look to the waters!—asleep on their breast,
Seems not the ship like an island of rest?
Bright and alone on the shadowy main,
Like a heart cherished home on some desolate plain!

Who—as she smiles in the silvery light,
Spreading her wings to the bosom of night,

Alone on the deep, as the moon in the sky,
A phantom of beauty—could deem, with a sigh,
That so lovely a thing is this mansion of sin,
And souls that are smitten lie bursting within!

Who, as he watches her silently gliding,
Remembers that wave after wave is dividing
Bosoms that sorrow and guilt could not sever,
Hearts that are parted and broken for ever?
Or dreams that he watches, afloat on the wave,
The death-bed of hope, or the young spirit's grave?

T. K. Hervey.

"A SQUALL, DEEP LOWERING."

A squall, deep lowering, blots the southern sky,
Before whose boisterous breath the waters fly.
Its weight the topsails can no more sustain:
"Reef topsails!—Reef!" the master calls again.
The halyards and top bowlines soon are gone;
To clewlines and reef-tackles next they run;
The shivering sails descend; the yards they square,
Then quick aloft the ready crew repair;
The weather-earings and the lee are passed,
The reefs enrolled, and every point's made fast.
Their task above thus finished, they descend,
And vigilant th' approaching squall attend.
It comes resistless, and with foaming sweep
Upturns the whit'ning surface of the deep!

. . . . . .

The clouds, with ruin pregnant, now impend,
And storm and cataract tumultuous blend!
Deep on her side the reeling vessel lies:
"Brail up the mizen quick!" the master cries;
"Man the clew-garnets! Let the mainsheet fly!"—
It rends in scores of shivering shreds on high!
The main-sail, all in streaming ruins tore,
Loud fluttering, imitates the thunder's roar!
The ship still labours in th' oppressive strain,
Low bending, as if ne'er to rise again.
"Bear up the helm a while!" young Rodmond cries;
Swift at the word the helm a-weather flies.
She feels its guiding power and veers apace;
And now the foresail right athwart they brace.

With equal sheets restrained, the bellying sail
Spreads a broad concave to the sweeping gale.
While o'er the foam the ship impetuous flies,
Th' attentive timoneer [1] the helm applies.
As in pursuit along the aerial way,
With ardent eye, the falcon marks his prey,
Each motion watches of the doubtful chase,
Obliquely wheeling through the liquid space;
So, governed by the steersman's glowing hands,
The regent helm her motion still commands.

FALCONER.

"WHERE LIES THE LAND?"

WHERE lies the land to which yon ship must go?
  Festively she puts forth in trim array,
  As vigorous as a lark at break of day.
Is she for tropic suns, or polar snow?—
What boots the inquiry? Neither friend nor foe
  She cares for : let her travel where she may,
  She finds familiar names, a beaten way
Ever before her, and a wind to blow.

Yet still I ask: What haven is her mark?
  And, almost as it was when ships were rare,
  (From time to time like pilgrims, here and there,
Crossing the waters) doubt, and something dark,
  Of the old sea some reverential fear,
Are with me at thy farewell, joyous bark.

WORDSWORTH.

THE PHANTOM-SHIP.

IN Mather's Magnalia Christi,
  Of the old colonial time,
May be found in prose the legend
  That is here set down in rhyme.

A ship sailed from New Haven;
  And the keen and frosty airs,
That filled her sails at parting,
  Were heavy with good men's prayers.

---

[1] The helmsman. Not to add here a bundle of notes on nautical terms, all of which would be but half-informative without actual experience or extensive diagrams, it is only right to say that in this descriptive passage Falconer proved his mastery in handling a square-rigged vessel.

"O Lord! if it be thy pleasure"
  (Thus prayed the old divine)
"To bury our friends in the ocean,
  Take them,—for they are thine."

But Master Lamberton muttered,
  And under his breath said he—
"This ship is so crank and walty,
  I fear our grave she will be!"

And the ships that came from England,
  When the winter months were gone,
Brought no tidings of this vessel,
  Nor of Master Lamberton.

This put the people to praying
  That the Lord would let them hear
What, in His greater wisdom,
  He had done with friends so dear.

And at last their prayers were answered:
  It was in the month of June,
An hour before the sunset
  On a windy afternoon;

When, steadily steering landward,
  A ship was seen below,—
And they knew it was Lamberton, Master,
  Who sailed so long ago.

On she came, with clouds of canvas,
  Right against the wind that blew,
Until the eye could distinguish
  The faces of the crew.

Then fell her straining topmasts,
  Hanging tangled in the shrouds;
And her sails were loosened and lifted,
  And blown away like clouds.

And the masts, with all their rigging,
  Fell slowly, one by one;
And the hulk dilated and vanished,
  As a sea-mist in the sun!

And the people who saw this marvel
  Each said unto his friend,
That this was the mould of their vessel,
  And thus her tragic end.

And the pastor of the village
  Gave thanks to God in prayer,
That, to quiet their troubled spirits,
  He had sent this Ship of Air.

LONGFELLOW.

THE SHIP-BUILDERS.

THE sky is ruddy in the east;
  The earth is grey below;
And, spectral in the river-mist,
  The ship's white timbers show.
Then let the sounds of measured stroke
  And grating saw begin,
The broad axe to the gnarlèd oak,
  The mallet to the pin.

Hark! Roars the bellows, blast on blast;
  The sooty smithy jars;
And fire-sparks, rising far and fast,
  Are fading with the stars.
All day for us the smith shall stand
  Beside that flashing forge;
All day for us his heavy hand
  The groaning anvil scourge.

From far-off hills the panting team
  For us is toiling near;
For us the craftsmen down the stream
  Their island barges steer.
Ring out for us the axeman's stroke
  In forests old and still;
For us the century-circled oak
  Falls crashing down his hill.

Up, up! In nobler toil than ours
  No craftsman bears a part:
We make of Nature's giant powers
  The slaves of human art.
Lay rib to rib and beam to beam,
  And drive the tree-nails free;
Nor faithless joint nor yawning seam
  Shall tempt the yearning sea!

Where'er the keel of our good ship
  The sea's rough field shall plough,
Where'er her tossing spars shall drip
  With salt-spray caught below,
That ship must heed her master's beck,
  Her helm obey his hand,
And seamen tread her reeling deck
  As if they trod the land.

Her oaken ribs the vulture-beak
  Of northern ice may seal;
The sunken rock and coral-peak
  May grate along her keel;
And know we well the painted shell,
  We give to wind and wave,
Must float, the sailors' citadel—
  Or sink, the sailors' grave.

Ho, strike away the bars and blocks,
  And set the good ship free!
Why lingers on these dusty stocks
  The young bride of the sea?
Look!—How she moves a-down the grooves
  In graceful beauty now!
How lowly, on the breast she loves,
  Sinks down her virgin prow!

God bless her! Wheresoe'er the breeze
  Her snowy wing shall fan,
Aside the frozen Hebrides,
  Or sultry Hindostan;
Where'er in mart or on the main,
  With peaceful flag unfurled,
She helps to wind the silken chain
  Of commerce round the world.

Speed on the ship!—But let her bear
  No merchandise of sin,
No groaning cargo of despair
  Her roomy hold within;
No Lethean drug for eastern lands,
  Nor poison-draught for ours;
But honest fruits of toiling hands
  And Nature's sun and showers.

Be hers the prairie's golden grain,
 The desert's golden sand,
The clustered fruits of sunny Spain,
 The spice of morning-land.
Her pathway on the open main
 May blessings follow free,
And glad hearts welcome back again
 Her white sails from the sea!

       WHITTIER.

SONG FOR ALL SEAS, ALL SHIPS.

TO-DAY a rude, brief recitative
Of ships sailing the seas, each with its special flag or
 ship-signal;
Of unnamed heroes in the ships; of waves spreading
 and spreading, as far as the eye can reach;
Of dashing spray, and the winds piping and blowing;
And out of these a chant for the sailors of all nations,
Fitful, like a surge:

Of sea-captains young or old, and the mates, and of all
 intrepid sailors;
Of the few, very choice, taciturn, whom fate can never
 surprise nor death dismay,
Pick'd sparingly without noise by thee, old ocean, chosen
 by thee—
Thou sea that pickest and cullest the race in time, and
 unitest nations,
Suckled by thee, old husky nurse, embodying thee:
(Ever the heroes on water or on land, by ones or twos
 appearing,
Ever the stock preserv'd, and never lost, though rare,
 enough for seed preserv'd.)

Flaunt out, O sea, your separate flags of nations!
Flaunt out visible, as ever the various ship's signals!
But do you reserve especially for yourself and for the
 soul of man one flag above the rest,
A spiritual woven signal for all nations, emblem of man
 elate above death—
Token of all brave captains and all intrepid sailors and
 mates,
And all that went down doing their duty,—

Reminiscent of them, twined from all intrepid captains
    young or old,—
A pennant universal, subtly waving all time, o'er all
    brave sailors,
All seas, all ships.

Whitman.[1]

IN CABIN'D SHIPS AT SEA.

In cabin'd ships at sea,—
The boundless blue on every side expanding,
With whistling winds and music of the waves, the large
    imperious waves;
Or some lone bark buoy'd on the dense marine,
Where joyous, full of faith, spreading white sails,
She cleaves the ether 'mid the sparkle and the foam of
    day, or under many a star at night:
By sailors young and old, haply will I, a reminiscence
    of the land, be read,[2]
In full rapport at last.

Here are our thoughts, voyagers' thoughts;
Here not the land, firm land, alone appears, may then
    by them be said;
The sky o'erarches here; we feel the undulating deck
    beneath our feet;
We feel the long pulsation, ebb and flow of endless
    motion,
The tones of unseen mystery, the vague and vast
    suggestions of the briny world, the liquid-flowing
    syllables,
The perfume, the faint creaking of the cordage, the
    melancholy rhythm—
The boundless vista and the horizon far and dim are all
    here,
And this is ocean's poem.

Whitman.

[1] and [2] I have heard Whitman spoken of as "The Martin Tupper of America." He was, is, and will continue to be, far more than that; yet it is a pity that he let his bombast and conceit go the length of naming this piece of work "A Song for all Seas, all Ships." If there was one thing that Whitman could not have done it was to have written a sea-song. Every characteristic he had was so much against his ever being known to seamen that I doubt if one in each ten thousand to-day has heard his name; I also doubt if any of his verse will ever be known in shipboard life.

THE SHIP STARTING.

Lo, the unbounded sea !
On its breast a ship starting, spreading all sails, carrying
    even her moon-sails.
The pennant is flying aloft as she speeds—she speeds
    so stately; below emulous waves press forward;
They surround the ship with shining, curving motions
    and foam.

WHITMAN.

"ABOARD AT A SHIP'S HELM."

ABOARD at a ship's helm—
A young steersman steering with care.

Through fog on a sea-coast dolefully ringing,
An ocean-bell—and a warning bell, rocked by the waves.

O you give good notice indeed, you bell by the sea-reefs
    ringing,
Ringing, ringing, to warn the ship from its wreck-place.

For as on the alert, O steersman, you mind the loud
    admonition;
The bows turn; the freighted ship, tacking, speeds
    away under her grey sails—
The beautiful and noble ship, with all her precious
    wealth, speeds away gaily and safe.

But O the ship, the immortal ship ! O ship aboard the
    ship !
Ship of the body, ship of the soul, voyaging, voyaging,
    voyaging !

WHITMAN.

THE STEAMBOAT.

SEE how yon flaming herald treads
    The ridged and rolling waves,
As, crashing o'er their crested heads,
    She bows her surly slaves !
With foam before and fire behind,
    She rends the clinging sea,
That flies before the roaring wind
    Beneath her hissing lee.

The morning spray, like sea-born flowers,
  With heaped and glistening bells,
Falls round her fast, in ringing showers,
  With every wave that swells;
And, burning o'er the midnight deep,
  In lurid fringes thrown,
The living gems of ocean sweep
  Along her flashing zone.

With clashing wheel and lifting keel,
  And smoking torch on high,
When winds are loud and billows reel,
  She thunders, foaming, by :
When seas are silent and serene,
  With even beam she glides—
The sunshine glimmering through the green
  That skirts her gleaming sides.

Now, like a wild nymph, far apart
  She veils her shadowy form,
The beating of her restless heart
  Still sounding through the storm;
Now answers, like a courtly dame,
  The reddening surges o'er,
With flying scarf of spangled flame,
  The Pharos of the shore.

To-night yon pilot shall not sleep,
  Who trims his narrowed sail;
To-night yon frigate scarce shall keep
  Her broad breast to the gale :
And many a foresail, scooped and strained,
  Shall break from yard and stay,
Before this smoky wreathe hath stained
  The rising mist of day.

Hark, hark !—I hear yon whistling shroud;
  I see yon quivering mast !
The black throat of the hunted cloud
  Is panting forth the blast !
An hour, and, whirled like winnowed chaff,
  The giant surge shall fling
His tresses o'er yon pennon-staff,
  White as the sea-bird's wing.

Yet rest, ye wanderers of the deep,—
   Nor wind nor wave shall tire
Those fleshless arms, whose pulses leap
   With floods of living fire :
Sleep on—and, when the morning light
   Streams o'er the shining bay,
Oh, think of those for whom the night
   Shall never wake in day !
O. W. HOLMES.

THE DISMANTLED SHIP.

IN some unused lagoon, some nameless bay,
In sluggish, lonesome waters, anchor'd near the shore,
An old, dismasted, grey and battered ship—disabled,
   done,
After free voyages to all the seas of earth, haul'd up at
   last and hawser'd tight—
Lies rusting, mouldering.
WHITMAN.

"IT COMES!—THE DIRE CATASTROPHE!"

IT comes !—The dire catastrophe draws near !
Lashed furious on by destiny severe,
The ship hangs hovering on the verge of death :
Hell yawns ; rocks rise, and breakers roar beneath !

   .   .   .   .   .   .

In vain the cords and axes were prepared,
For now th' audacious seas insult the yard ;
High o'er the ship they throw a dreadful shade,
Then on her burst in terrible cascade,
Across the foundering deck o'erwhelming roar,
And foaming, swelling, bound upon the shore !
Swift up the mounting billow now she flies,
Her shattered top half-buried in the skies :
Borne o'er a latent reef the hull impends,
Then, thundering, on the marble crags descends !
Her ponderous bulk the dire concussion feels,
And, o'er upheaving surges, wounded, reels.
Again she plunges ! Hark !—a second shock
Bilges the splitting vessel on the rock !

Down on the vale of death, with dismal cries,
The fated victims, shuddering, cast their eyes
In wild despair; while yet another stroke,
With strong convulsion, rends the solid·oak.
Ah, Heaven!—behold her crashing ribs divide!
She loosens, parts, and spreads in ruin o'er the tide!

FALCONER.

ON THE LOSS OF THE *ROYAL GEORGE*.[1]

TOLL for the Brave!
  The brave that are no more!
All sunk beneath the wave
  Fast by their native shore!

Eight hundred of the brave,
  Whose courage well was tried,
Had made the vessel heel,
  And laid her on her side.

A land-breeze shook the shrouds,
  And she was overset;
Down went the *Royal George*
  With all her crew complete.

Toll for the Brave!
  Brave Kempenfelt is gone;
His last sea-fight is fought;
  His work of glory done.

It was not in the battle;
  No tempest gave the shock;
She sprang no fatal leak,
  She ran upon no rock.

His sword was in its sheath;
  His fingers held the pen,
When Kempenfelt went down
  With twice four hundred men.

Weigh the vessel up,
  Once dreaded by our foes!
And mingle with the cup
  The tear that England owes.

[1] This is said to have been written to the mournful march in "Scipio," immediately Cowper heard of the loss of the vessel, September 1782.

Her timbers yet are sound,
  And she may float again
Full charged with England's thunder,
  And plough the distant main :

But Kempenfelt is gone,
  His victories are o'er ;
And he and his eight hundred
  Shall plough the wave no more.

COWPER.

THE WRECK

ALL night the booming minute gun
  Had pealed along the deep,
And mournfully the rising sun
  Looked o'er the tide-worn steep.
A bark from India's coral strand,
  Before the raging blast,
Had vailed her topsails to the sand,
  And bowed her noble mast.

The queenly ship !—Brave hearts had striven,
  And true ones died with her !—
We saw her mighty cable riven,
  Like floating gossamer.
We saw her proud flag struck that morn,
  A star once o'er the seas—
Her anchor gone, her deck uptorn—
  And sadder things than these !

We saw her treasures cast away,—
  The rocks with pearls were sown,
And strangely sad, the ruby's ray
  Flashed out o'er fretted stone.
And gold was strewn the wet sands o'er,
  Like ashes by a breeze ;
And gorgeous robes.—But, oh ! that shore
  Had sadder things than these !

We saw the strong man still and low,
  A crushed reed thrown aside ;
Yet by that rigid lip and brow,
  Not without strife he died.

And near him on the seaweed lay—
  (Till then we had not wept)—
But well our gushing hearts might say,
  That there a mother slept !

For her pale arms a babe had prest,
  With such a wreathing grasp,
Billows had dashed o'er that fond breast,
  Yet not undone the clasp.
Her very tresses had been flung
  To wrap the fair child's form,
Where still their wet long streamers hung,
  All tangled by the storm.

And beautiful, midst that wild scene,
  Gleamed up the boy's dead face,
Like slumber's, trustingly serene,
  In melancholy grace.
Deep in her bosom lay his head,
  With half-shut violet eye—
He had known little of her dread,
  Nought of her agony !

Oh ! human love, whose yearning heart
  Through all things vainly true,
So stamps upon thy mortal part
  Its passionate adieu—
Surely thou hast another lot,
  There is some home for thee,
Where thou shalt rest, remembering not
  The moaning of the sea !
                    FELICIA HEMANS.

THE LIGHTHOUSE.

THE rocky ledge runs far into the sea,
  And on its outer point, some miles away,
The Lighthouse lifts its massive masonry,
  A pillar of fire by night, of cloud by day.

Even at this distance I can see the tides,
  Upheaving, break unheard along its base—
A speechless wrath, that rises and subsides
  In the white lip and tremor of the face.

And as the evening darkens, lo ! how bright,
　Through the deep purple of the twilight air,
Beams forth the sudden radiance of its light
　With strange, unearthly splendour in its glare !

Not one alone; from each projecting cape
　And perilous reef along the ocean's verge,
Starts into life a dim, gigantic shape,
　Holding its lantern o'er the restless surge.

Like the great giant Christopher, it stands
　Upon the brink of the tempestuous wave,
Wading far out among the rocks and sands,
　The night-o'ertaken mariner to save.

And the great ships sail outward and return,
　Bending and bowling o'er the billowy swell;
And, ever joyful as they see it burn,
　They wave their silent welcomes and farewells.

They come forth from the darkness, and their sails
　Gleam for a moment only in the blaze;
And eager faces, which the light unveils,
　Gaze at the tower, and vanish while they gaze.

The mariner remembers, when a child,
　On his first voyage, he saw it fade and sink;
And when, returning from adventures wild,
　He saw it rise again o'er ocean's brink.

Steadfast, serene, immovable, the same
　Year after year, through all the silent night,
Burns on for evermore that quenchless flame,
　Shines on that inextinguishable light !

It sees the ocean to its bosom clasp
　The rocks and sea-sand with the kiss of peace;
It sees the wild winds lift it in their grasp,
　And hold it up, and shake it like a fleece.

The startled waves leap over it; the storm
　Smites it with all the scourges of the rain,
And steadily against its solid form
　Press the great shoulders of the hurricane.

The sea-bird wheeling round it, with the din
　Of wings and winds and solitary cries,
Blinded and maddened by the light within,
　Dashes him against the glare, and dies.

I 2

A new Prometheus, chained upon the rock,
　　Still grasping in his hand the fire of Jove,
It does not hear the cry, nor heed the shock,
　　But hails the mariner with words of love.

"Sail on!" it says, "sail on, ye stately ships!
　　And with your floating bridge the ocean span;
Be mine to guard this light from all eclipse,
　　Be yours to bring man nearer unto man!"

　　　　　　　　　　　　LONGFELLOW.

FORGING THE ANCHOR.[1]

THE windlass strains the tackle chains; the black mound
　　heaves below,
And red and deep a hundred veins burst out at every
　　throe :
It rises, roars, rends all outright—O Vulcan, what a
　　glow !
'Tis blinding white; 'tis blasting bright—the high sun
　　shines not so !
The high sun sees not, on the earth, such fiery fearful
　　show;
The roof-ribs swarth, the candent hearth, the ruddy
　　lurid row
Of smiths that stand, an ardent band, like men before
　　the foe :
As, quivering through his fleece of flame, the sailing
　　monster slow
Sinks on the anvil; while the ring of faces fiery grow—
"Hurrah!" they shout. "Leap out, leap out!" Bang,
　　bang! the sledges go.
Hurrah! The jetted lightnings are hissing high and
　　low;
A hailing fount of fire is struck at every squashing blow.
The leathern mail rebounds the hail; the rattling cinders
　　strow
The ground about; at every bound the sweltering foun-
　　tains flow;

---

[1] Although there is no breath, nor even a glimpse of the sea in these lines, I venture to think that the subject is sufficient excuse for their inclusion here ; especially as I have been unable to find any really worthy song on the forging of an anchor.

And thick and loud the swinking crowd, at every stroke,
    pant "Ho!"
In livid and obdurate gloom he darkens down at last;
A shapely one he is and strong as e'er from cat [1] was
    cast.
O trusted and trustworthy guard, if thou hadst life like
    me,
What pleasures would thy toils reward beneath the deep
    green sea!

S. FERGUSON.

[1] The cathead, from which the anchor hangs at a vessel's bow, when
ready to be cast.

BALLADS, SONGS AND CHANTIES

CLOWN. . . . *I love a ballad but even too well, if it be doleful matter merrily set down, or a very pleasant thing indeed and sung lamentably. . . . What hast here?—ballads?*

MOPSA. *Pray now, buy some. I love a ballad in print. A' life: for then we are sure they are true.*

AUTOLYCUS. *Here's one to a very doleful tune—How a usurer's wife was brought to bed of twenty money-bags at a burden. . . .*

MOPSA. *Is it true, think you?*

AUTOLYCUS. *Very true, and but a month old.*

DORCAS. *Bless me from marrying a usurer!*

. AUTOLYCUS. *Here's the midwife's name to 't—one Mistress Taleporter—and five or six honest wives that were present. Why should I carry lies abroad?*

MOPSA. *Pray you now, buy it.*

CLOWN. *Come on, lay it by; and let's first see more ballads,—we'll buy the other things anon.*

AUTOLYCUS. *Here's another ballad, of a fish that appeared upon the coast . . . and sung this ballad against the hard hearts of maids: It was thought she was a woman, and was turned into a cold fish, for she would not exchange flesh with one that loved her. The ballad is very pitiful, and as true.*

DORCAS. *Is it true, think you?*

AUTOLYCUS. *Five justices' hands at it, and witnesses more than my pack will hold!*

CLOWN. *Lay it by too,—another.*

AUTOLYCUS. *This is a merry ballad, but a very pretty one.*

MOPSA. *Let's have some merry ones.*

AUTOLYCUS. *Why, this is a passing merry one, and goes to the tune of "Two maids wooing a man." There's scarce a maid westward but she sings it; 'tis in request, I can tell you.*

CLOWN. *We'll have this song. . . . Come, bring away thy pack after me.—Wenches, I'll buy for you both.—Pedlar, let's have the first choice.—Follow me, girls.*

From *A Winter's Tale*, ACT iv., scene 3.

More solid things do not show the complexion of the times so well as ballads and libels.

JOHN SELDEN.

She fell in love with the ballad of a sailor—
  Heigh-ho, and the wind it blew!
Her mother and her father stood by the tailor—
  Heigh-ho, and the wind it blew!

OLD SONG.

SIR PATRICK SPENS.[1]

THE king sits in Dunfermline town,
    Drinking the blude-red wine :
"Oh, where will I get a skeely [2] skippèr
    To sail this new ship o' mine? "

Oh, up and spak' an eldern knight
    There at the king's right knee,—
"Sir Patrick Spens is the best sailòr
    That ever sailed the sea."

Our king has written a braid lettèr,
    And sealed it wi' his hand,
And sent it to Sir Patrick Spens,—
    Was walking on the strand.

"To Noroway, to Noroway
    To Noroway o'er the faem;
The king's daughtèr to Noroway,—
    'Tis thou maun tak' her hame." [3]

The first word that Sir Patrick read,
    Sae loud, loud laughèd he :
The neist that Sir Patrick read,
    Salt tears blindit his e'e.

"Oh, wha is this ha'e done this deed,
    And tauld the king o' me?—
To send us out at this time o' year,[4]
    To sail across the sea !

    .   .   .   .[5]

Be it wind, be it weet, be it hail, be it sleet,
    Our ship must sail the faem;
The king's daughtèr to Noroway,—
    'Tis we must tak' [6] her hame."

[1] *See* Appendix, p. 369.   [2] Skilful.   [3] and [6] Often rendered "O' Noroway" and "fetch her hame." (*See* Appendix.)   [4] Sometime between the day of SS. Simon and Jude and Candlemas. About two hundred years after this incident the Scots Parliament made it illegal for vessels to sail with staple goods during the above-named period. [5] Here the thread of the narrative appears to be broken; possibly a stanza has been lost. This peculiar sort of illusion, however, is frequent in the oldest metrical tales that we have in English.

They hoysed their sails on Monenday morn
  Wi' a' the speed they may :
And they ha'e landed in Noroway
  Upon a Wodensday.

They hadna been a week, a week,
  In Noroway but twae,
When that the lords o' Noroway
  Began aloud to say,—

"Ye Scottishmen spend a' our king's goud
  And a' our queenis fee,"—
"Ye lie, ye lie, ye liars loud !
  Fu' loud I hear ye lie !

"For I brought as mickle white moniè
  As gane [1] my men and me,
And I brought a half-fou [2] o' gude red goud
  Out o'er the sea wi' me.

"Mak' ready, mak' ready, my merry men a' !
  Our gude ship sails the morn."—
"Now ever, alake, my master dear,
  I fear a deadly storm.

"I saw the new moon late yestreen,
  Wi' the auld moon in her arm ; [3]
And if we gang to sea, mastèr,
  I fear we'll come to harm."

They hadna sailed a league, a league,
  A league but barely three,
When the lift [4] grew dark, and the wind blew loud,
  And gurly grew the sea.

The ankers loosed, and the topmasts lap ; [5]
  It was sic a deadly storm :
And the waves cam' ower the broken ship,
  Till a' her sides were torn.

---

[1] and [2] As will be enough.   [3] An old superstition, equivalent to a ring around the moon foretelling bad weather. [4] Welkin. [5] Leapt—sprung, as when a sailing-vessel labours close-hauled and her topmasts spring fore and aft ; in which case they are often "sprung," *i. e.* split, or go by the cap.

"Oh, where will I get a gude sailòr
   To tak' my helm in hand,
Till I gae up to the tall top-màst
   To see if I can spy land? "

"Oh, here am I, a sailor gude,
   To tak' the helm in hand,
Till you gae up to the tall top-màst,—
   But I fear ye'll spy nae land."

He hadna gane a step, a step,
   A step but barely ane,
When a bout [1] flew out o' the goodly ship,
   And the salt sea it cam' in.

"Gae fetch a web o' the silken claith, [2]
   Anither o' the twine,
And wap them into our ship's side,
   And letna the sea cam' in."

They fetched a web o' the silken claith,
   Anither o' the twine,
And they wapped them into that gude ship's side,
   But still the sea cam' in.

Oh, laith, laith were our gude Scots lords
   To weet their milk-white hands !
But lang ere a' the play was ower
   They wat their gouden bands.

Oh, laith, laith were our gude Scots lords
   To weet their cork-heeled [3] shoon !
But lang ere a' the play was play'd
   They wat their hats aboon.

And many was the feather-bed
   That flattered [4] on the faem,
And many was the gude lord's son
   That never more cam' hame.

The ladies wrang their fingers white;
   The maidens tore their hair,
A' for the sake o' their true-loves,—
   For them they'll see nae mair.

[1] Bolt.   [2] and [3] *See* Appendix, pp. 369-70.   [4] Floated.

Oh lang, lang will the ladies sit,
  Wi' their fans into their hand,
Before they see Sir Patrick Spens
  Come sailing to the strand!

And lang, lang may the maidens sit,
  Wi' their good kaims in their hair,
Awaiting for their ain dear loves,—
  For them they'll see nae mair.

Half ower, half ower fra Aberdour,[1]
  'Tis fifty fathoms deep;
And there lies gude Sir Patrick Spens,
  Wi' the Scots lords at his feet.

THE LASS OF LOCH ROYAN.[2]

"O wha will shoe my bonny foot?
  And wha will glove my hand?
And wha will lace my middle jimp[3]
  Wi' a lang, lang linen band?

"O wha will kame my yellow hair
  Wi' a new-made silver kame?
And wha will father my young son,
  Till Lord Gregory cam' hame?"

"Thy brother will kame thy yellow hair;
  Thy mother will glove thy hand;
Thy sister will lace thy middle jimp,
  Till Lord Gregory cam' to land.

"Thy brother will kame thy yellow hair
  Wi' a new-made silver kame;
And God will be they bairn's father,
  Till Lord Gregory cam' hame."

---

[1] This has been written "Aberdeen"; but it appears very plainly to have been an error. Reasons for this are given in the Appendix, pp. 372-3.

[2] Lochroyan is in Galloway; and the ruined castle "situated on the sea," and supposed to have been enchanted, is said to be very ancient. Different versions of this ballad, mostly picked-out stanzas, are known under other names, the most common one being "Love Gregory." The first full rendering was issued by Sir Walter Scott; it consisted of thirty-nine stanzas. Since then other stanzas have crept in, but they are generally of doubtful origin. [3] A loose kind of stays.

"But I will get me a bonny boat,
  And I will sail the sea;
And I will gang to Lord Gregorỳ,
  Since he canna cam' to me."

Syne she's gar't [1] built a bonny boat,
  To sail the saut, saut sea:
The sails war o' the light green silk,
  The tows [2] o' taffety.

She hadna sail'd but twenty leagues—
  But twenty leagues and three,
When she met wi' a rank robbèr
  And a' his company.

"Now are ye fair the Queen herself?—
  For so ye weel might be.
Or are ye the Lass o' Loch Royàn,
  Seekin' Lord Gregorỳ?"

"Oh, I am neither the Queen," said she,
  "Nor sic I seem to be;
But I am the Lass o' Loch Royàn,
  Seekin' Lord Gregorỳ."

"Oh, seé na thou yon bonny bower?
  It's a' covered o'er wi' tin.
When thou hast sail'd it round about
  Thy lord thou'lt find within."

And when she saw the stately tower
  Shinin' sae clear and bright,
Whilk stood aboon the jawin' [3] wave
  Upon a rock of height;

Says—"Row the boat, my mariners!
  And bring me to yon land;
For there I see my love's castlè,
  Close by the saut sea strand."

She sail'd it round and sail'd it round,
  And loud, loud crièd she—
"Now break, now break, ye fairy charms,
  And set my true love free!"

---

[1] Made, probably meaning here that Annie had a boat built for her purpose.   [2] Ropes.   [3] Pouring, rushing.

She's ta'en her young son in her arms,
  And to the door she's gane;
And lang she knocked, and sair she ca'd;
  But answer got she nane.

"O open the door, Lord Gregorỳ!
  O open and let me in!
For the wind blows thro' my yellow hair,
  And the rain draps o'er my chin!

"O open, open, dear my lord!
  O open and let me in!
For I'm the Lass o' Loch Royàn,
  Cam' far frae kith and kin!"

Up then and spak' his ill mothèr:
  (An ill death may she dee!)
"Ye're no the Lass o' Loch Royàn;
  She's far out on the sea!

"Awa', awa', ye ill womàn!
  Ye're no come here for good!
Ye're but some witch or wil' warlòck,
  ·Or mermaid o' the flood!"

"I am neither witch nor wil' warlòck,
  Nor mermaid o' the sea;
But I am Annie o' Loch Royàn,—
  O open the door to me!"

Up then and spak' his ill mothèr,
  (An ill death may she find!)
In a' the voice o' Lord Gregorỳ,
  Wha slept and couldna mind:

"Gin thou be Annie o' Loch Royàn,
  (As I trow thou binna she)
Now tell me some o' the love-tokèns
  That pass'd 'twixt thee and me."

"Oh, dinna ye mind, Lord Gregorỳ,
  As we sat at the wine,
We changèd rings frae our fingèrs?—
  And I can show thee thine.

"Oh, yours was gude, and gude enow;
  But aye the best was mine:
For yours was o' the gude red gowd,
  But mine o' the diamond fine."

"If thou be she o' Loch Royàn,
  (As I kennà thou be,)
Tell me some mair o' the love-tokèns
  That pass'd 'twixt thee and me."

"Oh, mind ye not, Lord Gregorỳ,
  As we sat on the hill,
Thou twined me o' my maidenhead?—
  Right sair against my will.

"Now open the door, Lord Gregorỳ!
  Open the door, I pray!
For thy young son is in my arms,
  And will be dead ere day!"

"Ye're fause, ye're fause, ye ill womàn!—
  So go ye hence and dee.
Ye're no the Lass o' Loch Royàn;
  Wha's far out on the sea!"

Fair Annie turned her round about:
  "Weel, since that it be sae;
May never a woman that's borne a son
  Hae a heart sae fou o' wae!

"Tak' down, tak' down that mast o' gowd!
  Set up a mast o' tree!
It disna become a forsaken ladỳ
  To sail sae royalliè!"

When the cock had crawn, and the day did dawn,
  And the sun began to peep;
Then up and raise him Lòrd Gregorỳ,
  And sair, sair did he weep.

"Oh, I hae dream'd a dream, mothèr—
  I wish it may prove true!
That the bonny Lass o' Loch Royàn
  Was at the gate e'en now.

"Oh, I hae dream'd a dream, mothèr:
  The thought o' it gars me greet![1]
That fair Anniè o' Loch Royàn
  Lay cauld dead at my feet!"

"Gin it be for Annie o' Loch Royàn
  That ye mak' a' this din,
She stood the night thro' at yon' door;
  But I wadna let her in."

[1] Makes me weep.

"Oh, wae betide ye, ill womàn!—
  An ill deid cam' to ye,
That wadna open the door to her!
  Nor yet wad waken me!"

Oh, he went down to yon shore-side
  As fast as he could fare:
He saw fair Annie in the boat;
  But the wind it toss'd her sair.

"And hey, Anniè! And how, Anniè!
  O Annie, winna ye bide?"
But aye the mair he cried Anniè,
  The braider grew the tide.

"And hey, Anniè! And how, Anniè!
  Dear Annie, speak to me!"
But aye the louder he cried Anniè,
  The louder roar'd the sea.

The wind blew loud; the sea grew rough,
  And dash'd the boat ashore:
Fair Annie floated thro' the faem;
  But her babie rose no more.

Lord Gregory tore his yellow hair,
  And made a heavy moan:
Fair Annie's corpse lay at his feet,—
  Her bonny young son was gone.

Oh, pallid, pallid was her cheek,
  And gowden was her hair;
But clay-cauld war her rosy lips—
  Nae spark o' life was there.

And first he kiss'd her whiten'd cheek,
  And syne he kiss'd her chin,
And syne he kiss'd her rosy lips—
  There was nae breath within.

"Oh, wae betide my cruel mothèr!—
  An ill death may she dee!
She turned my true love frae my door,
  Wha cam' sae far to me.

"Oh, wae betide my cruel mothèr!—
  An ill death come to ye,
Wha's been the death of a' o' us—
  My Annie, babe and me!"

ANONYMOUS.

SIR WALTER RALEIGH SAILING IN
LOW LANDS.[1]

Sir Walter Raleigh has built a ship—in the Nether-
lands,
Sir Walter Raleigh has built a ship—in the Netherlands,
And it is called the *Sweet Trinity,*
And it was taken by a false gallaley—
    Sailing in the Low Lands, O.

"Is there never a seaman bold—in the Netherlands,
Is there never a seaman bold—in the Netherlands,
That will go take this false gallaley,
All to redeem the *Sweet Trinity,*
    Sailing in the Low Lands, O?"

Then spoke the little ship-boy—in the Netherlands,
Then spoke the little ship-boy—in the Netherlands:
"Master, what will you give, an I take this false
gallaley,
And release the *Sweet Trinity*— .
    Sailing in the Low Lands, O?"

"I'll give thee gold, and I'll give thee fee—in the
Netherlands,
I'll give thee gold, and I'll give thee fee—in the
Netherlands,
And my eldest daughter thy wife shall be—
    Sailing in the Low Lands, O."

[1] There is a number ot versions of this ballad, the most of which
vary in the fate of the cabin-boy. Its first appearance seems to have
been on broadsides from 1680 to 1685, or later ; but it is thought to
have had an earlier origin. (Raleigh died on Oct. 29, 1618.) Some
versions are called "The Golden Vanity" or "Goulden Vanitee"; in
these there is no mention of Raleigh, the story being of a *north-
country vessel* bearing the name "Golden Vanity," and meeting with
a French galley while sailing in the Lowlands. One version has it
"Turkish gallee"—in the Lowlands at that date ! In all probability the
story of the ship "boy" had a foundation in fact ; and this version very
likely came into existence towards the end of the seventeenth century,
when time had made Raleigh's name, even in the north of England,
synonymous with adventure at sea. In its repetition of the first line
and its half-detached refrain the ballad is curiously reminiscent of the
chanties of centuries later.

K

He set his breast, and away he did swim—in the Nether-
    lands,
He set his breast, and away he did swim—in the Nether-
    lands,
Until he came to the false gallaley—
        Sailing in the Low Lands, O.

He had an augur fit for the nonce—in the Netherlands,
He had an augur fit for the nonce—in the Netherlands,
The which did bore fifteen good holes at once [1]—
        Sailing in the Low Lands, O.

Some were at cards and some at dice—in the Nether-
    lands,
Some were at cards and some at dice—in the Nether-
    lands,
Until the salt-water flashed in their eyes—
        Sailing in the Low Lands, O.

Some cut their hats, and some cut their caps—in the
    Netherlands,
Some cut their hats, and some cut their caps—in the
    Netherlands,
All for to stop the salt-water gaps—[2]
        Sailing in the Low Lands, O.

He set his breast, and away he did swim—in the
    Netherlands,
He set his breast, and away he did swim—in the
    Netherlands,
Until he came to his own ship again—
        Sailing in the Low Lands, O.

"I have done the work I promised to do—in the Nether-
    lands,
I have done the work I promised to do—in the Nether-
    lands;
For I've sunk the false galley and released the *Sweet
    Trinity*—
        Sailing in the Low Lands, O.

[1] This must be taken as meaning that the augur would bore fifteen
holes without sharpening.   One of the "Golden Vanity" versions has
"bore two holes at twice!"   [2] This reminds one of the "silken
claith" and the canvas to stop the leak in "Sir Patrick Spens."

"You promised me gold, and you promised me fee—
in the Netherlands,
You promised me gold, and you promised me fee—in
the Netherlands:
Your eldest daughter my wife she must be—
Sailing in the Low Lands, O."

"You shall have gold, and you shall have fee—in the
Netherlands,
You shall have gold, and you shall have fee—in the
Netherlands;
But my eldest daughter your wife shall never be—
Sailing in the Low Lands, O."

"Then fare you well, you cozening lord—in the Nether-
lands,
Then fare you well, you cozening lord—in the Nether-
lands,
Seeing you are not as good as your word—
Sailing in the Low Lands, O."

And thus I will conclude my song of sailing in the Low
Lands,
Wishing all happiness to all seamen, old and young,
In their sailing in the Low Lands, O.

ANONYMOUS.

THE SPANISH LADY'S LOVE.[1]

WILL you hear a Spanish lady,
How she wooed an English man?
Garments gay and rich as may be,
Decked with jewels, she had on.
Of a comely countenance and grace was she,
And by birth and parentage of high degree.

[1] There are several old ballads with much the same burthen as this one carries, one instance being "The Beautiful Lady of Kent"; but this, which was first published in *The Garland of Good-will*, 1631, by Thomas Deloney, is supposed to have been the earliest of them all. There is a tradition that the captain was Sir Richard Levison, of Trentham, Staffordshire, who did excellent work against the Spaniards towards the end of the sixteenth century. Another story, long current in western counties, had it that he was one of the Popham family, by whom, it was said, a painting of the inamorato and her gold bracelets and chain were kept long after the affair, which was dramatised by Thomas Hull, set to music, and played in Covent Garden Theatre, 1765.

K 2

As his prisoner he kept her,
　In his hands her life did lie;
Cupid's bands did hold them faster
　In the liking of an eye.
His courteous company was to her all joy;
To favour him in anything she was not coy.

But at length there came commandment
　For to set the ladies free,
With their jewels still adornèd—
　None to do them injury.
Then said this beauty mild: "Full woe is me!
Oh, let me still sustain this loved captivity!

"Gallant captain show some pity
　To a lady in distress;
Leave me not within this city,
　Or I die in heaviness.
Thou hast set this present day my body free;
But my heart in prison still remains with thee."

"Why dost thou, fair lady, love me,
　Whom thou knowest thy country's foe?
These strange words make me suspect thee,—
　Serpents lie where flowers grow."
"All the harm I wish to thee, most courteous knight,
God grant the same upon my head may fully light.

"Blessèd be the time and season
　When you came on Spanish ground:
If our foes you may be termèd,
　Gentle foes we have you found.
With our city you have gained our hearts each one;
Then to your country bear away what you have won."

"Rest you here, most gallant lady;
　Rest you still and weep no more:
Of brave lovers there is plenty—
　Spain doth yield a wondrous store."
"Spaniards fraught with jealousy we often find;
But English men thro' all the world are counted kind.

"Leave me not unto a Spaniard;
　You alone enjoy my heart.
I am lovely, young and tender—
　Love should likewise be my part.

Still to serve thee day and night my mind is pressed—
The wife of ev'ry English man is counted blest."

"It would be a shame, sweet lady,
   For to bear a woman hence;
English sailors never carry
   Any such without offence."
"I will quickly change myself, if it be so;
And like a page I'll follow you, where'er you go."

"I have neither gold nor silver
   To maintain thee in such case;
And to travel is great charges,
   As thou know'st, in ev'ry place."
"My jewels and my chains ev'ry one shall be thine own,
And eke five hundred pounds in gold that lies unknown."

"On the sea are many dangers;
   Mighty storms do there arise,
Which will be to ladies dreadful,
   And force tears from their fair eyes."
"Well, in troth, I shall endure extremity;
For I could find in heart to lose my life for thee."

"Courteous lady, leave this fancy—
   Here comes all that breeds this strife:
I, in England, have already
   A sweet woman to my wife.
I will not falsify my vow for gold or gain,
Nor yet for all the fairest dames that ever lived in Spain."

"Oh, how happy is that woman
   That enjoys so true a friend!
Many glorious days God send her!—
   Of my suit I make an end.
On my knees I pardon crave for mine offence,
Which did from love and true affection first commence.

"Commend me to thy lovely lady;
   Bear to her this chain of gold
And these bracelets, for a token,—
   Grieving that I was so bold:
All my jewels in like sort take thou with thee;
For they are fitting for thy wife, but not for me.

"All my days I'll spend in prayer—
  Love and all his laws defy :
In a nunnery will I shroud me,
  Far from any company.
But ere my prayers have an end, be sure of this—
To pray for thee and for thy love I will not miss.

"Thus farewell, most gallant captain !
  Farewell, too, my heart's content !
Count not Spanish ladies wanton,—
  Tho' to thee my love was bent.
Joy and true prosperity go still with thee ! "
"The like fall ever to thy share, most fair lady ! "

ANONYMOUS.

THE BEAUTIFUL LADY OF KENT; OR, THE SEAMAN OF DOVER.[1]

A SEAMAN of Dover, whose excellent parts,
For wisdom and learning, had conquered the hearts
Of many young damsels, of beauty so bright,—
Of him this new ditty in brief I shall write ;

And show of his turnings and windings of fate,
His passions and sorrows, so many and great ;
And how he was blessèd with true love at last,
When all the rough storms of his troubles were past.

Now, to be brief, I shall tell you the truth :
A beautiful lady, whose name it was Ruth,—
A squire's young daughter, near Sandwich, in Kent,
Prov'd all his heart's treasure, his joy and content.

Unknown to her parents in private they met,
Where many love lessons they conn'd and reset ;
With kisses, and many embraces likewise,
She granted him love, and thus gainèd the prize.

"My love, I consent to be thy sweet bride,
Whatever becomes of my fortune," she cried :
"The frowns of my father I never will fear ;
But freely will go through the world with my dear."

[1] See Appendix, p. 373.

A jewel he gave her in token of love,
And vow'd, by the sacred Powers above,
To wed the next morning; but they were betray'd,
And all by the means of a treacherous maid;

Who told the girl's parents what purpose was meant.
With that they fell into a passion intent,
And said ere a seaman their daughter should have,
They rather would follow her corpse to the grave.

The lady was straight to her chamber confin'd,
Where long she continued in sorrow of mind;
And so did her love, for the loss of his dear,—
No sorrow was ever so sharp and severe.

When long he had mourn'd for his love and delight,
Close under the window he came in the night,
And sung forth this ditty:—"My dearest, farewell!
Behold, in this nation no longer I dwell.

"I am going from hence to the kingdom of Spain;
Because I am willing that thou shouldst obtain
Thy freedom once more; for my heart it will break,
If longer thou liest confin'd for my sake."

The words which he utter'd, they caus'd her to weep;
Yet, nevertheless, she was forcèd to keep
Deep silence that minute—that minute, for fear
Her honourèd father and mother should hear.

Soon after, bold Henry he enter'd on board;
The heavens a prosperous gale did afford,
And brought him with speed to the kingdom of Spain,
There he with a merchant some time did remain.

The merchant, finding him both faithful and just,
Preferr'd him to places of honour and trust.
He was there made great as his heart could request;
Yet, wanting his Ruth, he with grief was oppress'd.

So great was his grief it could not be conceal'd,
Both honour and riches no pleasure could yield.
In private he often would weep and lament
For Ruth, the fair, beautiful lady of Kent.

Now, while he lamented the loss of his dear,
A lady of Spain did before him appear,
Bedecked with rich jewels both costly and gay,
Who earnestly sought for his favour that day.

Said she, "Gentle swain, I am wounded with love;
And thou art the person I honour above
The greatest of nobles that ever was born;—
Then pity my tears, and my sorrowful mourn!"

"I pity thy sorrowful tears," he repli'd,
"And wish I were worthy to make thee my bride;
But, lady, thy grandeur is greater than mine,
Therefore, I am fearful my heart to resign."

"O! never be doubtful of wedding with me—
No manner of danger will happen to thee.
At my own disposal I am, I declare:
Receive me with love, or destroy me with care."

"Dear madam, don't fix thy affection on me;
Thou art fit for some man of a noble degree,
That is able to keep up thine honour and fame,—
I'm but a poor sailor, from England who came.

"A man of mean fortune, whose substance is small,
I have not wherewith to maintain thee withal,
Sweet lady, according to honour and state:
Now this is the truth, which I freely relate."

The lady she lovingly squeezèd his hand,
And said, with a smile, "Ever blest be the land
That bred such a noble, brave seaman as thee:
I value no honours,—thou'rt welcome to me.

"My parents are dead: I have jewels untold,
Besides in possession a million of gold;
And thou shalt be lord of whatever I have,—
Grant me but thy love, which I earnestly crave."

Then turning aside, to himself he repli'd,
"I am courted with riches and beauty beside:
This love I may have; and my Ruth is deni'd."
Wherefore he consented to make her his bride.

The lady she cloth'd him both costly and great.
His noble deportment was proper and straight;
It charmèd the innocent eye of his dove,
And added a second new flame to her love.

Then marri'd they were without longer delay.
Now here we will leave them, both glorious and gay,
To speak of fair Ruth; who in sorrow was left
At home with her parents, of comfort bereft.

WHEN under the window, with an aching heart,
He told his fair Ruth he so soon must depart,
Her parents they heard, and well pleasèd they were;
But Ruth was afflicted with sorrow and care.

Now, after her lover had quitted the shore,
They kept her confin'd a full twelvemonth or more;
And when they were pleas'd for to set her at large,
With laying upon her this wonderful charge—

To fly from a seaman as she would from death.
She promis'd she would, with a faltering breath:
Yet, nevertheless, the truth you shall hear,
She found out a way for to follow her dear.

Then, taking her gold and her silver also,
In seaman's apparel [1] away she did go,
And found out a master, with whom she agreed
To carry her over the ocean with speed.

Now when she arriv'd at the kingdom of Spain,
From city to city she travell'd amain,
Enquiring about everywhere for her love,
Who now had been gone seven [2] years and above.

[1] There is quite a number of old ballads and songs on sweethearts going as sailors or cabin-boys in their lovers' vessels, rather than be parted. (*See* note to "Constance and Anthony," p. 150.) One—of which I remember a portion, as sung by my paternal grandfather, but have been unable to find in print—was called "The Handsome Cabin-boy," and told how the captain fell in love with, but was repulsed by, his "female cabin-boy." In the "Two Faithful Lovers" she refused gold, servants, etc., to stay at home; so the lover took her with him the vessel was wrecked; he was saved, and she was drowned.
[2] This, also, is an ever-recurrent feature in amatory verse-tales of the sixteenth, seventeenth and eighteenth centuries : even to-day amongst illiterate classes, particularly in agricultural districts, there is an idea that a seven years' absence sets wife or husband free. Probably this notion was an outcome of the old ballad feature.

In Cadiz, as she walk'd along in the street,
Her love and his lady she happen'd to meet;
But in such a garb as she never had seen,—
She look'd like an angel, or beautiful queen.

With sorrowful tears she turn'd her aside:
"My jewel is gone; I shall ne'er be his bride.
Yet, nevertheless, though my hopes are in vain,
I'll never return to old England again.

"But here, in this place, I will now be confin'd;
It will be a comfort and joy to my mind
To see him sometimes, though he thinks not of me,—
Since he has a lady of noble degree."

Now while in the city fair Ruth did reside,
Of a sudden this beautiful lady she died;
And, though he was in the possession of all,
Yet tears from his eyes in abundance did fall.

As he was expressing his piteous moan,
Fair Ruth came unto him, and made herself known.
He started to see her, but seemèd not coy,
Said he, "Now my sorrows are mingled with joy."

The time of the mourning he kept it in Spain,
And then he came back to old England again,
With thousands and thousands which he did possess;
Then glorious and gay was sweet Ruth in her dress.

WHEN over the seas to fair Sandwich he came,
With Ruth and a number of persons of fame,
Then all did appear most splendid and gay,
As if it had been a great festival day.

Now when they took up with their lodgings, behold,
He stripp'd off his coat of embroidery and gold!
And presently borrow'd a mariner's suit,
That he with her parents might have some dispute,

Before they were sensible he was so great;
And when he came in and knock'd at the gate,
He soon saw her father and mother likewise
Expressing their sorrow, with tears in their eyes.

To them, with obeisance, he modestly said,
"Pray where is my jewel, that innocent maid,
Whose sweet lovely beauty doth thousands excel?
I fear, by your weeping, that all is not well!"

"No, no! she is gone—she is utterly lost!
We have not heard of her a twelvemonth at most!
Which makes us distracted with sorrow and care,
And drowns us in tears at the point of despair."

"I'm grievèd to hear these sad tidings!" he cried.
"Alas! honest young man," her father replied,
"I heartily wish she'd been wedded to you,
For then we this sorrow had never gone through."

Sweet Henry he made them this answer again—
"I am newly come home from the kingdom of Spain;
From whence I have brought me a beautiful bride,
And am to be marri'd to-morrow!" he cried.

"And if you will go to my wedding," said he,
"Both you and your lady right welcome shall be."
They promis'd they would, and accordingly came,
Not thinking to meet with such persons of fame.

All deck'd with their jewels and rubies and pearls,
As equal companions of barons and earls,
Fair Ruth, with her love, was as gay as the rest,
So they in their marriage were happily blest.

Now as they return'd from the church to an inn,
The father and mother of Ruth did begin
Their daughter to know, by a mole they had loath'd,
Although in a garment of gold she was cloth'd.

With transports of joy they flew to the bride,
"O! where hast thou been, sweetest daughter?" they
        cried,
"Thy tedious absence has grievèd us sore,
As fearing, alas! we should see thee no more."

"Dear parents," said she, "many hazards I ran
To fetch home my love, this rare prize of a man:
Receive him with joy; for 'tis very well known,
He seeks not your wealth—he's enough of his own."

Her father repli'd, and he merrily smil'd,
"He's brought home enough, as he's brought home my
    child.
A thousand times welcome thou art, I declare,
Whose presence disperses both sorrow and care!"

Full seven long days in feasting they spent;
The bells in the steeple they merrily went;
And many fair pounds were bestow'd on the poor,—
The like of this wedding was never before!

ANONYMOUS.

CAPTAIN GLEN.[1]

THERE was a ship and a ship of fame,
Launch'd from the stocks and bound to the main,
With a hundred and fifty brisk young men,
All pick'd and chosen every one.

William Glen was her captain's name;
He was a tall and fine young man,
As good a sailor as went to sea,
And he was bound to New Barbarỳ.

'Twas first of April we set sail,
Blest with a sweet and pleasant gale;
For we were bound to New Barbarỳ
With merchandise and gold in fee.

We had not sail'd one day but two—
One day but two, when our jovial crew
All fell sick but sixty-three,
As he went to New Barbarỳ.

One night the Captain he did dream
There came a voice and said to him—
"Prepare you and your company,
To-morrow night [2] you must with me."

---

[1] This—an undoubtedly genuine ballad that was probably monotoned through villages and small towns by "turnpike" sailors about one hundred and forty years ago, and retailed by them at a penny apiece—is one of the best material representations of the "Jonah" superstition which is still found in sailing craft, particularly amongst seamen of the Upper Baltic.   [2] This summoning on the night before death is a common feature in the morality folk-pieces of the sixteenth and seventeenth centuries.

This wak'd the Captain in a fright—
It being third [1] watch of the night;
Then for his boatswain [2] he did call
And told his deadly secrets all.

"When I in England did remain
God's holy day I did profane;
In drunkenness I did delight,
Which now my trembling soul doth fright.

"There's one thing more I must rehearse,
Of all things else it is the worse :
A knight I slew in Staffordshire,
All for the love of a lady fair.

"Now this is his ghost, I'm much afraid,
That hath in me such terror made;
Altho' the King hath pardon'd me,
This ghost will be my tragedy."

"Oh, worthy Captain, since 'tis so,
No mortal of it e'er shall know;
So hold the secret in your breast,
And pray to God to give you rest."

We had not sail'd a league but three—
But three, when raging grew the sea;
There rose a tempest in the skies,
That fill'd us all with dumb surprise.

Our main-mast sprung at break of day,
Which caus'd our rigging to give way;
The seamen were in sore affright
At terrors of that fatal night.

Up then and spake our fore-mast man, [3]
As he did by the fore-yard stand;
He cried, "O Lord, receive my soul !"
And to the deck he did down fall.

[1] From four o'clock to eight in the morning.   [2] It may seem to be curious that the master should call the boatswain and not the mate ; but in old literature we seldom find an instance of brotherly ties between master and mate, and not more often is the thing seen afloat to-day, especially under sail. If the mate and the boatswain are not on comrade-like terms, it is ten to one that the master has a leaning to the latter. [3] In a man-o'-war this would have been the captain of the foretop, a petty officer that was not carried by merchantmen towards the end of the eighteenth century ; and it is open to some doubt if he was known a hundred years earlier, to which time certain internal evidences of the ballad seem to say that it belongs.

The sea did wash both fore and aft,
Till scarce a soul on board was left;
Our yards were split, our rigging was tore—
The like was never seen before.

The boatswain then he did declare
The Captain was a murderèr,
Which did so anger all the crew,
They up and overboard him threw.

Our treacherous Captain being dead,
Within that hour gone was our dread;
The wind did drop, and calm the sea
As we sailed on to Barbarỳ.

Now, when we reach'd the Spanish shore.
Our sore-tri'd ship for to repair,
The people all were 'maz'd to see
Our dismal case and misery.

So when our ship she was repair'd
To fair England our course was steer'd;
And when we came to London Town,
Our dismal case was there made known.

For many wives had husbands lost,
Whom they lamented, to their cost;
And caus'd them weep full bitterly—
These tidings from New Barbarỳ.

A hundred and fifty brisk young men
Had to our goodly ship belong'd;
And now of all our company
There did remain but sixty-three.

Now, seamen all, where'er you be
I pray a warning take by me;[1]
You love your lives, so have a care
Never to sail with a murderèr.

'Tis never more that I again
Intend to cross the raging main;
But live in peace in my countrỳ—
And so here ends my tragedỳ.

ANONYMOUS.

[1] " Now . . . where'er you be, I pray a warning take by me ":
These words, exactly as here, are found in many of the inferior ballads
of the seventeenth and eighteenth centuries, especially in the verse-
stories of young women being betrayed by men who loved awhile, then
sailed or rode away.

THE FAIRE MAID'S CHOICE.[1]

Being a pleasante new songe of a saylor,
Who excells a miller, a weaver, and a taylor,
Likewise brave gallants that goe fine and rare—
For none of them with saylors can compare.

As I through old Sandwych towne lately did pass,
I heard this new songe by a blooming faire lass;
   'Twas the praise of a saylor she sunge gallantly—
   "Of all sorts of traders a seaman for me!
Of all sorts of traders a seaman for me!"

I gave strict attention to her freshe ditty,
And thought it most wondrous gallant and pretty;
   With a voice sweete and pleasante soe neatly sunge
     she—
   "Of all sorts of traders a seaman for me!"
And this was the songe that she sang cheerily.

"Come all you faire maydens in countrie and towne,
Now lende your attention to what I sett downe,
   And lett your opinions with mine owne agree—
   Of all sorts of traders a seaman for me.

"The brave hardy saylor, God blesse him, I say;
He is a great pains-taker both night and day;
   When he is affoat soe hard worketh he,
   That of all sorts of traders a seaman for me.

"And of all sorts of gallants soe gaudy and fine,
That with gold and with silver soe mightily shine,
   The seaman doth outstrip them all in degree—
   Soe of all sorts of traders a seaman for me.

"For a saylor will venture hys life and hys blood
For the sake of hys kyng and hys countrie's good;
   He is brave and he's gallant in every degree,
   Soe of all sorts of traders a seaman for me.

"He ventures for traffik uppon the salte seas,
To pleasure our gentrie, whych lives at its ease;

[1] This is the best of several ballads of this kind; it is also one of the oldest with this burthen, its date being probably about the time of the Restoration. In a more modern form, but with the same refrain, it was sung by east coast seamen when I was a boy amongst them.

Thro' manye great dangers he goes cheerily—
Soe of all sorts of traders a seaman for me.

"Amongst all your merchants and tradesmen that be
I'll ne'er sett my fancy—there's none such for me;
   But a saylor I'll have my dear husband to be—
   For of all sorts of traders a seaman for me.

"With a thievyng younge miller I never will deal,
For out of a bushel a peck he will steal,—
   I'll have noe love-tradyng with such knaves as he;
   But of all sorts of traders a seaman for me.

"Now a fine pimpyng taylor, or lousie weavèr,
To steal cloth and yarn from their graveyards would
      stir;
   O such fellowes are not for my companiè,
   For of all sorts of traders a seaman for me.

"Also the carpenter and the shoemàker,
The blacksmith, the brewer, the pastieface'd baker,—
   The moste they are knaves with noe honostiè,
   Soe of all sorts of traders a seaman for me.

"For *I* love a saylor as *I* love my life,
And I am resolvèd to be a sea wife;
   Noe man else in England my husbande shall be,
   For of all sorts of traders a seaman for me.

"Now I'll tell you why I love seamen soe,—
I have to my sweeteheart a saylor, oh—oh;
   He's a stout, proper lad, as you shall soone see—
   Soe of all sorts of traders a seaman for me.

"If that I were worthe a greate shipp full of gold,
My love should possess it, and with it make bold;
   I would make him the mastcr of ev'ry penniè,
   For of all sorts of traders a seaman for me.

"Thro' fire and thro' water I'de goe, I doe sweare,
For the sake of my sweeteheart that I love soe deare;
   If I might have an earl I'de forsake hym for he—
   For of all sorts of traders a seaman for me.

"Here's a healthe to my dear, come pledge me who
  please,
And to all gallant saylors that sayle on the seas!
  Pray God blesse and keepe them from all dangers
  free—
  For of all sorts of tradesmen a seaman for me!"

ANONYMOUS.

THE SEAMAN'S HAPPY RETURN.[1]

WHEN Sol did cast no light,
  Being darken'd over;
And the deep time of night
  The far skies did cover—
Running a river by,
  Whereon ships were sailing,
A most fair maid spy'd I,
  A-crying and a-wailing.

Up to this maid I stept,
  Asking what had griev'd her;
She answered me, and wept,
  . Fate it had deceiv'd her.
"My love is press'd," quoth she,
  "To cross yon ocean;
And proud waves make the ship
  Be ever in motion.

"We lov'd for seven years or more,
  Both of us so sure;
But I am now left on shore,
  My grief alone t' endure.
He promis'd back to turn
  If life was spar'd him;
With grief I constant mourn
  That death hath lair'd him."

---

[1] Under the title "The Welcome Sailor," Mr. Ashton ("Real
Sailor-Songs") has a much later version of this ballad—so late, in fact,
that I heard it sung on the east coast thirty years ago, with certain
"improvements" which are lacking in his copy. It will be evident to
the reader that this version was written by a man of education.

Straight a brisk lad she spy'd—
  He made her admire;
And a keepsake, he untied,
  Pleasèd her desire.
"Is my love safe?" quoth she:
  "Will he come near me?"
That young man did answer make—
  "Virgin, do pray hear me.

"Beneath one banner bright,
  For old England's glory,
Your dear love and I did fight—
  Mark you well my story.
But by an unhappy shot
  We two friends were parted,
And his death's-wound there he got
  Though so valiant-hearted.

"All of this I witness can,
  For 'twas I stood by him;
And for courage, I must say,
  None could e'er outvye him.
Still he would the foremost be,
  Striving for his honour;
But Dame Fortune is a bitch—
  Vengeance black upon her!

"But before he was quite dead,
  Or his heart was broken,
Up to me these words he said:
  'Pray you give this token
To my love, if you her find—
  There be none that's fairer;
Tell her that she must be kind
  And sure to love the bearer.'

"In his grave he now doth lie
  In a stately manner,
'Cause he fought so valiantly
  For sweet love and honour.
All the right he had in you
  Unto me he gave it;
And now since it is my due,
  Pray you let me have it."

Raging she here flung away,
    Like to one distracted,
Not e'en knowing what to say,
    Nor like what she acted :
All along she curs'd her fate,
    And seem'd to need a warder,
Saying—"Friend, you come too late,—
    I'll have no man on order !

"You to your house return,—
    Here I shall be pleasèd
My dear, dead love to mourn,
    Since he is deceasèd.
In sabl'st weeds I'll go—
    Let who will come jeer me;
Since foul death hath serv'd me so,
    None shall come a-near me.

"The chaste Penelope
    Did mourn for her Ulysses;
And I've more grief than she,
    Robb'd of all my blisses.
I'll ne'er love man again,—
    Therefore pray you hear me;
I'll pour on you disdain
    If once you come a-near me !

"I know he lov'd me well,
    For when we two parted
None could his grief excel—
    Both were most true-hearted.
Those promises we made
    Shall be broken never,
And what to me he said
    Shall fill my heart for ever."

Now hearing this she said
    Made his love wax stronger,
So off disguise he laid,
    And kept the hoax no longer.
When her dear love she knew,
    In sweet wanton fashion
Into his arms she flew !—
    Such is love's own passion.

L 2

He ask'd her how she lik'd
　　His late counterfeiting—
If or not she was well pleas'd
　　With such like a-greeting?
Quoth she—"You made much go
　　In your several speeches :
Could you coin bright guineas so,
　　How soon we would have riches !

"O favouring gale of wind
　　That here hath waft thee over !
May Heaven preserve that ship
　　That brought my constant lover.
Come kiss me now, my sweet—
　　True love is no slander :
Thou shalt hence my Hero be,
　　And I'll be thy Leander.

"Dido, Queen of Carthage,
　　Lov'd devout Æneas ;
But my true love is found
　　Far more true than he was.
Venus never fonder was
　　Of her young Adonis,
Than, my love, I'll be of thee
　　Since my dear so known is."

Then hand-in-hand they walked,
　　With gaiety and pleasure ;
They laugh'd, they kiss'd, they talk'd—
　　Love knoweth not of measure.
Now down they sit and sing,
　　But she 'tis sings the clearest,
Like nightingale in spring—
　　"O welcome home, my dearest ! "
　　　　　　　　　　　　ANONYMOUS.

BLACK-EYED SUSAN.

ALL in the Downs the fleet was moor'd,
　　The streamers waving in the wind,
When black-eyed Susan came on board :
　　"Oh ! where shall I my true love find?

Tell me, ye jovial sailors, tell me true,
If my sweet William sails among your crew? " [1]

William, who, high upon the yard,
  Rock'd by the billows to and fro,
Soon as her well-known voice he heard,
  He sighed and cast his eyes below :
The cord glides swiftly through his glowing hands,
And quick as lightning on the deck he stands.

So the sweet lark, high-pois'd in air,
  Shuts close his pinions to his breast,
If chance his mate's shrill call he hear,
  And drops at once into her nest :
The noblest captain in the British fleet
Might envy William's lips those kisses sweet.

"O Susan, Susan, lovely dear,
  My vows shall ever true remain !
Let me kiss off that falling tear,—
  We only part to meet again :
Change as ye list, ye winds, my heart shall be
The faithful compass that still points to thee !

"Believe not what the landsmen say,
  Who tempt, with doubts, thy constant mind :
They'll tell thee, sailors, when away,
  At every port a mistress find.—
Yes, yes !—believe them when they tell thee so ;
For thou art present wheresoe'er I go.

"If to fair India's coast we sail,
  Thine eyes are seen in diamonds bright ;
Thy breath is Afric's spicy gale,—
  Thy skin is ivory so white :
Thus every beauteous object that I view
Wakes in my soul some charm of lovely Sue.

"Though battle calls me from thy arms,
  Let not my pretty Susan mourn ;
Though cannons roar, yet, free from harms,
  William shall to his dear return :

---

[1] An old song, "The Sailor Boy"—possibly not so old as to be anterior to Gay's time—has :

    "O sailor, sailor, send me word,
      If my true love William be on board."

Love turns aside the balls that round me fly,
Lest precious tears should drop from Susan's eye."

The boatswain gives his dreadful word,—
　　The sails their swelling bosoms spread;
No longer may she stay on board:
　　They kiss: She sighs: He hangs his head.
Her lessening boat unwilling rows to land:
"Adieu!" she cries, and waves her lily hand.

GAY.

"'TWAS WHEN THE SEAS WERE ROARING."

'TWAS when the seas were roaring
　　With hollow blasts of wind,
A damsel lay deploring,
　　All on a rock reclin'd.
Wide o'er the foaming billows
　　She cast a wistful look;
Her head was crowned with willows
　　That trembled o'er the brook.

"Twelve months are gone and over,
　　And nine long tedious days:
Why didst thou venturous lover—
　　Why didst thou trust the seas?
Cease, cease, thou cruel ocean,
　　And let my lover rest!
Ah! what's thy troubled motion
　　To that within my breast?

"The merchant, robb'd of treasure,
　　Views tempests in despair;
But what's the loss of treasure,
　　To losing of my dear?
Should you some coast be laid on,
　　Where gold and diamonds grow,
You'll find a richer maiden—
　　But none that loves you so.

"How can they say that Nature
  Has nothing made in vain?
Why, then, beneath the water
  Do hideous rocks remain?
No eyes those rocks discover
  That lurk beneath the deep,
To wreck the wandering lover,
  And leave the maid to weep."

All melancholy lying,
  Thus wail'd she for her dear,—
Repaid each blast with sighing,
  Each billow with a tear;
When, o'er the white wave stooping,
  His floating corpse she spied;
Then, like a lily drooping,
  She how'd her head and died.

GAY.

CONSTANCE AND ANTHONY:[1]

AN ADMIRABLE STORY FROM THE NORTH COUNTREE.

Two lovers in the north,
  Constance and Anthony—
Of them I'll now set forth
  A gallant history:
They lov'd exceeding well,
  As plainly doth appear;
But that which I shall tell
  The like you ne'er did hear.
    Still she cries: "Anthony—
    My bonnie Anthony!
    Gang thou by land or sea
    I'll bear thee companie—
    O my own Anthony!"

[1] This is a very fair example of the ballad that pictures a sweetheart going to sea, as a boy, with her lover; some of them end in wreck and the death of the couple, or of one of them, while the other is left to die speedily of a broken heart. From the frequency of this story, in verse and prose, especially during the eighteenth century, it is very evident that the venture was made often enough for the idea to have obtained a permanent place in the popular mind, at a time when sentiment had a far greater hold on the people than it has now.

Anthony he must to sea,
   His calling doth him bind :
"My Constance, dear," quoth he,
   "I must leave thee behind.
But prithee do not grieve—
   Thy tears will not avail;
I'll think of thee, sweetheart,
   When we are under sail."
      Still she cries : "Anthony,
      I'll wend along with thee—
      Oh—oh, my Anthony ! "

"How that may be," said he—
   "Consider well the case."
Quoth she—"Sweet Anthony,
   I'll bide not in this place :   .
If thou goest, so go I ;
   As for means, do not doubt
A woman's policie
   Great matters will find out—
      "My bonnie Anthony," etc.

"I would be very glad,—
   But, prithee, tell me how? "
"I'll dress me like a lad—
   What sa'st thou to me now? "
"The seas thou can'st not brook "—
   "Yes, very well," quoth she ;
"I'll scullion to the cook
   For thy sweet companie—
      "My bonnie Anthony," etc.

Anthony's leave she had ;
   And, dress'd in man's array,
She was the brightest lad
   Seen on a summer's day.
(Oh, see what love will do !
   At home she will not bide ;
With her true love she'll go,
   Let weal or woe betide—
      Still crying : "Anthony—
      My bonnie Anthony ! " etc.)

On the ship 'twas her lot
  To be the under-cook,
And at the fire hot
  Great pains she took;
She servèd every one,
  As fitted his degree;
And now and then alone
  She kissèd Anthony—
      Saying : "O Anthony ! " etc.

Alack and well-a-day,
  By tempest on the main
Their ship was cast away
  Upon the coast of Spain :
To th' mercy of the wave
  They all committed were;
She did her own self save,
  Then cried for her dear—
      "O my own Anthony ! " etc.

By swimming on a plank
  She got to Bilbo's shore,
Where first she Heaven did thank,
  Then she lamented sore :
"O woe is me ! " cried she,
  "The saddest lass alive,—
On my dear Anthony
  The cruel sea doth thrive !
      "O bonnie Anthony ! " etc.

"What shall become of me?
  Why did I strive for shore,
Sith my sweet Anthony
  I never shall see more ! "
Fair Constance, do not grieve;
  The same kind Providence
Hath spar'd thy lover dear;
  But he is far from hence.
      Still she cries : "Anthony ! " etc.

A rich merchànt of Spain
  Saw this fair seeming lad,
That did lament in pain,
  And was so grievous sad :

He had in England been,
  And English understood;
And, having heard and seen,
  He in amazement stood,
      As she cried: "Anthony!" etc.

The merchant askèd her
  Who was that Anthony.
Said she: "My brother, sir,
  Who came from thence with me."
He did her entertain,
  In thought she was a boy:
Two years she did remain,
  Before she found her joy—
      Still she cried: "Anthony!" etc.

For Anthony was ta'en
  By an English renegade,
Who forc'd him to remain
  At the sea-roving trade.
I' th' nature of a slave
  He did i' th' galley row;
Thus he his life did save,
  But Constance did not know,
      Though she cried: "Anthony!" etc.

Now mark what came to pass,—
  See how the Fates did work;
A ship that her master's was
  Surpris'd the English-Turk;
And into Bilbo brought
  All that on board her were:
Constance full little thought
  Her Anthony so near,
      As she cried: "Anthony!" etc.

When they were come ashore,
  Anthony and the rest;
She, who so sad before,
  Was now with joy possess't.
The merchant much did muse
  At this too sudden change;
He did demand the news—
  Which unto him was strange,
      For she sang: "Anthony!" etc.

Down on her knees she fell
  Unto her master kind,
And all the truth did tell—
  No word she kept behind;
Whereat he blest the pair,
  And in a ship of Spain,
Not asking them for fare,
  He sent them home again,
    While she sang: "Anthony!" etc.

That Spanish merchant rich
  Did from his bounty give
A sum of gold, on which
  They now do bravely live:
For now in Westmoreland
  They are join'd hand-in-hand—
Constance and Anthony,
  They live in love and glee—
    As she sings: "Anthony,
      My bonnie Anthony!
    God's providence, we see,
    Guarded both thee and me—
      O my own Anthony!"

ANONYMOUS.

JACK ROBINSON.[1]

(AIR—"COLLEGE HORNPIPE.")

THE perils and dangers of the voyage past,
And the ship into Portsmouth come at last,
The sails all furl'd, and the anchor cast—
  The merriest of all was Jack Robinson.
For his Poll he had trinkets and gold galore,
Besides of prize-money quite a store;
So along with his mates he went ashore,
  As cox'un of the boat—Jack Robinson.

---

[1] This ballad, so very unusual that it might have been taken from actual life yesterday, has been ascribed to Thomas Hudson, a portrait painter of the eighteenth century who had Reynolds for a pupil; but the evidence is too slight to rely on.

He met there a man and said to him—"I say,
Mayhap you know of one Polly Gray;
She lives somewhere about."   The man said—"Nay,
  I do not, indeed," to Jack Robinson.
So Jack says unto him—"I've left my ship,
And all my messmates I've given the slip;
So p'r'aps you'll share in a good can of flip—
  For you're a hail sort of fellow," says Jack Robinson.

In a public-house then they sat them both down
And talk'd of admirals of high renown,
And drank as much grog as cost half-a-crown—
  This here strange man and Jack Robinson.
Then Jack call'd out for the reckoning to pay;
The landlady came in, in spanking array ·
"My eyes and limbs, why, here's Polly Gray!
  How the deuce did you get here?" cries Jack
    Robinson.

The landlady stagger'd against the near wall
And mutter'd, at first, she didn't know him at all.
"Shiver me," says Jack—"well, here's a pretty squall!
  Damn it!—Don't you know me?—I'm Jack Robinson.
Don't you know this handkerchief you giv'd me?—
Just three year ago, before I went to sea:
Ev'ry day I've look'd at it, then thought of thee—
  Upon my soul I have!" says Jack Robinson.

Says the lady quick, says she—"I've now chang'd my
    state."—
"Why, you don't mean," cries Jack, "that you've got a
    mate?
You know you promis'd me."—Says she—"I couldn't
    wait;
  For no tidings could I gain of you, Jack Robinson:
And one day someb'dy came up to me and said,
So somebody else had somewhere read
In some newspaper, as how you were dead."—
  "I've not been dead at all!" cries Jack Robinson.

Then he turn'd his quid and finish'd his glass,
Hitch'd up his trousers and said—"Alas,
That ever I liv'd to be made such an ass!—
  To be bilk'd [1] by a woman!" says Jack Robinson.

---

[1] This is the earliest use I have found of this slang descendant of
"balk"; it, the reference to newspapers—as recording the death of an

"But to fret and stew about it's all in vain :
I'll get a ship for Holland, France or Spain—
No matter where—to Portsmouth I'll never come
    again ! "
And he was off before you could say Jack Robinson.
ANONYMOUS.

BRYAN AND PEREENE.[1]

THE north-east wind did briskly blow;
    The ship was safely moor'd;
Young Bryan thought the boat's crew slow,
    And so leapt overboard.

Pereene, the pride of Indian dames,
    His heart long held in thrall;
And whoso his impatience blames,
    I wot, ne'er loved at all.

A long, long year, a month and day
    He'd dwelt on English land;
Nor once in thought or deed did stray,—
    Though ladies sought his hand.

For Bryan he was tall and strong,—
    Right blythsome roll'd his een;
Sweet was his voice whene'er he sung;
    He scant had twenty seen.

But who the countless charms can draw
    That graced his mistress true?
Such charms the old world seldom saw,
    Nor oft, I ween, the new.

Her raven hair plays round her neck,
    Like tendrils of the vine;
Her cheeks red, dewy rosebuds deck;
    Her eyes like diamonds shine.

---

able seaman—and the last six words of the ballad seem to say that the piece is not more than 150 to 170 years old.

[1] This very pathetic ballad is said to have been founded on a distressing occurrence in the island of St. Christopher, West Indies, where the tragedy happened much as it is described here.

Soon as his well-known ship she spied,
  She cast her weeds away : [1]
And to the palmy shores she hied,
  All in her best array.

I' sea-green silk, so neatly clad,
  She there impatient stood,—
The crew, with wonder, saw the lad
  Repel the foaming flood.

Her hands a handkerchief display'd,
  Which he at parting gave;
Well-pleased, the token he survey'd,
  And manlier beat the wave.

Her fair companions, one and all
  Rejoicing, crowd the strand;
For now her lover swam in call,
  And almost touched the land.

Then through the white surf did she haste,
  To clasp her handsome swain;
When, ah, a shark bit through his waist!
  His heart's blood dyed the main.

He shrieked! His half sprang from the wave,
  Streaming with purple gore;
But soon it found a living grave,
  And, ah, was seen no more!

Now haste, now haste, ye maids, I pray!
  Fetch water from the spring :
She falls; she swoons; she dies away,—
  And soon her knell they ring.

Now each fresh morning round her tomb,
  Ye fair, fresh flowerets strew,—
So may your lovers 'scape his doom,
  Her helpless fate 'scape you !

                              J. GRAINGER.

[1] Contrast the two lines in Gay's " Black-Eyed Susan " :

    " Soon as her well-known voice he heard,
      He sigh'd and cast his eyes below."

THE GALLANT SEAMAN'S RETURN FROM THE INDIES.

I am a stout seaman newly come on shore;
I have been a long voyage, where I ne'er was before;
But now I am return'd, I'm resolv'd to see
My own dearest honey, whose name it is Betty.

I have been absent from her full many a day;
But yet I was constant in every way:
Though many beautiful dames I did see,
Yet none pleas'd me so well as pretty Betty.

Now I am intended, whatever may betide,
For to go and see her, and make her my bride;
And if that she and I together can agree,
I never will love none but pretty Betty.

HIS SONG ON MEETING BETTY.

Well met, pretty Betty, my joy and my dear;
I now am returnèd thy heart for to cheer;
Though long I've been absent, I still thought on thee—
O, my heart it was always with pretty Betty.

Then come, my own dearest, to the tavern let's go,
Whereas we'll be merry for an hour or two;
So lovingly together we both will agree,
And I'll drink a good health to my pretty Betty.

And when we have done, to the church we will hie,
Whereas we'll be joinèd in matrimony;
And always I'll be a kind husband to thee,
If thou wilt be my wife, pretty Betty.

I will kiss thee and hug thee all night in my arms;
I'll be careful of thee, and keep thee from harms;
I will love thee dearly in every degree,
For my heart it is fixed on pretty Betty.

For thee will I rove and sail far and near;
The dangerous rough sea shall not put me in fear;
And if I get treasure, I'll bring it to thee;
And I'll venture dear life for pretty Betty.

And more than all this I'll tell thee, my dear,
I will bring thee safe home rich jewels to wear;

And many new fashions I will provide thee,
So that none shall compare with my pretty Betty.

Then come, mine own dearest, and grant me thy love;
Both loving and constant to thee I will prove; .
If but thou wilt put all thy trusting in me,
I vow to love none but pretty Betty.

BETTY'S REPLY.

O welcome, my dearest! O welcome to shore!
Thy absence so long hath troubl'd me sore;
But since thou'rt returnèd, this I'll assure thee,
'Tis thou art the man that my husband shall be.

Altho' that some maids now-a-days prove untrue,
Yet *I*'ll never change my old love for a new;
My promise I'll keep while life is in me,
For 'tis thou art the man that my husband shall be.

I have been courted by many a proper youth—
If thou wilt believe me, I'll tell thee the truth;
For all my affections I have set on thee,
And thou art the man that my husband shall be.

Then, dearest, be not discontented in mind;
To thee I will always prove loving and kind;
No lord nor knight I'll have, if they would have me,
For thou art the man that my husband shall be.

If that I might have a shipload of money,
I would not forsake my own true love and honey;
No wealth and no honour shall force or tempt me
To forsake him who ever my true love shall be.

THE MORAL.

This lusty brave seaman and his dearest dear
Were married full speedily, as I did hear;
And now they together do live happily,
And he vows to love his pretty Betty.

He is overjoy'd now he has gained his mate;
They do love and live without strife or debate;
He is kindness unto her in every degree,
So I wish him well to enjoy pretty Betty.

All young men and maidens pray learn by my song
To be true to your sweethearts and do them no wrong;
Prove constant and just, and not false-hearted be,—
And thus I will now conclude my new ditty.

ANONYMOUS.

POOR LYCON.

HARD by the Hall, our master's house,
   Where Mersey flows into the main,—
Where woods and winds and waves dispose
   A lover to complain;

With arms across, along the strand,
   Poor Lycon walked and hung his head;
Viewing those footsteps in the sand,
   Which a bright nymph had made.

"The tide," said he, "will soon erase
   The marks so lightly here imprest;
But time or tide will ne'er deface
   Her image in my breast.

"Am I some savage beast of prey?
   Am I some horrid monster grown,
That thus she flies so swift away,
   Or meets me with a frown?

"That bosom soft, that lily-skin
   (Trust not the fairest outside show!)
Contain a marble heart within,
   A rock hid under snow.

"Ah me! the flints and pebbles wound
   Her tender feet, from whence there fell
These crimson drops which stain the ground,
   And beautify each shell.

"Oh, fair one, moderate thy flight!
   I will no more in vain pursue;
But take my leave for a long night:
   Adieu, lov'd maid, adieu!"

With that he took a running leap,—
   He took a Lover's Leap, indeed,
And plunged into the sounding deep,
   Where he had sailed with speed!

M

The melancholy hern stalks by;
    Around the squalling sea-gulls yell;
Aloft the croaking ravens fly,
    And toll his funeral bell.

The waters roll above his head;
    The billows toss it o'er and o'er;
His ivory bones lie scatterèd,
    And whiten all the shore.

ANONYMOUS.

SOLDIER AND SAILOR.

I LOVE contemplating, apart
    From all his homicidal glory,
The traits that soften to our heart
    Napoleon's story !

'Twas when his banners at Boulogne
    Armed in our Island every freeman,
His navy chanced to capture one
    Poor British seaman.

They suffered him, I know not how,
    Unprisoned on the shore·to roam;
And aye was bent his longing brow
    On England's home.

His eye, methinks, pursued the flight
    Of birds to Britain half-way over
With envy; *they* could reach the white
    Dear cliffs of Dover.

A stormy midnight watch, he thought,
    Than this sojourn would have been dearer,
If but the storm his vessel brought
    To England nearer.

At last, when care had banished sleep,
    He saw one morning—dreaming—doting,
An empty hogshead from the deep
    Come shoreward floating;

He hid it in a cave, and wrought
   The live-long day laborious; lurking,
Until he launched a tiny boat
   By mighty working.

Heaven help us! 'twas a thing beyond
   Description, wretched: such a wherry
Perhaps ne'er ventured on a pond,
   Or crossed a ferry.

For ploughing in the salt-sea field,
   It would have made the boldest shudder;
Untarred, uncompassed, and unkeeled,
   No sail—no rudder.

From neighbouring woods he interlaced
   His sorry skiff with wattled willows;
And thus equipped he would have passed
   The foaming billows—

But Frenchmen caught him on the beach,
   His little argo sorely jeering;
Till tidings of him chanced to reach
   Napoleon's hearing.

With folded arms Napoleon stood,
   Serene alike in peace and danger;
And, in his wonted attitude,
   Addressed the stranger :—

"Rash man, that wouldst yon channel pass
   On twigs and staves so rudely fashioned;
Thy heart with some sweet British lass
   Must be impassioned."

"I have no sweetheart," said the lad;
   "But—absent long from one another—
Great was the longing that I had
   To see my mother."

"And so thou shalt," Napoleon said,
   "Ye've both my favour fairly won;
A noble mother must have bred
   So brave a son."

He gave the tar a piece of gold,
   And, with a flag of truce, commanded
He should be shipped to England Old,
   And safely landed.

Our sailor oft could scantly shift
    To find a dinner, plain and hearty;
But *never* changed the coin and gift
    Of Bonaparté.

CAMPBELL.

THE INCHCAPE ROCK.

No stir in the air,—no stir in the sea;
The ship was as still as she could be,
Her sails from heaven received no motion,
Her keel was steady in the ocean.

Without any sign or sound of their shock
The waves floated over the Inchcape Rock:
So little they rose, so little they fell,
They did not move the Inchcape Bell.

The worthy Abbot of Aberbrothok
Had placed that bell on the Inchcape Rock;
On a buoy in the storm it floated and swung
And over the waves its warning rung.

When the rock was hid by the surges' swell,
The mariners heard the warning bell;
And then they knew the perilous rock,
And blest the Abbot of Aberbrothok.

The sun in heaven was shining gay;
All things were joyful on that day;
The sea-birds screamed, as they wheeled around,
And there was joyance in their sound.

The buoy of the Inchcape Bell was seen,
A darker speck on the ocean green:
Sir Ralph the rover walked his deck,
And he fixed his eye on the darker speck.

He felt the cheering power of spring,—
It made him whistle, it made him sing;
His heart was mirthful to excess :
But the rover's mirth was wickedness.

His eye was on the Inchcape float :
Quoth he—"My men, put out the boàt,
And row me to the Inchcape Rock,
And I'll plague the Abbot of Aberbrothok."

The boat is lowered; the boatmen row,
And to the Inchcape Rock they go:
Sir Ralph bent over from the boat,
And he cut the bell from the Inchcape float.

Down sunk the bell, with a gurgling sound;
The bubbles rose and burst around:
Quoth Sir Ralph—"The next who comes to the rock,
Won't bless the Abbot of Aberbrothok."

Sir Ralph the rover sailed away;
He scoured the seas for many a day:
And, now grown rich with plundered store,
He steers his course for Scotland's shore.

So thick a haze o'erspreads the sky,
They cannot see the sun on high;
The wind hath blown a gale all day—
At evening it hath died away.

On deck the rover takes his stand,—
So dark it is they see no land:
Quoth Sir Ralph—"It will be lighter soon,
For there is the dawn of the rising moon."

"Canst hear," said one, "the breakers roar?
For methinks we should be near the shore."
"Now where we are I cannot tell;
But I wish I could hear the Inchcape Bell."

They hear no sound; the swell is strong;
Though the wind hath fallen, they drift along,
Till the vessel strikes with a quivering shock,—
"Oh, Christ, it is the Inchcape Rock!"

Sir Ralph the rover tore his hair;
He cursed himself in his despair;
The waves rush in on every side;
The ship is sinking beneath the tide.

But even in his dying fear
One dreadful sound could the rover hear—
A sound as if with the Inchcape Bell
The Devil below was ringing his knell.

SOUTHEY.

THE HIGH TIDE ON THE COAST OF LINCOLNSHIRE, 1571.

THE old mayor climbed the belfry-tower,
  And ringers ran by two, by three :
" Pull,—if ye never pulled before !
  Good ringers, pull your best," quoth he.
" Play uppe, play uppe, O Boston bells !
Ply all your changes, all your swells ;
  Play uppe ' The Brides of Enderby ' ! "

Men say it was a stolen tyde—
  The Lord that sent it, He knows all ;
But in myne ears doth still abide
  The message that the bells let fall :
And there was nought of strange, beside
The flights of mews and peewits pied,
  By millions crouched on the old sea wall.

I sat and spun within the doore ;
  My thread brake off,—I raised myne eyes ;
The level sun, like ruddy ore,
  Lay sinking in the barren skies ;
And dark against day's golden death
She moved where Lindis wandereth,
  My sonne's faire wife, Elizabeth.

            .   .

If it be long, ay, long ago,—
  When I beginne to think how long,
Again I hear the Lindis flow,
  Swift as an arrowe, sharpe and strong ;
And all the aire, it seemeth mee,
Bin full of floating bells (sayth shee)
  That ring the tune of Enderby.

        .   .   .

¹ At the risk of some condemnation I have deemed it necessary to
my purpose here to leave out the purely lyrical milking-song, and the
pastoral stanzas seven and eight.   Jean Ingelow was no impressionist ;
and in this extremely fine piece of work her aim was to give a com-
plete picture of the happening, with more landward than seaward
detail, and with, for absolute art's sake, a little too much of "my
sonne's wife."

Then some looked uppe into the sky,
  And all along where Lindis flows
To where the goodly vessels lie,
  And where the lordly steeple shows.
They sayde—"And why should this thing be?
What danger lowers by land or sea?
    They ring the tune of Enderby!—

"For evil news from Mablethorpe,
  Of pyrate galleys warping down;
For shippes ashore beyond the scupe,
  They have not spared to wake the towne.
But while the west bin red to see,
And storms be none, and pyrates flee,
    Why ring 'The Brides of Enderby'?"

I looked without; and, lo! my sonne
  Came riding down with might and mayne.
He raised a shout, as he drew on,
  Till all the welkin rang again—
"Elizabeth! Elizabeth!"
(A sweeter woman ne'er drew breath
    Than my sonne's wife, Elizabeth.)

"The old sea wall," he cried, "is downe!
  The rising tide comes on apace;
And boats adrift in yonder towne
  Go sailing up the market-place!"
He shook as one that looks on death.
"God save you, mother!" straight he saith.
    "Where is my wife, Elizabeth?"

"Good sonne, where Lindis winds away,
  With her two bairns I marked her long;
And, ere yon bells began to play,
  Afarre I heard her milking song."
He looked across the grassy lea,
To right, to left: "Ho Enderby!"—
    They rang "The Brides of Enderby!"

With that he cried and beat his breast;
  For, lo! along the river's bed
A mighty eygre reared his crest,
  And uppe the Lindis raging sped.
It swept, with thunderous noises loud,
Shaped like a curling snow-white cloud,
    Or like a demon in a shroud.

And rearing Lindis, backward pressed,
  Shook all her trembling bankes amayne;
Then madly at the eygre's breast
  Flung up her weltering walls again:
Then bankes came down with ruin and rout;
Then beaten foam flew round about;
  Then all the mighty floods were out.

So farre, so fast the eygre drave,—
  The heart had hardly time to beat,
Before a shallow seething wave
  Sobbed in the grasses at oure feet;
The feet had hardly time to feel,
Before it brake against the knee,—
  And all the world was in the sea!

Upon the roofe we sate that night;
  The noise of bells went sweeping bye;
I marked the lofty beacon-light
  Stream from the tower, red and high—
A lurid mark and dread to see!
And awsome bells they were, to mee,
  That in the dark rang "Enderby."

They rang the sailor-lads to guide
  From roofe to roofe, who fearless rowed:
And I—my sonne was at my side.
  And yet the ruddy beacon glowed;
And yet he moaned beneath his breath,
"Oh, come in life, or come in death!—
  O lost, my love, Elizabeth!"

And didst thou visit him no more?
  Thou didst, thou didst, my daughter deare:
The waters layde thee at his doore,
  Ere yet the early dawn was clear,—
Thy pretty bairns in fast embrace;
The lifted sunne shone on thy face—
  Downe drifted to thy dwelling place.

That flow strewed wrecks about the grass;
  That ebbe swept out the flocks to sea:
A fatal ebbe and flow, alas!
  To manye more than myne and mee.

But each will mourn his own, she saith;
And sweeter woman ne'er drew breath
  Than my sonne's wife, Elizabeth.

  .   .   .   .   .   .

                                JEAN INGELOW.

THE WRECK OF THE *HESPERUS*.

IT was the schooner *Hesperus*
  That sailed the wintry sea;
And the skipper had taken his little daughter
  To bear him company.

Blue were her eyes as the fairy flax,
  Her cheeks like the dawn of day;
And her bosom white, as the hawthorne buds
  That ope' in the month of May.

The skipper he stood beside the helm;
  His pipe was in his mouth,
And he watched how the veering flaw did blow
  The smoke, now west, now south.

Then up and spake an old sailor,
  Had sailed the Spanish main,
"I pray you put into yonder port,
  For I fear a hurricane.

"Last night the moon had a golden ring,[1]
  And to-night no moon we see!"
The skipper he blew a whiff from his pipe,
  And a scornful laugh laughed he.

Louder and louder blew the wind,
  A gale from the north-east;
The snow fell hissing in the brine,
  And the billows frothed like yeast.

Down came the storm, and smote amain
  The vessel in its strength;
She shuddered and paused, like a frightened steed,
  Then leaped her cable's length.

"Come hither! come hither! my little daughter,
  And do not tremble so;
For I can weather the roughest gale
  That ever wind did blow."

      [1] *See* note 2, "It is the midnight hour," p. 9.

He wrapped her warm in his seaman's coat,
    Against the stinging blast;
He cut a rope from a broken spar,
    And bound her to the mast.

"Oh, father, I hear the church-bells ring!
    Oh, say what may it be?"
"'Tis a fog-bell on a rock-bound coast!"—
    And he steered for the open sea.

"Oh, father, I hear the sound of guns!
    Oh, say what may it be?"
"Some ship in distress, that cannot live
    In such an angry sea!"

"Oh, father, I see a gleaming light!
    Oh, say what may it be?"
But the father answered never a word,—
    A frozen corpse was he.

Lashed to the helm, all stiff and stark,
    With his face turned to the skies;
The lantern gleamed, through the gleaming snow,
    On his fixed and glassy eyes.

Then the maiden clasped her hands and prayed
    That savèd she might be;
And she thought of Christ, who stilled the wave
    On the Lake of Galilee.

And fast through the midnight dark and drear,
    Through the whistling sleet and snow,
Like a sheeted ghost the vessel swept
    Tow'ds the reef of Norman's Woe.

And ever, the fitful gusts between,
    A sound came from the land;
It was the sound of the trampling surf
    On the rocks and the hard sea-sand.

The breakers were right beneath her bows,—
    She drifted a dreary wreck;
And a whooping billow swept the crew,
    Like icicles, from her deck.

She struck where the white and fleecy waves
  Looked soft as carded wool;
But the cruel rocks, they gored her side,
  Like the horns of an angry bull.

Her rattling shrouds, all sheathed in ice,
  With the masts went by the board;
Like a vessel of glass, she stove and sank,—
  Ho! Ho! the breakers roared.[1]

At daybreak, on the bleak sea-beach,
  A fisherman stood aghast,
To see the form of a maiden fair
  Lashed close to a drifting mast.

The salt sea was frozen on her breast;
  The salt tears in her eyes;
And he saw her hair, like the brown seaweed,
  On the billows fall and rise.

Such was the wreck of the *Hesperus*,
  In the midnight and the snow;
Christ save us all from a death like this,
  On the reef of Norman's Woe!

LONGFELLOW.

SIR HUMPHREY GILBERT.

SOUTHWARD with fleet of ice
  Sailed the corsair Death:
Wild and fast blew the blast,
  And the east wind was his breath.

His lordly ships of ice
  Glistened in the sun;
On each side, like pennons wide,
  Flashing crystal streamlets run.

---

[1] Banality on tragedy, says the reader, probably. Yes, this line is, indeed, a false and jarring note. Yet, although Longfellow did write with that "fatal facility" in which there is always weakness, and is commonly the high road to mawkish sentiment and other defects, he still had that affinity to the external verities of the sea which the majority of greater writers have not had. And here, where he unmistakably rings the masses' note of popularity, it cannot be denied that, despite the superior person's disdain of his work generally, he is true to the purpose of his lines, both as a sea picture and as an imitation of much older things.

His sails of white sea-mist
  Dripped with silver rain;
But where he passed there were cast
  Leaden shadows o'er the main.

Eastward from Compobello
  Sir Humphrey Gilbert sailed;
Three days or more seaward he bore,—
  Then, alas! the land-wind failed.

Alas! the land-wind failed,
  And ice-cold grew the night;
And never more, on sea or shore,
  Should Sir Humphrey see the light.

He sat upon the deck;
  The Book was in his hand:
"Do not fear,—Heaven is near,"
  He said, "by water as by land."

In the first watch of the night,
  Without a signal's sound
Out of the sea, mysteriously,
  The fleet of Death rose all around.

The moon and the evening star
  Were hanging in the shrouds;
Every mast, as it passed,
  Seemed to rake the passing clouds.

They grappled with their prize,
  At midnight black and cold:
As of a rock was the shock!
  Heavily the ground-swell rolled.

Southward, through day and dark,
  They drift in close embrace,
With mist and rain o'er the open main;
  Yet there seems no change of place.

Southward, for ever southward,
  They drift through dark and day;
And, like a dream in the Gulf stream
  Sinking, vanish all away.

LONGFELLOW.

THE SANDS OF DEE.

"Oh, Mary! go and call the cattle home—
  And call the cattle home,
  And call the cattle home,
    Across the sands of Dee." [1]
The western wind was wild and dank with foam :
  And all alone went she.

The western tide crept up along the sand,—
  And o'er and o'er the sand,
  And round and round the sand,
    As far as eye could see.
The rolling mist came down and hid the land :
  And never home came she.

"Oh ! is it weed, or fish, or floating hair?—
  A tress of golden hair,
  A drownèd maiden's hair,
    Above the nets at sea ! "
Was never salmon yet that shone so fair
  Among the stakes of Dee.

They rowed her in across the rolling foam—
  The cruel, crawling foam,
  The cruel, hungry foam,
    To her grave beside the sea.
But still the boatmen hear her call the cattle home,
  Across the sands of Dee.

KINGSLEY.

[1] For some time this beautifully expressed piece of pathos was supposed to relate to the mouth of the Scottish Dee ; but " western wind" and " western tide " prove the river to have been the Chester Dee.

SONGS

"NOW SAFE MOOR'D."

Now safe moor'd, with bowl before us,
 Messmates, heave a hand with me;
Lend a brother-sailor chorus,
 While he sings our lives at sea.

O'er the wide wave-swelling ocean,
 Tossed aloft or tumbled low;
As to fear, 'tis all a notion—
 When our time's come, we must go.

DIBDIN.

A TUDOR SAYLORS' SONG.

WEE be three poore mariners,
 Newlie come from the seas;
Wee spende oure lives in jeopardy,
 While others live at ease.
  Shal wee goe dance the rounde, the rounde?—
  Shal wee goe dance the rounde?
   And hee that is a bullyboy [1]
  Come pledge mee on this grounde!

Wee care not for those martial men
 That doe oure states [2] disdain;
But we care for the marchante men
 That doe oure states maintaine.
  To them wee dance this rounde arounde,—
  To them wee dance this rounde;
   And hee that is a bully-boy
  Come pledge mee on this grounde!

SONG: A SAYLOR'S VANITE.

LUSTELY, lustely, lett us sayle forthe;
The winde trim doth serve us—itt blowes from the
  north:
All things wee have readie, and nothing wee want,
 To furnish oure shipp that rydeth herebye,—
Victals and weapons ther bee nothing scant;
 Leeke [3] worthie mariners oureselves wee wil trie.

Her flagges bee new-trimmed, sett fauntyng alofte;
 Oure shipp for swift swimmyng—oh, she doth excell!
Wee feare noe enemys—wee have scaped them ofte;
 Of all shipps that swimmeth she beareth the bell. [4]
  Lustely, lustely, lustely, etc.

---

[1] How modern!—one might cry. For the same term, meaning an able and friendly fellow, occurs again and again in sailors' songs and chanties of the past century, such as "Blow the Man Down." [2] Their condition. The "martial men" were no doubt the captains of warships, as opposed to the merchants and the masters of their vessels. [3] Like. [4] This may, or may not, have been a slang phrase of those days (the time was when "piece" was quite a respectable description of a

And here is a mayster [1] excelleth in skill;
  And oure mayster's mate—hee is not to seeke; [2]
And here is a lesta-swayne wil doe his goode wil;
  And here is a shippe-boye we never had leeke.
        Lustely, lustely, lustely, etc.

If fortune then fail not, and our next voiage prove,
  Wee wil returne merely and make goode cheare;
And hold al together, as frinds linkt in love;
  The cannes shal be filled with wine, ale and beer.
        Lustely, lustely, lustely, etc.

                                    ANONYMOUS.

TO HER SEAFARING LOVER. [3]

SHAL I thus longe, and be no whit the neare? [4]
And shal I still complaine to thee, the which me will
    not hear?
Alas! say "Nay"—say "Nay"! and be no more so
    dumb;
But open thou thy manlye mouth and say that thou
    wilt come;
  Wherebye my hart may thinke, although I see not
    thee,
  That thou wilt come—thy worde so sware—if thou
    a live man be.
The roaring, hugy waves they threaten my pore ghoste, [5]
And tosse thee upp and downe the seas in daunger to
    be loste.

---

woman); but how closely allied it is to that colourful expression of to-day, "she takes the cake"!—which, a hundred years ago, was "give him the basket."
  [1] Master is still spelt and pronounced "maister" in north-country dialects.   [2] This phrase is in dialect use to-day, in the sense of being quite up to the mark in intelligence, work, etc.   [3] Under the sub-title of "Uncertain Authors" this poem first saw the light in *Songs and Sonnets*, which was published by Richard Tottel in 1557. In that year Tottel also issued a first collection of the poems of Surrey (1517–47) and Wyatt (1503–42). Those two friends—who produced a sort of sister and brother in poetry—brought the sonnet to England and naturalised the form; and an examination of both the form and the expression of the above lines, along with Surrey's acknowledged work, added to the fact that Tottel saw them all through the press, makes it easy to think that this piece came from Surrey's hand.   [4] Nearer.
  [5] Daunts the spirit.

Shal they not make me feare that they have swolowed
    thee?—
But as thou arte most sure alive, so wilt thou come to
    me;
    Wherebye I shal go see thy shipp ride on the strand,
    And thinke and sai—"So, there he comes!" and
    "Sure here wil he land."
    And then I shal lifte upp to thee my litle hand;
    And thou shalt thinke thine hart in ease, in health
    to see me stand.

And if thou come indede (as Christ thee sende to do),
These arms, which misse thee now, shal then embrace
    (and hold) thee too:
    Each vein to every joynt the lively bloode shal spreade,
    Which now, for want of thy glad sighte, doth shew
    ful pale and dead.
But if thou slip[1] thy troth, and do not come at all;
As minutes in the clock do strike, so call for deathe I
    shal:
    To pleas both thy false hart, and rid myself from woe,
    The rather had I die in troth than live forsaken so.
                            ANONYMOUS.

SONG.

THE maister, the swabber, the boteswayn and I
    The gunner and hys mate
Lov'd Mall, Meg and Marian and Margerie;
    But none of us car'd for Kate.
    For she had a tongue with a tange,
    Wuld cry to a saylor—"Go hange!"
She lov'd not the savor of tarre nor of pytche;
Yet a taylor myght scratche her wher'er shee did itche:
    Then to sea, boies, and lett her go hange!
                           SHAKESPEARE.

THE MAYDE OF AMSTERDAM.[2]

    IN Amsterdam there dwelt a mayde—
    Marke well what I doe sai!
    In Amsterdam there dwelt a mayde,
    And she was mistresse of her trade—

---

[1] Break, as break away from it.
[2] I have recently seen this written as a chanty, but never heard it
sung as such. In my youth I did hear, from a formerly deep-water

And I'le goe no more a roving with you, fayre mayde,
 A roving, a roving;
 Since roving's beene my ruin,
I'll goe no more a roving with you, fayre mayde.

 Her cheek was red, her eye was browne—
  Marke well what I doe sai!
 Her cheek was red, her eye was browne—
But I'le goe no more a roving with you, fayre mayde,
 A roving, a roving;
 Since roving's beene my ruin,
I'll goe no more a roving with you, fayre mayde.
THOMAS HEYWOOD.

THE LOWLANDS O' HOLLAND.[1]

 "THE love that I ha'e chosen
  Sall ever me content;
 The saut sea sall be frozen
  Before I do repent:
 Repent it sall I never
  Until the day I dee; '
 But the Lowlands o' Holland
  Ha'e ta'en my love frae me.

 "My love he built a bonny ship
  And set her on the main,
 Wi' twenty-four brave mariners
  To sail her out an' hame:
 But, O, the wind it 'gan to rise;
  The sea began to rout;
 And my love and his bonny ship
  Turned withershins[2] about.

---

sailor, the refrain sung to other solo-lines; unfortunately, I can only remember that they were about a "fair maid." As a matter of fact the song is from "The Rape of Lucrece" (1608), where more of it can be seen. Heywood (1575–1648) was one of the most prolific writers that have lived; in addition to a number of serious books entirely from his own pen, he had by far the greater share in 220 plays; but besides the above song his chief point of interest here is that he wrote of sea-fights like one who had taken part in them.

[1] There are other versions of this ballad, both in English and in Lowland Scots; but it is impossible to say which is the oldest. As for quality, there is little or no choice. There are, of course, ballads by the dozen on the same subject, most of them being very poor things, and the majority showing that the sweetheart died for her lover lost at sea. [2] The wrong way round, *i.e.* turned over.

"There sall nae mantle deck my back,
  No kaime gae in my hair;
Neither sall coal or candlelight
  Gleam in my bower fair:
Nor will I choose anither love
  Till down I lay to dee;
Sin' the Lowlands o' Holland
  Ha'e ta'en my love frae me."

"Noo haud your tongue, my docthre dear;
  Be still, an' bide content:
There is ither lads in Galloway,—
  Ye needna sair lament."
"O there is nane in Galloway—
  There's nane at a' for me:
I ne'er ha'e lo'ed a lad but ane,
  An' he's drown'd i' the sea."

ANONYMOUS.

TO LUCASTA:[1]
ON HIS GOING BEYOND THE SEAS.

IF to be absent were to be
Away from thee;
  Or that when I am gone
  You and I were alone;
Then, my Lucasta, might I crave
Pity from blustering wind or swallowing wave.

But I'll not sigh one blast or gale
To swell my sail,
  Nor pay a tear to 'suage
  The blue god's rage;
For, whether he will let me pass
Or no, I'm still as happy as I was.

Though seas and land betwixt us both—
Our faith and troth,
  Like separated souls,
  All time and space controls;

---

[1] Lovelace—pitifully unfortunate in love, politics and in life gener-
ally—was far too much of a soldier ever to be anything of a sailor; per-
haps that was why he put nothing of the sea really into this cavalier-
like yet manly lyric, with his resolution not to swell the sail of his
heartache by so much as a sigh.   Still it is not an unfitting leaf in a
chaplet of the sea's verse.

N 2

Above the highest sphere we meet
Unseen, unknown, and greet as angels greet.

So then we do anticipate
Our after-fate
   And are alive i' the skies
If thus our lips and eyes
Can speak, like spirits unconfined
In Heaven, their earthy bodies left behind.

RICHARD LOVELACE.

THE SPANISH LADIES.[1]

FAREWEL and adieu to you, Spanish ladies—
Farewel and adieu to you, ladies of Spain,
We have received orders for to sail to old England;
   But we hope by-and-by for to see you again.

We'll rant and we'll roar [2] like true British heroes!
   We'll rant and we'll roar across the salt seas,
Until we strike soundings in the Channel of England:
   From Ushant to Scilly 'tis thirty-five leagues.

.   .   .   .   .

Then we hove our ship to, with the breeze at sou'-west,
     sirs—
We hove our ship to, for to take soundings clear.
And soundings we got, sirs, in ninety-five fathom,
   And bold up the channel our course we did steer.

The first land we made it was callèd the Deedman;
   Next Ram's Head of Plymouth, Start, Portland and
     Wight:
We passed under Beachy, by Fairleigh and Dungeness;
   And hove-to again, off the South Foreland light.

---

[1] This song is used by Captain Marryat in *Poor Jack*, and he adds that it is an old one. It is also in J. H. Dixon's Percy Society volume, *Ancient Poems, Ballads and Songs*, and is to be found on broadsides in different versions; but how old the song really is there appears to be no means of ascertaining. The wording and song generally seem to point to the latter part of the seventeenth or early in the eighteenth century; yet it was sung by sailors up to twenty or thirty years ago, the air being a plaintive one in a minor key and certainly not fitting to the song.   [2] In the later versions of more polite times this is usually " We'll range and we'll rove."

Then a signal was made for the grand fleet to anchor,
All in the fair Downs, that night for to sleep:
'Twas "stand by your stoppers! Let go your shank
painters!
Haul up your clew-garnets! Stick out tacks and
sheets!"

. . . . .

So let every man toss off a full bumper—
Let every man here toss off his full bowls:
We'll drink and be jolly, and drown melancholy;
So here's a good health to all true-hearted souls!

ANONYMOUS.

"I AM A BRISK AND SPRIGHTLY LAD."

I AM a brisk and sprightly lad
But just come home from sea, sir;
Of all the lives I ever led,
A sailor's life for me, sir.

With a yeo, yeo, yeo!
Whilst the boatswain pipes all hands,—
Yeo, yeo, yeo!

What girl but loves the merry tar?
We o'er the ocean roam, sir;
In every clime we find a port,
In every port a home, sir.
With a yeo, yeo, yeo!

But when our country's foes are nigh,
Each hastens to his guns, sir;
We make the boasting Frenchmen fly,
And bang the haughty Dons, sir.
With a yeo, yeo, yeo!

Our foes reduced, once more on shore
We spend our cash with glee, sir;
And when all's gone, we drown our care
And out again to sea, sir.
With a yeo, yeo, yeo!

ANONYMOUS.

THE PITTENWEEM FISHER-WIFE'S SONG.

OH, blythely shines the bonnie sun
    Upon the Isle o' May,
An' blythely comes the morning tide
    Into St. Andrew's Bay!
Then up, gude man!—the breeze is fair.
    An' up, my braw bairns three!
There's bonnie gold in yonder boat
    That sails so well the sea.

    When life's last sun gaes feebly down,
      An' death cam's to our door—
    When a' the world's a dream to us,
      Ye'll gae to sea no more.

Ye've seen the waves as blue as air,
    Ye've seen them green as grass,
But ne'er have feared their heaving yet
    From Fife Ness to the Bass:
Ye've knawn the sea black-like as pitch,
    Ye've knawn it like the snaw;
But ye never feared its raging yet,
    Howe'er the winds did blaw.

Were I a man I'd off 'to sea,—
    This earth is aye the same:
Gie me the ocean for my dower,
    My vessel for my hame;
Gie me the fields that no share ploughs,
    The farm that pays no fee;
Gie me the bonnie fish, that flash
    So gaily thro' the sea.

The bright sun's up, an' roond the Ness
    The breeze does softly blaw:
Our gude man has the lines aboard—
    Awa', my bairns, awa'!
An' ye'll be back by gloaming grey,
    When red the fire I'll low;
An' in your songs an' tales ye'll tell
    How weel the boat ye row!

ANONYMOUS.

HEAVING THE LEAD.

For England when, with favouring gale,
  Our gallant ship up Channel steered;
And, scudding under easy sail,
  The high blue western land appeared,—
To heave the lead the seaman sprung,
And to the pilot cheerly sung:
    "By the deep—*Nine!*"

And, bearing up to gain the port,
  Some well-known object kept in view,—
An abbey-tower, a harbour-fort,
  Or beacon to the vessel true;
While oft his lead the seaman flung,
And to the pilot cheerly sung
    "By the mark—*Seven!*"

And, as the much-loved shore drew near,
  With transport we beheld the roof
Where dwelt a friend or partner dear,
  Of faith and love a matchless proof,—
His lead once more the seaman flung,
And to the watchful pilot sung:
    "Quarter less *five!*"

Now to her berth the ship draws nigh; [1]
  We shorten sail,—she feels the tide.
"Stand clear the cable!" is the cry:
  The anchor's gone. . . . We safely ride.
The watch is set, and through the night
.We hear the seaman, with delight,
    Proclaim: "All's well!"

Anonymous.

[1] To my mind this stanza is an addition to the original song, which is printed by Douce and some others in three stanzas only. These seven lines serve as a natural and well-expressed epilogue to the song; but neither in expression, feeling, nor atmosphere—perhaps "mood" would be better—are they really continuous with the former stanzas. Besides, the song proper—as I look at it—is so admirably correct both in its statements and in its further suggestions that it must have come from the hand of one who knew how to be accurate yet retain illusion; while the concluding stanza contains such an unseamanlike error as the confusion of "berth" with a temporary "anchorage." Mark how Dibdin rang the changes on this song, p. 198.

"BLOW, BOREAS, BLOW."

Blow, Boreas, blow, and let thy surly winds
  Make the billows foam and roar!
Thou canst no terror breed in valiant minds;
  For, spite of thee, we'll live and find a shore.
Then cheer, my hearts, and be not awed,
  But keep the gun-room clear;
Tho' hell's broke loose, and devils roar abroad,
  Whilst we have sea-room here, boys, never fear!

Hey, how she tosses up!—how far!
The mounting topmast touched a star!
The meteors blazed, as thro' the clouds we came,
And, salamander-like, we lived in flame.
But now we sink!—Now, now we go
Down to the deepest shades below!
Alas! where are we now?—who, who can tell?—
Sure 'tis the lowest room of hell!—
Or where the sea-gods dwell:
With them we'll live,—with them we'll live and reign,—
With them we'll laugh and sing and drink amain.
But see, we mount! See, see, we rise again!
Tho' flashes of lightning and tempests of rain
Do fiercely contend who shall conquer the main;
Tho' the captain does swear, instead of a prayer,
And the sea is all fired by demons of air;
    Yet we'll drink, and defy
    The mad spirits that fly
    From the deep to the sky,
  And sing whilst the thunders here bellow!
For Fate will still have a kind home for the brave,
And ne'er make his grave of a salt-water wave,—
  To drown—no, never to drown a good fellow!
               R. Bradley.

THE SAILOR'S RESOLUTION.

How little do the landsmen know
  Of what we sailors feel
When waves do mount and winds do blow,—
  But we have hearts of steel.

No danger can affright us;
  No enemy shall flout:
We'll make the monsieurs fight us —
  So toss the can about!

Stick stout to orders, messmates,—
  We'll plunder, burn and sink.
Then, France, have at your first-rates—
  For Britons never shrink.
We'll rummage all we fancy;
  We'll bring them in by scores,
And Moll and Kate and Nancy
  Shall roll in louis d'ors!

While here at Deal we're lying,
  With our noble commodore,
We'll spend our wages freely, boys,
  And then to sea for more.[1]
In peace we'll drink and sing, boys;
  In war we'll never fly.
Here's a health to George our King, boys,
  And the royal family.

                                          ANONYMOUS.

"ALL HANDS ALOFT."

ALL hands aloft!
Swab the coach [2] fore and aft,
For the Punch Clubbers [3] straight will be sitting:
  For fear the ship roll
  Sling up a full bowl—
To our honour let all things be fitting.

[1] This and the last stanza of "I am a brisk and sprightly lad" remind me of a song that I sometimes heard on the east coast, but never saw in print, and of which I can, unfortunately, remember only:
      "I've spent all my tin
      With the girls a-drinking gin,
      Now on the briny ocean I must wander."

[2] An after cabin of a frigate.   [3] Officers, called "Punch Clubbers" here, probably in derision; punch clubs were then a feature of London life.   It would appear that the singer was an A.B., or a petty officer, who, while being one of a party cleaning out the cabin, pretended to imitate his betters at table after dinner, as is common enough when a joker finds himself in such a situation.   The song was first published in Durfey's *Wit and Mirth: or Pills to Purge Melancholy*, 1719, and was written, apparently, by one who had only a passing acquaintance with his subject.

In an ocean of punch
  We to-night will all sail;
In the bowl there is sea-room,
  So much we ne'er fail.
Here's to thee, messmate—
"Thanks, honest Tom "—
  And a health to the king :
Whilst the larboard man drinks,
  Let the starboard man sing.

With full double-cups
We'll liquor our chaps;
And then we'll turn out,
With a "Who-up, who-who ! "
But let's drink ere we go—
Let's drink ere we go !

The wind 's veering aft—
  Then loose ev'ry sail;
She'll bear all her topsails a-trip; [1]
Heave the log from the poop,
  (It blows a fresh gale)
And a just account on the board keep.
She runs eight knots—
And eight cups, to my thinking;
  That's a cup for each knot
Must be filled for our drinking.
  Here's to the skipper—
    "Thanks, honest John " :
  'Tis a health to the king;
  Whilst one is drinking,
    The other shall fill.
      With full double-cups, etc.

The quartier must con, [2]
Whilst the foremost man steers : [3]
Here's a health to each port where we're bound;
  Who delays—'tis a bumper—
Shall be drubb'd at the gears, [4]
The depth of each cup therefore sound :

[1] An anchor is a-trip when it leaves the ground ; so that an old-fashioned single-topsail would be a-trip when it left the cap, which would make it simply a bag.   [2] The quarter-master must keep a look-out and direct the course.   [3] I have seen this phrase elsewhere, and can make no sense of it, unless it means the captain of the foretop.

[4] The running gear generally, belayed to a pipe-rail around the foot of a mast.

To our noble commander,
　To his honour and wealth—
May he drown and be damn'd
　That refuses the health.
Here's to thee, honest Harry—
　"Thanks, honest Will "—
Old true-penny still;
　Whilst the one is a-drinking,
The other shall fill.
　　　With full double-cups, etc.

　What news on deck, ho?—
It blows a mere storm :
She lies a try [1] under the mizen.
　Why, what tho' she does,
Will it do any harm?—
If a bumper more does us all reason?
　The bowl must be filled, boys,
In spite of the weather :
Yea, huzza !   Let's howl altogether !
　Here's to thee, Peter—
　　"Thanks, honest Joe."
　About let it go !
　In the bowl still a calm is,
　Where'er the winds blow !
　　With full double-cups, etc.

　　　　　　　　　　　　ANONYMOUS.

BRITAIN'S BULWARKS.

WHEN Britain on her sea-girt shore
　Her ancient Druids erst addressed,
"What aïd," she cried, "shall I implore?—
　What best defence, by numbers pressed? "
"The hostile nations round thee rise,"
　The mystic oracle replied,
"And view thine isle with envious eyes :
　Their threats defy, their rage deride,
Nor fear invasion from those adverse Gauls,—
Britain's best bulwarks are her wooden walls.

"Thine oaks, descending to the main,
　With floating forts shall stem the tide;
Asserting Britain's liquid reign,
　Where'er her thundering navies ride.

[1] Lying-to temporarily, as a try, to see how the vessel behaves.

Nor less to peaceful arts inclined
  Where commerce opens all her stores,
In social bonds shall league mankind,
  And join the sea-divided shores :
Spread thy white wings where naval glory calls,—
Britain's best bulwarks are her wooden walls.

"Hail, happy isle ! What though thy vales
  No vine-impurpled tribute yield,
Nor fanned with odour-breathing gales,
  Nor crops spontaneous glad the field?
Yet liberty rewards the toil
  Of industry to labour prone,
Who jocund ploughs the grateful soil,
  And reaps the harvest she has sown :
While other realms tyrannic sway enthralls,—
Britain's best bulwarks are her wooden walls ! "
                                    T. A. ARNE.[1]

"IN STORMS, WHEN CLOUDS."

In storms, when clouds obscure the sky,
And thunders roll, and lightnings fly—
In midst of all these dire alarms
I think, my Sally, on thy charms :
      The troubled main,
      The wind and rain
  My ardent passion prove :
      Should seas o'erwhelm,
      Lashed to the helm,
  I'd think on thee, my love.

But should the gracious pow'rs be kind,
Dispel the gloom and still the wind,
And waft me to thy arms once more,
Safe on my long-lost native shore,
      Then ne'er again
      I tempt the main,

---

[1] Arne (1710–78) was a doctor of music. His sister had an excellent voice, for which reason he, when he was eighteen years of age, specially wrote her a part in "Rosamund," which was a success. She became the very young wife of Colley Cibber, who was largely instrumental in getting Arne's operas staged at Drury Lane.

But tender joys improve :
  I then with thee
  Will happy be,
And think on nought but love.

ANONYMOUS.

BEN BACKSTAY.

BEN BACKSTAY was a boatswain—
  A very jolly boy;
No lad than he more merrily
  Could pipe all hands, ahoy :
And when unto his summons
  We did not well attend,
No lad than he more merrily
  Could handle a rope's-end.
      Singing chip-cho, cherry-cho,
      Fol-de-riddle-ido !

It chanced one day our captain—
  A very jolly dog—
Served out to all the company
  A double share of grog.
Ben Backstay he got tipsy
  Unto his heart's content;
And being half-seas-over,—
  Why, overboard he went.
      Singing chip-cho, cherry-cho, etc.

A shark was on the larboard-bow,—
  Sharks don't on manners stand,
But grapple all that they come near,
  Just like your sharks on land.
We hove Ben out some tackling,
  Of saving him in hopes;
But the shark he bit off his head,
  So he couldn't see the ropes.
      Singing chip-cho, cherry-cho, etc.

Without his head his ghost appeared
  All on the briny lake;
He piped all hands on deck and said—
  "Lads, warning by me take :

By drinking grog I lost my life;
    So, lest my fate you meet,—
Why, never mix your liquors, lads;
    But always drink them neat." [1]
        Singing chip-cho, cherry-cho, etc.
                                ANONYMOUS.

HEART OF OAK.

COME, cheer up, my lads, 'tis to glory we steer,
To add something new to this wonderful year;
To honour we call you, not press you like slaves,—
For who are so free as the sons of the waves?
Heart of oak are our ships; heart of oak are our men:
    We always are ready—
    Steady, boys, steady:
We'll fight and we'll conquer again and again!

We ne'er meet our foes but we wish them to stay;
They never meet us but they wish us away:
If they run, then we follow, and drive them ashore;
For if they won't fight us, we cannot do more.
                                Chorus.

Monsieur Thurot,[2] in the absence of Boyce,[3]
Went over to Ireland to brag the dear boys:
Near Man,[4] Elliot met him, and gave him a blow
Which sent him to tell it to Pluto below.
                                Chorus.

---

[1] The date of this song is unknown; but it must have been fairly soon after 1740, seeing that the "moral" is a satire on "grog," which Admiral Vernon brought into existence in that year—one year after his success on Porto Bello, and the year before his disastrous expedition to Cartagena.
[2] François Thurot, son of a small innkeeper at Nuito, in Côte d'Or; he was a privateer, a smuggler, and was suspected of piracy; he crossed the Channel in a small open boat, with a pair of oars and a sail made of his shirt; he spent a year in Dover prison, studied mathematics and music, and attracted the attention of the Maréchal de Belle Isle, who induced him to take to navigation and join the French Navy.   [3] Commodore Boys, whose squadron had been told off to keep Thurot bottled up in Dunkirk; but the former corsair evaded him, went round by Gottenburg and Bergen, met with foul weather, and put into Islay, Argyllshire, to repair, then sailed down the Irish Sea to mischief and capture. (*See* p. 191). Curiously enough William Boyce wrote the music for this song, which made its first appearance in one of Garrick's pantomimes, and the name is spelt Boyce in the earliest obtainable copies of the song.
[4] The Isle of Man.   On this occasion (February 1760), Thurot had

They talk to invade us, these terrible foes;
They frighten our women, our children, our beaux;
But in their flat bottoms in darkness come o'er,
Sure Britons they'll find to receive them on shore.

Chorus.

We'll make them to run, and we'll make them to sweat,
In spite of the Devil and *Russell's Gazette:*
Then cheer up, my lads; with one heart let us sing—
Our soldiers, our sailors, our statesmen, our king.

Chorus.

GARRICK.

THE BAY OF BISCAY, O!

LOUD roar'd the dreadful thunder;
   The rain a deluge pours;
The clouds were rent asunder
   By lightning's vivid pow'rs!
The night both drear and dark—
Our poor deluded bark,
     Till next day
     There she lay
In the Bay of Biscay, O!

Now, dashed upon a billow,
   Her op'ning timbers creak!
Each fears a watery pillow,—
   None stop the dreadful leak!

---

command of two frigates and a sloop—his other vessels having left him
for different reasons—with which, and the 1200 soldiers he had aboard,
he was to invade Ireland. He had already taken and abandoned Car-
rickfergus when Hawke—who was then operating off Brest and Vannes
—detached three frigates from his fleet, under the command of Captain
Elliot, who came upon the enemy at 3 a.m. on the 28th, off the Mull
of Galloway, and overcame them, after an hour and a half's engage-
ment, in which Thurot was killed. Elliot got his three prizes safely to
anchor in Ramsey Bay, Isle of Man; and the victory was signalised by
a number of inferior broadsides. It may be added that Garrick wrote
"Heart of Oak." "Hearts of Oak" was old in his day. "Old Meg
of Herefordshire," 1609, has "Yonkers that have hearts of oake at
fourscore yeares"; and in the epilogue to her "Cruel Gifte," 1717,
Mrs. Centlivre wrote:

"Where are the rough, brave Britons to be found
With Hearts of Oak, so much of old renowned?"

To cling to slippery shrouds
Each breathless seaman tries
  As she lay,
  Till the day,
In the Bay of Biscay, O!

At length the wished-for morrow
 Broke through the hazy sky;
Absorbed in silent sorrow,
 Each heaved a bitter sigh.
The dismal wreck to view
Struck horror to the crew,
  As she lay,
  On that day,
In the Bay of Biscay, O!

Her yielding timbers sever;
 Her pitchy seams are rent—
When Heaven (all bounteous ever)
 Its boundless mercy sent!
A sail in sight appears,—
We hail her with three cheers!
  Now we sail,
  With the gale,
From the Bay of Biscay, O!

ANDREW CHERRY.

THE SEA-FISHER'S LIFE.[1]

WHAT joys attend the fisher's life—
  Blow, winds, blow!
The fisher and his faithful wife—
  Row, boys, row!
He drives no plough on stubborn land;
His fields are ready to his hand;
No nipping frosts his orchards fear;
He has his autumn all the year—
  Blow, winds, blow!

The husbandman has rent to pay—
  Blow, winds, blow!
And seed to purchase every day—
  Row, boys, row!

[1] This song was not written by a sea-fisher, nor by any one who knew a tithe of what a sea-fisher's life is; the whole thing is in opposition to the fisherman's spirit towards the facts of his life. But as a song, with its refrain, it is worthy of inclusion here.

But he who farms the rolling deeps,
Though never sowing, always reaps;
The ocean's fields are fair and free;
There are no rent-days on the sea—
     Blow, winds, blow!

ANONYMOUS.

THE ZETLAND FISHERMAN'S GOOD-BYE.

FAREWELL, merry maidens, to song and to laugh,
For the brave lads of Westra are bound to the Haaf;
And we must have labour and hunger and pain,
Ere we dance with the maids of Dunrossness again.

For now, in our trim boats of Norroway deal,
We must dance on the waves, with the porpoise and
     seal:
The breeze it may pipe, so it pipe not too high,
And the gull be our songstress whene'er she flits by.

Sing on, my brave bird, while we follow, like thee,
By bank, shoal and quicksand, the swarms of the sea;
And when twenty-score fishes are straining our line,
Sing louder, brave bird, for the spoils shall be thine.[1]

We'll sing while we bait, and we'll sing while we haul,—
For the deeps of the Haaf have enough for us all:
There is torsk[2] for the gentle, and skate for the carle—
And there's wealth for bold Magnus, the son of the earl.

Huzza! my brave comrades, give way for the Haaf—
We shall sooner come back to the dance and the laugh;
For life without mirth is a lamp without oil,—
Then mirth and long life to the bold Magnus Troil!

SCOTT.

THE SAILOR'S WIFE.

AND are ye sure the news is true?
     And are ye sure he's weel?
Is this a time to think o' wark?—
     Ye jades, lay by your wheel!

---

[1] Gulls of different kinds follow fishing vessels night and day, because the offal and the useless small fry are thrown overboard after each catch.   [2] A large, deep-water fish of the cod family, common to the upper parts of the North Atlantic, and very plentiful around the Shetlands and Faroes.

O

Is this the time to spin a thread,
    When Colin's at the door?
Reach down my cloak,—I'll to the quay,
    And see him come ashore!
For there's nae luck about the house,—
    There's nae luck at a';
There's little pleasure in the house,
    When our gudeman's awa'.

And gie to me my bigonet,
    My bishop's-satin gown;
For I maun tell the baillie's wife
    That Colin's in the town.
My Turkey slippers maun gae on,
    My stockin's, pearly blue—
It's a' to pleasure our gudeman,
    For he's baith leal and true.

Rise, lass, and mak' a clean fireside!—
    Put on a muckle pot;
Gie little Kate her button-gown,
    And Jock his Sunday coat:
And mak' their shoon as black as slaes,
    Their hose as white as snaw—
It's a' to please my ain gudeman,
    For he's been long awa'.

There's twa fat hens upo' the coup,—
    Been fed this month and mair;
Mak' haste and thraw their necks about,
    That Colin weel may fare:
And spread the table neat and clean,—
    Gar ilka thing look braw;
For wha can tell how Colin fared
    When he was far awa'?

Sae true his heart, sae smooth his speech,
    His breath like caller air:
His very foot has music in't,
    As he comes up the stair!
And will I see his face again?
    And will I hear him speak?
I'm downright dizzy wi' the thought,—
    In troth, I'm like to greet!

If Colin's weel, and weel content,
　　I hae nae mair to crave;
And gin I live to keep him sae,
　　I'm blest aboon the lave.
And will I see his face again?
　　And will I hear him speak?
I'm downright dizzy wi' the thought,—
　　In troth, I'm like to greet!
For there's nae luck about the house,—
　　There's nae luck at a';
There's little pleasure in the house,
　　When our gudeman's awa'.
　　　　　　　　　　　W. J. Mickle.[1]

TOM BOWLING.

Here, a sheer hulk, lies poor Tom Bowling,[2]
　　The darling of our crew;
No more he'll hear the tempest howling,
　　For death has broached him to.[3]
His form was of the manliest beauty,
　　His heart was kind and soft;
Faithful below, he did his duty;
　　But now he's gone aloft.

Tom never from his word departed,
　　His virtues were so rare;
His friends were many and true hearted;
　　His Poll was kind and fair:
And then he'd sing so blithe and jolly, —
　　Ah, many's the time and·oft!
But mirth is turned to melancholy,
　　For Tom has gone aloft.

Yet shall poor Tom find pleasant weather,
　　When He, who all commands,
Shall give, to call life's crew together,
　　The word to pipe all hands.

[1] William Julius Mickle (1734–78) was chief proof reader at the Clarendon Press. During his employment there he wrote an imitation of Spenser, called, at first, "The Concubine," afterwards altered to "Sir Martyn.". Ills best work, however, is an excellent translation of Camoens' "Lusiad," which was published three years before his death.
　[2] This *g* was, of course, put on to make "bowline," or "bowlin'," rhyme with "howling."　　[3] A ship is broached-to when she is hauled off a running course, and laid to the wind; *i.e.* stopped in her flight.

Thus Death, who kings and tars despatches,
    In vain Tom's life has doffed;
For, though his body's under hatches,
    His soul has gone aloft.

DIBDIN.

"A LIFE ON THE OCEAN WAVE."

A LIFE on the Ocean wave!
    A home on the rolling deep!
Where the scattered waters rave,
    And the winds their revels keep!
Like an eagle cag'd I pine
    On this dull, unchanging shore.
Oh, give me the flashing brine,
    The sea and the tempest's roar!

Once more on the deck I stand
    Of my own swift gliding craft!
Set sail! farewell to the land,
    The gale [1] follows fair abaft.
We shoot through the sparkling foam,
    Like an ocean bird set free;
Like the ocean bird, our home
    We'll find far out on the sea.

The land is no longer in view,
    The clouds have begun to frown,
But with a stout vessel and crew,
    We'll say, "Let the storm come down!"
And the song of our hearts shall be,
    While the winds and the waters rave,
A life on the heaving sea!
    A home on the bounding wave!

EPES SARGENT. [2]

[1] This word was rarely used with its literal meaning in the sea songs or the eighteenth and the early part of the nineteenth centuries; it generally meant, as it does here, a smart breeze. [2] One of a family whose men were prominent in Massachusetts from about 1760 to 1880. He was born at Gloucester, Mass., September 27, 1813, and died on December 31, 1880, at Boston, Mass., where he had long lived as a journalist and littérateur. He had various literary gifts, and was very successful as a dramatist.

THE NAVAL SUBALTERN.[1]

BEN BLOCK was a veteran of naval renown,
  And renown was his only reward;
For the Board still neglected his merits to crown—
  As no int'rest had he with my lord.

Yet brave as old Benbow was sturdy old Ben, —
  Ay, he laughed at the cannon's loud roar,
When the death-dealing broadsides made worm's-meat
    of men,
  And the scuppers were streaming with gore.

Nor could a lieutenant's poor stipend provoke
  This staunch tar to despise scanty prog;
For his biscuit he'd crack, turn his quid, crack his
    joke,
  And drown care in a jorum of grog.

Thus year after year, in a subaltern state,
  Poor Ben for his king fought and bled;
Till time had unroof'd all the thatch from his pate,
  And the hair from his temples had fled.

When humbly saluting, with *sinciput* bare,
  The first Lord of the Admiralty once,
Says his lordship—"Lieutenant, you've lost all your
    hair
  Since I last had a peep at your sconce!"

"Why, my lord," replied Ben, "it with truth may be
    said
  That while a bald pate I've stood under,
So many young captains have walked o'er my
    head,
  That to see me quite scalp'd were no wonder."
                                    ANONYMOUS.

[1] This song was probably written towards the end of the eighteenth century. It is practically the only one that deals with its particular phase of naval life, a phase that is still known, unfortunately, although to a less extent.

TACK AND HALF-TACK.

THE Yarmouth Roads are right ahead,
    The crew with ardour burning;
Jack sings out as he heaves the lead,
    On tack and half-tack [1] turning,—
      "By the dip [2] eleven!"
Lashed in the chains, the line he coils,
    Then round his head 'tis swinging;
And thus to make [3] the land he toils,
    In numbers quaintly singing,—
      "By the mark seven!"
And now, lest we run bump ashore,
He heaves the lead and shouts once more,—
      "Quarter less four!"

"About ship, lads!—tumble up there! Can't you see?
Stand-by well! Hark, hark, helm's a-lee!
Here she comes!—Up tacks and sheets! Haul,
               Mainsail haul! . . .
Haul off all!"
And as the lessening shore they view,
Exulting shout the happy crew;
Each singing, as some sail he furls,—
"Hey for the fiddles and the girls!"

    The next tack we run [4] out to sea,
      Old England scarce appearing;
    Again we tack, and Jack, with glee,
      Sings out, as land we're nearing,—
        "By the dip eleven!"
    And as they name some beauty dear,
      To tars of bliss the summit,
    Jack joins the jest, the jibe, the jeer,
      And heaves the ponderous plummet,—
        "By the mark seven!"

---

[1] Expressed nowadays more by the term "a long leg and a short one"—*i. e.* a long board and a short board.   [2] Deep.   Every fathom on the lead-line is known by "deeps" and "marks" alternately, thus in the first ten fathoms: one is a deep; two and three are marks; four, six, eight and nine are deeps; and five, seven and ten are marks. [3] Making the land is drawing close enough in to locate the position. [4] "Run" should be "stand"—another instance of Dibdin's landsmanship; a vessel "stands" to the wind—*i. e.* on tacks—and "runs" before it.

And now, while dangerous breakers roar,
Jack cries, lest we run bump ashore,—
   "Quarter less four!"
    "About ship, lads," etc.

Thus tars at sea, like swabs at home,
  By tack and tack are biassed;
The farthest way about we roam
  To bring us home the nighest,—
   By the deep eleven!
For one tack more, and 'fore the wind,[1]
  Shall we in a few glasses,
Now make the land both true and kind,
  To find our friends and lasses,—
   By the mark seven!
Then heave the lead, my lad, once more,
Soon shall we gaily tread the shore,—
   And a half four![2]
    "About ship, lads," etc.

DIBDIN.

THE MID-WATCH.

WHEN 'tis night, and the mid-watch is come,
  And chilling mists hang o'er the darkened main,
Then sailors think of their far distant home,
  And of those friends they ne'er might see again,
    But when the fight's begun,
    Each serving at his gun,
Should any thought of them come o'er our mind,
We think, should but the day be won,
    How 'twill cheer
    Their hearts to hear
That their old companion he was one!

Or, my lad, if you a mistress kind
  Have left on shore, some pretty girl and true,
Who many a night doth listen to the wind,
  And sighs to think how it may fare with you,—
    O when the fight's begun,
    Each serving at his gun,

---

[1] What Dibdin meant here Dibdin alone could tell. Each ha of the line has the opposite meaning of the other. Mark the wholesale difference between "Heaving the Lead" and this version.

[2] Half a fathom less than four fathoms.

Should any thought of her come o'er your mind,
Think, only should the day be won,
　　　How 'twill cheer
　　　Her heart to hear
That her own true sailor he was one!

SHERIDAN.

THE ANCHOR'S WEIGH'D.[1]

THE tear fell gently from her eye,
　When last we parted on the shore;
My bosom heav'd with many a sigh
　To think I ne'er might see her more.

"Dear youth," she cried, "and canst thou haste away?
My heart will break!—One little moment stay!
Alas, I cannot, cannot part from thee!"
"The anchor's weigh'd,—farewell."
"Farewell,—remember me!"

"Weep not, my love," I trembling said;
　"Doubt not a constant heart like mine:
I ne'er can meet another maid,
　Whose charms can fix this heart like thine."

"Go then," she cried; "but let thy constant mind
Oft think of her you leave in tears behind."
"Dear maid, this last embrace my pledge shall be,—
The anchor's weigh'd—farewell, remember me!"

S. J. ARNOLD.

SWEET ANNIE.[2]

SWEET Annie frae the sea-beach came,
　Where Jockey's speel'd[3] the vessel's side,
Ah! who can keep her heart at hame,
　When Jock is toss'd aboon the tide?

"Far off 'till distant realms he gangs;
　But I'se be true, as he ha'e been;
And when ilk lass around him thrangs,
　He'll think on Annie's faithful een.

---

[1] *See* Appendix, p. 368.
[2] This excellent song, with its wealth of suggested story, first saw
the light in *The Skylark*, which was published in Edinburgh in 1803,
and contains an Irish, applauding, humorous song on Nelson.
[3] Climbed.

"Our wealthy laird I met yestreen;
　Wi' gowd i' hand he tempted me;
He prais'd my brow and rowan een,
　And made a brag o' what he'd gie.

"But tho' Jack is far away,
　Blow'd up an' doon the awesome main,
I'se keep my heart anither day—
　Syne Jockey may return again.

"Nae mair, fause Jamie—sing nae mair,
　And fairly cast your pipe away;
Thy Jock he wad be troubl'd sair
　To see his friend his lo'e betray.

"Your sangs and a' your verse is vain,
　While Jockey's notes do faithful flow;
To him my heart shall true remain—
　I'se keep it for my constant Jo'.

"Blow saft, ye gales, round Jockey's head;
　An' gar the waves be cawn an' still;
His hameward sails with breezes speed,
　An' dinna a' my pleasures spill.

"Tho' full o'erlang will be his stay,
　Yet then he'll braw in siller shine,—
I'se keep my heart anither day,
　Syne Jockey will again be mine."

ANONYMOUS.

"OUR LINE WAS FORM'D."

OUR line was formed; the French lay-to;
　One sigh I gave to Poll ashore
(Too cold I thought our last adieu;
Our parting kisses seem'd too few,
　If we should meet no more.)
But, Love, avast!—My heart is oak;
　Howe's [1] gallant signal floats on high;
I see, through roaring cannon's smoke,
Their awful line subdu'd and broke.—
　They strike! They sink! They fly!

[1] A great naval tactician, and twice First Lord of the Admiralty. On June 1, 1794, when about 500 miles off Ushant, with a fleet of twenty-five ships of the line he fell in with a French fleet of twenty-six, seven of which he soon captured, and dismasted ten more.

Now, fighting's over, drink and joke!
Sing "Rule Britannia," "Hearts of Oak"! [1]
And toast before each martial tune:

"Howe, and the Glorious First of June!"
My limb's struck off—let soothing art
　　The chance of war to Poll explain;
Proud of the loss, I feel no smart,
'Cept as it wrings my Poll's true heart
　　With sympathetic pain.
Yet she will think—with love for guide—
　　Each scar a beauty on my face;
And as I strut, with martial pride,
On timbertoe, by Polly's side,
　　She'll call my limp a grace.
　　　　Now fighting's over, etc.

Now farewell every sea delight—
　　The cruise, with eager watchful days;
The skilful chase by glim'ring night;
The well-worked ship; the gallant fight;
　　The lov'd Commander's praise.
Yet Poll's dear care and constancy,
　　With prattling babes, more joy shall bring;
Proud when my boys shall first to sea
And follow Howe to victory,
　　And serve our noble King.
　　　　　　　　EARL OF MULGRAVE.

THE SAILOR'S ADIEU.

THE topsails shiver in the wind,
　　The ship she casts to sea;
But yet my soul, my heart, my mind,
　　Are, Mary, moor'd with thee:
For though thy sailor is bound afar,
Still love shall be his guiding star.

[1] It is curious that "Heart of Oak"—as Garrick wrote the phrase during his control of Drury Lane Theatre, 1747-76—had then been made plural by the popular voice, as it is maintained to-day.

Should landsmen flatter, when we've sailed,
  O doubt their artful tales;
No gallant sailor ever fail'd,
  If love breathed constant gales:
Thou art the compass of my soul,
Which steers my heart from pole to pole!

Sirens in every port we meet,
  More fell than rocks or waves;
But such as grace the British fleet
  Are lovers, and not slaves;
No foes our courage shall subdue,
Altho' we've left our hearts with you.

These are our cares; but if you're kind,
  We'll scorn the dashing main,
The rocks, the billows and the wind,
  The power of France and Spain:
Now England's glory rests with you,—
Our sails are full—sweet girls, adieu!

MICHAEL ARNE.

NELSON.[1]

O'ER Nelson's tomb, in silent grief opprest,
Britannia mourns her hero now at rest;
But those bright laurels will not fade with years,
Whose leaves are watered by a nation's tears.

    'Twas in Trafalgar's Bay
    We saw the Frenchmen lay,
      Each heart was bounding then;
    We scorn'd the foreign yoke,
    Our ships were British oak,
    And hearts of oak our men:

---

[1] This national favourite, from the same pen as "The Anchor's Weigh'd," made its appearance in "The Americans," at the Lyceum —which was then an opera-house—April 27, 1811. The music of the play was mostly the work of John Braham, a London-born Jew, who was trained by Leoni, an Italian. At the age of eleven he was singing *bravura* songs in grand opera. He was great in "The Bay of Biscay," and composed the music of "The Anchor's Weigh'd," but not of this song, which was the work of Matthew Peter King (1773–1823), who collaborated with him in "The Americans."

Our Nelson marked them on the wave;
Three cheers our gallant seamen gave,
    Nor thought of home or beauty;
Along the line the signal ran—
"England expects that every man
    This day will do his duty!"

And now the cannons roar
Along the affrighted shore—
    Our Nelson led the way:
His ship the *Victory* named,
Long be that *Victory* famed,
    For victory crown'd the day!
But dearly was that conquest bought;
Too well the gallant hero fought
    For England, home and beauty:
He cried, as 'midst the fire he ran—
"England expects that every man
    This day will do his duty!"

At last the fatal wound,
Which spread dismay around,
    The hero's breast received.
"Heav'n fights upon our side!
The day's our own!" he cried.
"Now long enough I've lived.
In honour's cause my life was pass'd,
In honour's cause I fall at last,
    For England, home and beauty."
Thus ending life as he began,
England confess'd that every man
    That day had done his duty.
                                   S. J. ARNOLD.

THE LARBOARD WATCH.

AT dreary midnight's restless hour,
    Deserted e'en by Cynthia's beam,
When tempests beat and torrents pour,
    And twinkling stars no longer gleam,
The wearied sailor, spent with toil,
    Clings firmly to the weather-shrouds;
And still the lengthen'd hour to guile,
    Sings, as he views the gathering clouds,
        "Larboard watch, ahoy!"

With anxious care he eyes each wave,
  That, swelling, threatens to o'erwhelm;
And, his storm-beaten bark to save,
  Directs with skill the faithful helm;
With joy he drinks the cheering grog,
  'Mid storms that bellow loud and hoarse;
With joy he heaves the rolling log,
  Marks the leeway and the course—
    "Larboard watch, ahoy!"

But who can speak the joy he feels,
While o'er the foam his vessel reels;
And, his tired eyelids slumbering fall,
He rouses at the welcome call
    Of—"Larboard watch, ahoy!"
                              ANONYMOUS.

NIGHT HYMN AT SEA.

NIGHT sinks on the wave;
  Hollow gusts are sighing;
Sea-birds to their cave
  Through the gloom are flying.
Oh! should storms come sweeping,
Thou, in Heaven unsleeping,
O'er Thy children vigil keeping,
    Hear, hear, and save!

Stars look o'er the sea,
  Few and sad and shrouded;
Faith our light must be,
  When all else is clouded.
Thou, whose voice came thrilling,
Wind and billow stilling,
Speak once more—our prayer fulfilling!
    Power dwells with Thee!
                          FELICIA HEMANS.

ROCK'D IN THE CRADLE OF THE DEEP.

ROCK'D in the cradle of the deep
I lay me down in peace to sleep;
Secure I rest upon the wave,
For Thou, O Lord, hast power to save.
I know Thou wilt not slight my call,
For Thou dost mark the sparrow's fall;
And calm and peaceful is my sleep—
Rock'd in the cradle of the deep.

And such the trust that still were mine,
Tho' stormy winds sweep o'er the brine;
Or tho' the tempest's fiery breath
Rouse me from sleep to wreck and death!
In ocean cave still safe with Thee,
The gem of immortality;
Thus calm and peaceful is my sleep—
Rock'd in the cradle of the deep.

EMMA WILLARD.[1]

THE ANGEL'S WHISPER.[2]

A BABY was sleeping,
Its mother was weeping,
Its father was far on the wild raging sea;
The tempest was swelling,
Round the fisherman's dwelling,
When she cried—"Dermot, darling, oh come back to
me!"

Her beads while she numbered,
The baby still slumbered
And smiled in her face, as she bended her knee—
"Oh, blest be the warning,
My child, thy sleep adorning,
For I know that the angels are whispering with thee!

[1] *Née* Hart, born at Berlin, U.S.A., February 23, 1787, died at
Troy, N.Y., April 15, 1870. She was a devoted educationist, a con-
temporary of James Gates Percival. *See* page 35. [2] To these lines
of beautiful, simple thought and feeling Lover composed a very suitable
air. As a song of the sea, the only excuse for its inclusion here is that
suggestion of storm and possible wreck and tragedy which underlies the
whole thing.

"And while they are keeping
    Bright watch o'er thy sleeping,
Oh, pray to them softly, my baby, with me!
    And say thou would'st rather
    They watched o'er thy father—
For I know that the angels are whispering with thee."

    The dawn of the morning
    Saw Dermot returning,
And his wife wept with joy her babe's father to see,
    And closely caressing
    Her child, with a blessing,
Said—"I knew that the angels were whispering with
    thee!"

SAMUEL LOVER.

THE PILOT.

"OH! pilot, 'tis a fearful night,
    There's danger on the deep;
I'll come and pace the deck with thee,
    I do not dare to sleep."
"Go down," the pilot cried, "go down
    This is no place for thee;
Fear not, but trust in Providence,
    Wherever thou may'st be."

"Ah! pilot, dangers often met
    We all are apt to slight,
And thou hast known these raging waves
    But to subdue their might."
"It is not apathy," he cried,
    "That gives this strength to me;
Fear not, but trust in Providence
    Wherever thou may'st be.

"On such a night the sea engulph'd
    My father's lifeless form;
My only brother's boat went down
    In just so wild a storm:
And such perhaps may be my fate,
    But still I say to thee,
Fear not, but trust in Providence
    Wherever thou may'st be."

T. H. BAYLY.

"THE SEA! THE SEA!"

THE Sea! the Sea! the open Sea!
The blue, the fresh, the ever free!
Without a mark, without a bound,
It runneth the earth's wide regions 'round;
It plays with the clouds; it mocks the skies;
Or like a cradled creature lies.

I'm on the Sea!   I'm on the Sea!
I am where I would ever be;
With the blue above, and the blue below,
And silence wheresoe'er I go;
If a storm should come and awake the deep,
What matter?   I shall ride and sleep.

I love (O! how I love) to ride
On the fierce foaming bursting tide,
When every mad wave drowns the moon,
Or whistles aloft his tempest tune,
And tells how goeth the world below,
And why the south-west blasts do blow.

I never was on the dull, tame shore,
But I loved the great Sea more and more,
And backwards flew to her billow breast,
Like a bird that seeketh its mother's nest;
And a mother she was, and is to me;
For I was born on the open Sea! [1]

The waves were white, and red the morn,
In the noisy hour when I was born;
And the whale it whistled, the porpoise rolled,
And the dolphins bared their backs of gold;
And never was heard such an outcry wild,
As welcomed to life the Ocean-child.

I've lived since then, in calm and strife,
Full fifty summers a sailor's life,
With wealth to spend, and a power to range,
But never have sought, nor sighed for change;
And Death, whenever he come to me,
Shall come on the wide unbounded Sea!

B. W. PROCTER.

[1] No; but dearly he wished that such had been the case. He was born in London, November 21, 1787; and with all his passionate love of the sea, and of Nature generally, he was one of the most genial and sincere men who ever lived.

"MY BOUNDING BARK."

My bounding bark, I fly to thee,—
　　I'm wearied of the shore;
I long to hail the swelling sea,
　　And wander free once more:
A sailor's life of reckless glee,
　　That only is the life for me!

I was not born for fashion's slave,
　　Or the dull city's strife;
Be mine the spirit-stirring wave,
　　The roving sailor's life:
A life of freedom on the sea,
　　That only is the life for me!

I was not born for lighted halls,
　　Or the gay revel's round;
My music is where Ocean calls,
　　And echoing rocks resound:
The wandering sailor's life of glee,
　　That only is the life for me!

ANONYMOUS.

A SEA-SONG.

A WET sheet and a flowing sea;
　　A wind that follows fast,
And fills the white and rustling sail,
　　And bends the gallant mast,—
And bends the gallant mast, my boys;
　　While, like the eager free,
Away the good ship flies, and leaves
　　Old England on the lee!

"Oh, for a soft and gentle wind!"
　　I heard a fair one cry:
But give to me the swelling[1] breeze,
　　And the white waves heaving high,—

---

[1] *See* Appendix, p. 375.

P

And white waves heaving high, my lads,
    The good ship tight and free :
This world of waters is our home,
    And merry men are we!

There's tempest in yon hornéd moon,
    And lightning in yon cloud;
But hark the music, mariners!
    The wind is wakening loud,—
The wind is wakening loud, my boys,
    The lightning flashes free :
While the hollow oak our palace is,
·   Our heritage the sea!

                        ALLAN CUNNINGHAM.

"TO SEA, TO SEA!"

To sea, to sea! The calm is o'er;
    The wanton water leaps in sport,
And rattles down the pebbly shore;
    The dolphin wheels; the sea cows snort,
And unseen mermaids' pearly song
Comes bubbling up, the weeds among.
    Fling broad the sail; dip deep the oar—
    To sea, to sea! The calm is o'er.

To sea, to sea! Our wide-winged bark
    Shall billowy cleave its sunny way,
And with its shadow, fleet and dark,
    Break the caved Triton's azure day,
Like mighty eagle soaring light,
Or antelopes o'er Alpine height.
    The anchor heaves; the ship swings free;
    The sails swell full,—to sea, to sea!

                        T. L. BEDDOES.[1]

[1] Thomas Lovell Beddoes (1803–49) was the son of a Clifton physician, a nephew to Maria Edgeworth and a close friend of B W. Procter's. He became an M.D. of Würzburg, and was banished by Bavarian, Prussian and Hanoverian governments for preaching democracy. As a dramatic poet he made a good start with "The Bride's Tragedy"; but his best work is "Death's Jest Book: or, The Fool's Tragedy."

WHEN THE WIND BLOWS FAIR.

FAR, far upon the sea—
The good ship speeding free—
Upon the deck we gather, young and old,
And view the flapping sail
Spreading out before the gale,
Full and round without a wrinkle or a fold;
Or watch the waves that glide
By the vessel's stately side,
Or the wild sea-birds that follow through the air :
Or we gather in a ring,
And with cheerful voices sing—
Oh, gaily goes the ship, when the wind blows fair !

Far, far upon the sea,
With the sunshine 'neath our lee,
We talk of pleasant days when we were young ;
And remember, though we roam,
The sweet melodies of home—
The songs of happy childhood which we sung.
And though we quit her shore,
To return to it no more,
Sound the glories that Britannia yet shall bear,—
That "Britons rule the waves,
And never shall be slaves."—
Oh, gaily goes the ship, when the wind blows fair !

Far, far upon the sea,
Whate'er our country be
The thought of it shall cheer us, as we go ;
And Scotland's sons shall join
In the song of "Auld Lang Syne,"
With voice by memory softened, clear and low ;
And the men of Erin's Isle,
Battling sorrow with a smile,   .
Shall sing "Saint Patrick's Morning," void of care :
And thus we pass the day,
As we journey on our way—
Oh, gaily goes the ship, when the wind blows fair !
                                   CHARLES MACKAY.[1]

[1] Mackay (1814–89) was the author of "Love-letters of a Violinist,"
"Cheer, Boys, Cheer," and "There's a Good Time Coming." In my
youth the songs were very popular, yet fame was all that Mackay got

TRANCADILLO.

OH, come, maidens, come o'er the blue rolling wave;
The lovely should still be the care of the brave—
   Trancadillo, Trancadillo !
With moonlight and starlight we'll bound o'er the
   billow—
   Bright billow, gay billow !
With moonlight and starlight we'll bound o'er the
   billow.

Wake the chorus of song, and our oars shall keep time,
While our hearts gently beat to the musical chime—
   Trancadillo, Trancadillo !
With oar-beat and heart-beat we'll bound o'er the
   billow—
   Bright billow, gay billow !
With oar-beat and heart-beat we'll bound o'er the
   billow.

As the waves gently heave under zephyrs' soft sighs,
So the waves of our hearts 'neath the glance of your
   eyes—
   Trancadillo, Trancadillo !
With eye-beam and heart-beam we'll bound o'er the
   billow—
   Bright billow, gay billow !
With eye-beam and heart-beam we'll bound o'er the
   billow.

See, the helmsman looks forth to yon beacon-lit isle;
So we shape our hearts' course by the light of your
   smile—
   Trancadillo, Trancadillo !
With love-light and smile-light we'll bound o'er the
   billow—
   Bright billow, gay billow !
With love-light and smile-light we'll bound o'er the
   billow.

---

out of them.   Whether or not the above song was ever set to music I
know not ; but I learnt it from an east coast seaman, who sang it to a
spirited air.

And when on life's ocean we turn our slight prow,
May the lighthouse of Hope beam like this on us now—
   Life's billow, frail billow.
With hope-light, the true-light, we'll bound o'er life's
     billow—
   Life's billow, frail billow;
With hope-light, the true-light, we'll bound o'er life's
     billow.

CAROLINE HOWARD.[1]

THE THREE FISHERS.

THREE fishers went sailing away to the west—
   Away to the west, as the sun went down;
Each thought on the woman who loved him best,—
   And the children stood watching them out of the
     town:
     For men must work, and women must weep;
     And there's little to earn, and many to keep,
     Though the harbour-bar be moaning.

Three wives sat up in the lighthouse-tower,
   And they trimmed the lamps—as the sun went down;
They looked at the squall, and they looked at the
     shower;
And the night-rack came rolling up, ragged and
     brown:
     But men must work, and women must weep,
     Though storms be sudden, and waters deep,
     And the harbour-bar be moaning.

Three corses lie out on the shining sands,
   In the morning gleam, as the tide goes down;
And the women are weeping and wringing their hands
   For those who will never come home to the town:
     For men must work, and women must weep;
     And the sooner it's over the sooner to sleep,
     And good-bye to the bar and its moaning.

KINGSLEY.

[1] *Née* Gilman, a Bostonian, U.S.A. (1794-1890); the wife of a lit-
térateur, the mother of another, and herself a voluminous writer of
considerable talent. How excellently she has caught the motion of
rowing in this song!—the conceits in which seem to bespeak an Irish
temperament.

DIRGE AT SEA.

SLEEP!—we give thee to the wave,
Red with life-blood from the brave.
Thou shalt find a noble grave.
    Fare thee well!

Sleep!—thy billowy field is won;
Proudly may the funeral gun,
'Midst the hush at set of sun,
    Boom thy knell!

Lonely, lonely is thy bed;
Never there may flowers be shed,
Marble reared, nor brother's head
    Bowed to weep.

Yet thy record on the sea,
Borne through battle high and free,
Long the red-cross flag shall be.
    Sleep! Oh, sleep!
FELICIA HEMANS.

THE WHITE SQUALL.

THE sea ran high and the barque rode well,
The breeze bore the tone of a vesper-bell;
'Twas a gallant barque with a crew as brave
As e'er was launched on the heaving wave.
She shone in the light of declining day;
Each sail was set, and each heart was gay.

They neared the land wherein beauty smiles,
The sunny shores of the Grecian Isles;
All thought of home and welcome dear,
Which soon should greet each wanderer's ear;
And in fancy joined the social throng,
In the festive dance and the joyous song.

A white cloud glides through the azure sky,—
What means that wild, despairing cry :
Farewell, the visioned scenes of home !
That cry is " Help ! " where no help can come.
For the white squall rides on the surging wave,
And the bark is 'gulfed in an ocean grave.

ANONYMOUS.

CHANTIES

The gondoliers of Venice while away their long midnight hours on the waters with the stanzas of Tasso. Fragments of Homer are sung by the Greek sailors of the Archipelago; the severe labour of the trackers in China is accompanied with a song which encourages their exertions and renders them simultaneous. Our sailors at Newcastle have their "Heave and ho!"

I. D'Israeli.

RIO GRANDE.[1]

(WINDLASS OR CAPSTAN.)

Oh, where are you bound to, my yaller gal?—
Heave-o, Rio!
Oh, where are you bound to, my yaller gal?—
We're bound to the Rio Grande!
Then it's heave-o, Rio! Heave-o, Rio!
And fare you well, my bonny young gal,
For we're bound to the Rio Grande!

Oh, where are you bound to, bully boys all?—
Heave-o, Rio!
Oh, where are you bound to, bully boys all?—
We're bound to the Rio Grande! etc.

Oh, what to do there, my bully boys all?—
Heave-o, Rio!
Oh, what to do there, my bully boys all?—
In that far away Rio Grande! etc.

To load up with gold, my bully boys all!—
Heave-o, Rio!
To load up with gold, my bully boys all!—
Away in the Rio Grande! etc.

Or die of the fever, bully boys all!—
Heave-o, Rio!
Or die of the fever, bully boys all!—
Away in the Rio Grande! etc.

THE FLASH PACKET.

(CAPSTAN.)

'Tis of a flash packet of bully-boy fame—
Bound away! Bound away!
She sails from the Mersey, and the Dreadnought's her
name—
Bound away! Bound away!

[1] These chanties are arranged as they would be sung on a round voyage out and home again. They are printed here as I wrote them down from the chanty-men at sea. The list is incomplete; but it is probably enough, for without the occasion, and the "roll and go" of ship and tongues and work, they are apt to seem to be merely foolish to landsmen's ears. Yet to hear them properly sung in their places, especially the hauling and capstan chanties, is a most inspiriting experience. The choruses are printed in italics and the solo parts in roman.

She sails from the Mersey where the broad waters flow;
She's a Liverpool packet,[1] O God, let her go!
  Bound away! Bound away, where the stormy winds
    blow!
  She's a Liverpool packet, O God, let her go!

O it's now we are leaving the Waterloo dock—
  Bound away! Bound away!
Where the girls and the boys on the pier-head do flock—
  Bound away! Bound away!
They give three loud cheers, while the tears down do
  flow;
Then away in the Dreadnought, O God, let us go!
  Bound away! Bound away, while the wages are low!
  She's a Liverpool packet, to the west'ard we go!

And when we go sailing up Long Island Sound—
  Bound away! Bound away!
With flags all a-flying and shore boats around—
  Bound away! Bound away!
Then the bands striking up "Yankee Doodle" will flow,
All to welcome the Dreadnought—O God, let us go!
  Bound away! Bound away, through gale, hail and
    snow!
  She's a Liverpool packet, O God, let her go!

WHISKEY! JOHNNY!

(HOISTING.[2])

O WHISKEY is the life of man—
  Whiskey![3] Johnny![4]
O Whiskey is the life of man—
  Whiskey for me, Johnny![5]

---

[1] No ships were ever worse driven than the Liverpool and New York packets, from about fifteen years before the advent of steam until steam drove them off the Atlantic. The average easterly passage was 23 days, and 39 on the westward run; but few of the vessels failed to make the former in sixteen days now and then. I can remember hearing the phrase "as hard to drown as a packet rat." "Packet rats" were the men who manned the vessels, and they grew to be known as, generally, the "hardest cases" that ever trod a deck. "Handspike hash," "marline-spike cracker," "belaying-pin soup" and similar phrases came into existence on those vessels.

[2] In all hoisting chanties the chanty man stands up and pulls on the leading part of the tackle, usually with the second or third mate; while the body of the men "tail on" to the fall after it has been "snatched" into a block on the deck thus forming two sides of a square. [3], [4] and [5] At

O Whiskey killed my poor old dad—
Whiskey! Johnny!
O Whiskey killed my poor old dad—
Whiskey for me, Johnny!

O Whiskey gave me two black eyes—
Whiskey! Johnny!
O Whiskey gave me two black eyes—
Whiskey for me, Johnny!

O Whiskey made me pawn my clothes—
Whiskey! Johnny!
O Whiskey made me pawn my clothes—
Whiskey for me, Johnny!

O Whiskey drowned my old grey aunt—
Whiskey! Johnny!
O Whiskey drowned my old grey aunt—
Whiskey for me, Johnny!

O Whiskey made me go to sea—
Whiskey! Johnny!
O Whiskey made me go to sea—
Whiskey for me, Johnny!

O Whiskey hot or whiskey cold—
Whiskey! Johnny!
O Whiskey hot or whiskey cold—
Whiskey for me, Johnny!

O Whiskey young or whiskey old—
Whiskey! Johnny!
O Whiskey young or whiskey old—
Whiskey for me, Johnny!

O Whiskey's a drink for a man with a heart—
Whiskey! Johnny!
O Whiskey's a drink for a man with a heart—
Whiskey for me, Johnny!

---

these words all hands pull together. This is one of our oldest chanties; it is supposed to have been known at the time of the Armada, with "malmsey" in the place of "whiskey." In all hauling chanties the men pull together at the end of each chorus.

BANKS OF SACRAMENTO.

(CAPSTAN.)

Now, my lads, get your beds and lie down—
To me hoodah! to me hoodah!
Now, my lads, get your beds and lie down—
To me hoodah, hoodah, O!
Blow, my bully-boys, blow,
For Californi-O!
There's plenty of gold,
So I've been told,
On the banks of Sacramento!

In the Black Ball [1] Line I served my time—
To me hoodah! to me hoodah!
In the Black Ball Line I served my time—
To me hoodah, hoodah, O!
Blow, my bully-boys, blow,
For Californi-O!
There's plenty of gold,
So I've been told,
On the banks of Sacramento!

O that was the line for cracking it on—
To me hoodah! to me hoodah!
O that was the line for cracking it on—
To me hoodah, hoodah, O!
Blow, my bully-boys, blow,
For Californi-O!
There's plenty of gold,
So I've been told,
On the banks of Sacramento!

(THE SAME: AS A HAULING CHANTY.)

Now, my lads, get your beds and lie down—
With a hoodah!
Now, my lads, get your beds and lie down—
With a hoodah, hoodah-day!

Blow, boys, blow for Californi-O—
With a hoodah!
There's plenty of gold, so I've been told—
On the banks of Sacramento!

[1] The first line of New York and Liverpool packets; the vessels had a huge black ball painted on the lower part of their topsails. *See* page 218.

We came to a land where the cocktail flows—
With a hoodah!
We came to a land where the cocktail flows—
With a hoodah, hoodah-day!

We came to a river where we couldn't get across
With a hoodah!
And the plenty of gold, as I'll have you told,
Was a bully, bully, bully loss—
With a hoodah, hoodah-day!

BOWLINE SONGS.

.

THE bully ship's a-rolling—
Haul away the bowline!
It's a-raining and a-snowing—
Haul away the bowline!
It's a-raining and a-snowing—
The bowline haul!   .

A Black Ball liner lies a-lee—
Haul away the bowline!
She'll lead us a chase, I'll bet a spree—
Haul away the bowline!
She'll lead us a chase, I'll bet a spree—
The bowline haul!

II [1]

Haul away the bowline, so early in the morning—
Haul away! haul away the bowline!
Haul away the bowline, so early in the morning—
Haul away, haul!   The bowline haul!

O London docks they are so fine, early in the morning—
Haul away! haul away the bowline!
O London docks they are so fine, early in the morning—
Haul away, haul!   The bowline haul!

[1] The original of this is said to have been sung in Tudor times, but it must have changed greatly since then.   In those days, when sails were not so well made as they are now, the bowline was a much more important rope than it is to-day.

And there lives Kitty on my half-pay, early in the
    morning—
    Haul away! haul away the bowline!
And there lives Kitty on my half-pay, early in the
    morning—
    Haul away, haul! The bowline haul!

When I get back I'll marry her, O, early in the
    morning—
    Haul away! haul away the bowline!
When I get back I'll marry her quick, O, early in the
    morning—
    Haul away, haul! The bowline haul!

And if she's married another man, O, early in the
    morning—
    Haul away! haul away the bowline!
And if she's married another man, O, early in the
    morning—
    Haul away, haul! The bowline haul!

I'll black his eyes and I'll off to sea, early in the
    morning—
    Haul away! haul away the bowline!
I'll black his eyes and I'll off to sea, early in the
    morning—
    Haul away, haul! The bowline haul!

STORM ALONG.[1]

(PUMPING.)

STORM along, and round she'll go—
    To me way-aye, storm along!
Storm along, and round she'll go—
    To me hi-hi-hi, Mister Storm-along!

Old Storm-along was a good old man—
    To me way-aye, storm along!
Old Storm-along was a good old man—
    To me hi-hi-hi, Mister Storm-along!

---

[1] The only time I heard this sung was at the pumps, after an Indian
Ocean hurricane. There is another version of it, with the second
chorus: "Come along, get along. Storm along, John"; but it is used
as a hauling chanty.

But now old Stormy's dead and gone—
To me way-aye, storm along!
But now old Stormy's dead and gone—
To me hi-hi-hi, Mister Storm-along!

He died when he blew our sails away—
To me way-aye, storm along!
He died when he blew our sails away—
To me hi-hi-hi, Mister Storm-along!

So we sunk him under a long, long roll—
To me way-aye, storm along!
So we sunk him under a long, long roll—
To me hi-hi-hi, Mister Storm-along!

Storm along through frost and snow—
To me way-aye, storm along!
Storm along through frost and snow—
To me hi-hi-hi, Mister Storm-along!

PADDY DOYLE.

(FURLING SAILS.)

To me aye-aye-aye—
And we'll *f-u-r-r-l!* [1]
Aye-aye-aye—
And pay Paddy Doyle for his *BOOTS!* [2]

To me aye-aye-aye—
And we'll *s-i-n-g!*
Aye-aye—
And we'll *h-e-a-v-e!*
Aye-aye—
And pay Paddy Doyle for his *BOOTS!*

To me aye-aye-aye—
And we'll *h-e-a-v-e!*
Aye-aye—
And we'll *s-w-i-n-g!*
Aye-aye—
And pay Paddy Doyle for his *BOOTS!*

[1] and [2] All hands join in and roll up the sail at the words in italics. This song is used only when stowing courses and topsails. For the furling of lighter sails and other short pieces of work, or where only three or four men are engaged, there are short chanties, such as: "Oho, Jew, roll him over!" "O bunt him, bunt him, boys!" "O rouse him, boys, rouse him, O!" etc.

ROLLING HOME.

(WINDLASS OR CAPSTAN.)

PIPE all hands to man the windlass,
　　See your cable-chain stowed clear—
　　　Rolling home! Rolling home!
For to-night we sail from Frisco,[1]
And for English shores we'll steer.
　　　Rolling home! Rolling home!
　　　Rolling home across the sea!
　　　Rolling home to dear old England!
　　　Rolling home, sweetheart, to thee!

If we all heave with a will, boys,
　　Soon our anchors we will trip—
　　　Rolling home! Rolling home!
And across the briny ocean
We will steer our gallant ship—
　　　Rolling home! Rolling home!
　　　Rolling home across the sea!
　　　Rolling home to dear old England!
　　　Rolling home, sweetheart, to thee!

Eighteen months away from England;
　　Now a hundred days or more—
　　　Rolling home! Rolling home!
On salt horse and cracker-hash, boys,
　　Peas and pork that make us sore—
　　　Rolling home! Rolling home!
　　　Rolling home across the sea!
　　　Rolling home to dear old England!
　　　Rolling home, sweetheart, to thee!

DIXIE LAND.[2]

(HOISTING.)

WAY down in Dixie,
In Dixie Land where de cotton grow—
　　Sing a song! Blow along—O!

---

[1] Or whatever port the ship is leaving.

[2] This chanty, like "Roll de Cotton Down," was no doubt originally a cotton-stowing song on the Mississippi, where the solo man was the leader of a gang, and the gang trolled out the chorus.

Way down in Dixie,
In Dixie Land I had a gal—
Sing a song! Blow along—O!

Way down in Dixie,
Her name it was Jemima-Joe—
Sing a song! Blow along—O!

Way down in Dixie,
She had black eyes and a lovely nose—
Sing a song! Blow along—O!

Way down in Dixie,
She dressed so smart she broke my heart—
Sing a song! Blow along—O!

Way down in Dixie,
There came a big buck nigger along—
Sing a song! Blow along—O!

Way down in Dixie,
He made love to my yaller gal—
Sing a song! Blow along—O!

Way down in Dixie,
I gave him one with a marline-spike—
Sing a song! Blow along—O!

Way down in Dixie,
So across the sea I had to go—
Sing a song! Blow along—O!

Way down in Dixie,
And now I am a sailorman—
Sing a song! Blow along—O!

SALLY BROWN.

(HOISTING.)

I SHIPPED aboard of a Liverpool liner—
Way O, roll and go!
I shipped aboard of a Liverpool liner—
Spend my money on Sally Brown!

Sally Brown was a gay mulatto—
Way O, roll and go!
Sally Brown was a gay mulatto—
Spend my money on Sally Brown!

Seven long years I courted Sally—
Way O, roll and go!
Seven long years I courted Sally—
Spend my money on Sally Brown!

Sally, I said, why don't you marry—
Way O, roll and go!
Sally, I said, why don't you marry—
Spend my money on Sally Brown!

She said I was no bone,[1] to tarry—
Way O, roll and go!
She said I was no bone, to tarry—
Spend my money on Sally Brown!

So round the Horn I went for Sally—
Way O, roll and go!
So round the Horn I went for Sally—
Spend my money on Sally Brown!

Sally Brown she married a baker—
Way O, roll and go!
Sally Brown she married a baker—
Spend my money on Sally Brown!

In New Orleans he took her dancing—
Way O, roll and go!
In New Orleans he took her dancing—
Spend my money on Sally Brown!

And now my Sally is gone for ever—
Way O, roll and go!
And now my Sally is gone for ever—
I'll spend no more on Sally Brown!

BLOW, BULLIES, BLOW.

(HOISTING.)

THERE's a Black Ball ship coming down the river—
Blow, bullies, blow!
There's a Black Ball ship coming down the river—
Blow, my bully-boys, blow!

And who d'ye think is the captain of her?—
Blow, bullies, blow!
And who d'ye think is the captain of her?—
Blow, my bully-boys, blow!

[1] No good.

Why, bully-man Hays is the captain of her—
Blow, bullies, blow!
Why, bully-man Hays is the captain of her—
Blow, my bully-boys, blow!

He'll hound you round from watch to watch—
Blow, bullies, blow!
He'll hound you round from watch to watch—
Blow, my bully-boys, blow!

And who d'ye think is the first mate of her?—
Blow, bullies, blow!
And who d'ye think is the first mate of her?—
Blow, my bully-boys, blow!

Santander Jones, he's a rocket from hell, boys—
Blow, bullies, blow!
Santander Jones, he's a rocket from hell, boys—
Blow, my bully-boys, blow!

He'll ride you down, as you ride the spanker—
Blow, bullies, blow!
He'll ride you down, as you ride the spanker—
Blow, my bully-boys, blow! [1]

DRUNKEN SAILOR. [2]

WHAT shall we do with a drunken sailor,
What shall we do with a drunken sailor,
What shall we do with a drunken sailor,
    Early in the morning?
    Way-aye, there she rises,
    Way-aye, there she rises,
    Way-aye, there she rises,
    Early in the morning!

[1] If the piece of work lasts long enough, this song continues through the whole list of officers, their attributes, what the men are fed on, what the ship is loaded with, etc., till the mate shouts "Belay!" and the halyards are made fast and coiled down. There is a variant of this song, which is sung to a quicker measure, and begins: "Blow, my boys, for I long to hear you."

[2] This is a "runaway" song; *i. e.* it is sung by all hands together, ramping hurriedly along the deck and pulling the line with them.

Chuck him in the long-boat till he gets sober,
Chuck him in the long-boat till he gets sober,
Chuck him in the long-boat till he gets sober,
Early in the morning !   .
Way-aye, there she rises,
Way-aye, there she rises,
Way-aye, there she rises,
Early in the morning !

BLOW THE MAN DOWN.

(HOISTING.)

Blow the man down, bullies, blow the man down—
Away-aye, blow the man down!
Blow the man down, bullies, blow him right down—
Give me some time to blow the man down!

Blow him right down from his feet to his crown—
Away-aye, blow the man down!
Blow him right down from his feet to his crown—
Give me some time to blow the man down!

As I was out walking in Paradise Street—
Away-aye, blow the man down!
As I was out walking in Paradise Street—
Give me some time to blow the man down!

A fine handsome girl there I chanced for to meet—
Away-aye, blow the man down!
A fine handsome girl there I chanced for to meet—
Give me some time to blow the man down!

This fine handsome girl then she said unto me—
Away-aye, blow the man down!
This fine handsome girl then she said unto me—
Give me some time to blow the man down!

" There's a spanking full-rigger just ready for sea "—
Away-aye, blow the man down!
" There's a spanking full-rigger just ready for sea "—
Give me some time to blow the man down!

That spanking full-rigger to Melbourne was bound—
Away-aye, blow the man down!
That spanking full-rigger to Melbourne was bound—
Give me some time to blow the man down!

She was very well-manned and very well-found—
Away-aye, blow the man down!
She was very well-manned and very well-found—
Give me some time to blow the man down!

But as soon as that packet was out on the sea—
Away-aye, blow the man down!
But as soon as that packet was out on the sea—
Give me some time to blow the man down!

I'd devilish bad treatment of every degree—
Away-aye, blow the man down!
I'd devilish bad treatment of every degree—
Give me some time to blow the man down!

So I give you this warning, afore we belay—
Away-aye, blow the man down!
So I give you this warning, afore we belay—
Give me some time to blow the man down!

Don't ever take heed now what handsome girls say—
Away-aye, blow the man down!
Don't ever take heed now what spanking girls say—
Give me some time to blow the man down!

RUBEN RANZO.

(HOISTING.)

SING a song of Ranzo, boys, sing—
Ranzo, boys, Ranzo!
Sing a song of Ranzo, boys, sing—
Sing a song of Ranzo!

O-o, you know my Ruben Ranzo—
Ranzo, boys, Ranzo!
O-o, you know my Ruben Ranzo—
Sing a song of Ranzo!

Ranzo took a notion to sail upon the ocean—
Ranzo, boys, Ranzo!
Ranzo took a notion to sail upon the ocean—
Sing a song of Ranzo!

He was a New York tailor, thought he'd be a sailor—
Ranzo, boys, Ranzo!
He was a New York tailor, thought he'd be a sailor—
Sing a song of Ranzo!

So he shipped himself on a Yankee whaler—
Ranzo, boys, Ranzo!
So he shipped himself on a Yankee whaler—
Sing a song of Ranzo!

She sailed away in a whistling breeze—
Ranzo, boys, Ranzo!
She sailed away in a whistling breeze—
Sing a song of Ranzo!

She was bound high up on the northern seas—
Ranzo, boys, Ranzo!
She was bound high up on the northern seas—
Sing a song of Ranzo!

O poor Ranzo, thought he'd be a sailor—
Ranzo, boys, Ranzo!
O poor Ranzo, thought he'd be a sailor—
Sing a song of Ranzo!

HAND-OVER-HAND.

(HAULING A LINE THAT COMES EASILY.)

A HANDY ship and a handy crew—
Handy, boys, so handy O!
A handy ship and a handy crew—
Handy, boys, so handy O!

A handy master, a handy mate—
Handy, boys, so handy O!
A handy master, a handy mate—
Handy, boys, so handy O!

A handy Bo'sun, a handy Sails [1]—
Handy, boys, so handy O!
A handy Bo'sun, a handy Sails—
Handy, boys, so handy O!

A handy Doc' [2] and a handy Chips [3]—
Handy, boys, so handy O!
A handy Doc and a handy Chips—
Handy, boys, so handy O!

[1] Sailmaker.   [2] Cook.   [3] Carpenter.

SÁNTA ANNA.[1]

SÁNTA ANNA gained the day—
Away Sánta Anna!
Sánta Anna gained the day—
All on the plains of Mexico!

Sánta Anna led the way—
Away Sánta Anna!
Sánta Anna led the way—
All on the plains of Mexico!

Sánta Anna was a good man—
Away Sánta Anna!
Sánta Anna was a good man—
All on the plains of Mexico!

In Mexico, as I've heard say—
Away Sánta Anna!
In Mexico, as I've heard say—
All on the plains of Mexico!

There's many a Señorita gay—
Away Sánta Anna!
There's many a Señorita gay—
All on the plains of Mexico!

And Sánta Anna shovels his gold!
Away Sánta Anna!
And Sánta Anna shovels his gold!
All on the plains of Mexico!

[1] Antonio Lopez de Sánta Anna was a Mexican general, born 1798, died 1876. He was the leader of the revolt against Emperor Iturbide. After being successful in this he led the chequered life of a military adventurer, an exile, a president of his country, a grand-marshal to Emperor Maximilian, a conspirator, and again a banished man. The reason of his being the subject of a chanty is no doubt due to the kind of influence which Mexico has always had over deep-water seamen, and to the fact that up to some fifty years ago such men often "jumped" their ships for the purpose solely of a Mexican—or other South American —adventure.

HANGING JOHNNY.

(HOISTING.)

THEY calls me " Hanging Johnny "—
  Away-i-oh!
They calls me " Hanging Johnny "—
  So hang, boys, hang!

First I hung my father—
  Away-i-oh!
First I hung my father—
  So hang, boys, hang!

Then I hung my brother—
  Away-i-oh!
Then I hung my brother—
  So hang, boys, hang!

Then I hung the parson [1]—
  Ho-ho! Aye-aye!
Then I hung the parson—
  So hang, boys, hang!

I would have hung my sister—
  Away-i-oh!
I would have hung my sister—
  So hang, boys, hang!

A rope, a beam, a ladder—
  Away-i-oh!
A rope, a beam, a ladder—
  So hang, boys, hang!

I'll hang you all together—
  Away-i-oh!
I'll hang you all together—
  So hang, boys, hang!

---

[1] There was generally a roar at this line, which was always followed by its own laughing chorus.

LEAVE HER, JOHNNY.[1]

(HAULING, HOISTING, OR PUMPING.)

Now we'll sing you a farewell song—
Leave her, Johnny, leave her!
A jolly old song, and it won't take long—
It's time for us to leave her!

You know you heard the captain say—
Leave her, Johnny, leave her!
You can go ashore and take your pay—
It's time for us to leave her!

The winds were foul, and the passage long—
Leave her, Johnny, leave her!
But before we go we'll sing this song—
It's time for us to leave her!

The winds were foul and the ship was slow—
Leave her, Johnny, leave her!
The grub was bad and the wages low—
So it's time for us to leave her!

She would neither steer nor wear nor stay—
Leave her, Johnny, leave her!
She shipped it green both night and day—
It's time for us to leave her!

She shipped it green and she made us curse—
Leave her, Johnny, leave her!
The mate is a devil, and the "old man" 's worse—
So it's time for us to leave her!

And so we'll wish that we never shall be—
Leave her, Johnny, leave her!
On a hungry bitch just the like of she—
It's time for us to leave her!

---

[1] This is never sung in its entirety except when mooring the vessel
at the end of the voyage, when the men know that they cannot—
or rather will not—be punished for candidly expressing their opinions
and very often, alas! the truth. On the only occasion on which I
heard it all sung I helped to swell the chorus, at the quayside in
Dundee, and well it was deserved.

NAVAL BATTLES AND SHIPS OF WAR

RULE, BRITANNIA.

When Britain first, at Heaven's command,
  Arose from out the azure main,
This was the charter of her land,
  And guardian-angels sung the strain:
Rule, Britannia! rule the waves!
Britons never will be slaves!

The nations, not so blest as thee,
  Must in their turn to tyrants fall;
Whilst thou shalt flourish, great and free,
  The dread and envy of them all.
      Rule, Britannia, etc.

Still more majestic shalt thou rise,
  More dreadful, from each foreign stroke;
As the loud blast that tears the skies
  Serves but to root thy native oak.
      Rule, Britannia, etc.

Thee haughty tyrants ne'er shall tame;
  All their attempts to bend thee down
Will but arouse thy generous flame,
  But work their woe and thy renown.
      Rule, Britannia, etc.

To thee belongs the rural reign;
  Thy cities shall with commerce shine;
All thine shall be the subject main,
  And every shore it circles thine.
      Rule, Britannia, etc.

The Muses, still with Freedom found,
*   Shall to thy happy coast repair;*
Blest Isle! with matchless beauty crowned,
*   And manly hearts to guard the fair:—*
Rule, Britannia! rule the waves!
Britons never will be slaves!

JAMES THOMSON.[1]

[1] This deservedly popular piece of patriotism was not originally thought to be Thomson's, but David Mallet's; it did not appear in any edition of his poems till long after his death. Its first appearance was as a song in Act ii., scene 5, of *Alfred: a Masque*, in which Thomson and Mallet collaborated. It was performed at Drury Lane, and published in 1740. It is now generally accepted as the work of Thomson. T. A. Arne was the composer of the music both of this and other popular pieces.

THE SEA-EYGHT IN THE ZWYN.[1]

LISTEN, and the batail I sal begyn,
Of Englishmen and Normandes in the Zwyn.

Minot[2] with mouth had meant to make
Sooth saws and sad for sum men's sake.
The words of Sir Edward[3] makes me to wake:
Wuld he salve as sune mi sorrow shuld slake?
    Were my sorrow slaked, sune wald I sing:
    When God will, Sir Edward shall us boot[4] bring.

Sir Philip the Valois cast was in care,
And said Sir Hugh Kyret to Flandres shuld fare
And have Normandes enough to leave on his lare,[5]
All Flandres to burn and mak it all bare;
But, unkind coward, wo was him there;
When he sailed in the Zwyn it sowed him sare,—
    Sare it them smarted that fared out of France,
    There learnt Englishmen them a new daunce.

The burgesses of Bruges war nothing to blame—
I pray Jesus save them from sin and from schame;
For they war sune at the Sluse all by a name,
Where many of the Normandes took mekil grame.[6]

[1] This battle was fought near Sluys, in the West Scheldt, not far from where Flushing now is; Edward III, in his series of efforts to possess himself of the crown of France, there met and defeated a fleet of 400 sail, June 24, 1340. The French lost 30,000 men and 230 vessels in the engagement. This is the earliest metrical account we have of a British naval battle; and it makes us sorry that we have not something of its kind, from a contemporary hand, on King Alfred's defeat of the 300 sail of Danish pirates, off the Dorset coast, with only ten galleys. [2] Minot, the author, seems to have flourished during the brilliant first half of Edward's reign; he wrote ten poems on that king's battles, and was one of the first writers after the Conquest to be worthy of being called a poet. From internal evidence he appears to have been present at some of the engagements. By his use of dialect terms and Yorkshire names it is probable that he hailed from the east, or perhaps the north-east, of that county, where his patronymic was then fairly common. It is thought that he was a soldier of fortune at Court. [3] The King. [4] Benefit. [5] Teaching; therefore one can only suppose that Sir Hugh was to have Normans enough to lay the country waste and to teach the English how better to behave themselves —that is, according to what Philip's notions were of such matters. [6] Much grief.

When Bruges and Ipres hereof herd tell,
They sent Edward to wit, that was in Arwell; [1]
Then had he no liking longer to dwell,
He hasted him to the Zwyn, with sergantes snell,[2]
To mete with the Normandes that false war and fell,
That had ment, if they might, all Flandres to quell.

King Edward unto sail was ful sune dight,
With earls and barons and many (a) kene knight;
They came by Blankenbergh on Saint John's night—
That was to the Normandes so sorry a sight : .
Yet trump'd they and daunc'd with torches ful bright—
In the wilde waniand [3] war their hertes light.

Upon the morn after, if sooth [4] I say,
A merry man, Sir Robert out of Morlay;
At half ebb in the Zwyn sought he the way—
Thare learnt the Normandes at bukler to play;
Helped them no prayer that they might pray—
The wretches are women, their weapon's away.

The Earl of Northampton help'd at that nede
All wise men of wordes and worthy in deed,—
Sir Walter the Mawnay, God give him mede,[5]
Was bold of body, in batail to bede.[6]

The Duke of Lancaster was dight for to drive,
With many moody men that thought for to thrive,—
Well and stalwartly stint [7] he that strife,
That few of the Normandes left they alive;
   Few left they alive but did them to leap—
   Men may find by the flood a hundred on heap.

Sir William of Klinton was easy to know,
Many stout bachelors he brought in a row;
It seemed with their schoting as if it did snow;
The boast of the Normandes broght they ful low.
   Their boast was abated and their mekil pride;
   For might they not flee, but there must they bide.

The gude Earl of Glowcester,—God make him glade—
Broght many bold men with bowes ful brade; [8]

---

[1] King Edward's fleet was probably lying at anchor in Orwell Haven—the mouths of the Orwell and the Stour.   [2] Eager, quick.
[3] A wailing, diminishing cry.   [4] Truth.   [5] Ale.   [6] Challenge.
Ended it.   [8] Long bows.

To bicker with the Normandes boldly they bade,
And in midst the flood forc'd them to wade—
　To wade war the wretches cast to the brim; [1]
　The kaitiffs came out of France to teach them to
　swim.

I praise John Badding as one of the best—
Faire came he sailing out of the south-west;
To prove those Normandes was he ful prest;
Till he had fought his fill he never did rest.

John of Aile, of the Sluse, with a squadron ful sheen
Was coming into Cajont [2] cantly [3] and kene;
But sune was his trumping turned to tene,—
Of him had Sir Edward his will, as I wene.

The schipmen of England sailed so swith, [4]
That none of the Normandes from them might skrith; [5]
Who so knew well his craft thare might it kith : [6]
Of all the gude that they got gave they no tithe.

Two hundred and more schippes on the sandes,
Had our English men won with their handes;
The koffes [7] of England war broght out of bandes,
And also the *Cristopher* that in the streme standes;
　In that stound they stood, with stremers ful still,
　Till they wist full well Sir Edward his will.

Sir Edward, owre gude king, worth in wall, [8]
Fought well on that flood, faire mot him fall; [9]
As it is custom of king to comfort them all,
So thankt he gudely the grate and the small;
　He thankt them gudely, God give him mede—
　Thus come owre King in the Zwyne to that gude dede.

[1] Up to the mouth; "up to his brim," said of one who has to hold his chin up to keep his mouth out of the water, is still a dialect term in the north of England. [2] A village on the river shore. [3] With cheery smartness; still in use on and about the border. [4] With speed. [5] To get away. [6] Show it off. This line makes one think that Minot had gained some practical experience of craft; only the seaman is aware how very necessary it is to know those hidden peculiarities which make up the temperament, in a way, of a vessel in order to get the best out of her in narrow waters and amongst opposing craft. [7] Merchant vessels which the enemy had made prisoners. [8] A good fighter, worth wailing for. [9] Have good fortune.

This was the bataile that fell in the Zwyn,
Where many Normandes made mekil din;
Well armed they war up to the chin:
But God and Sir Edward gert their boast blin [1]—
Thus blinned their boast, as we well ken:
God assoyle their souls, sais all,—Amen.

LAURENCE MINOT.

THE WYNCHYLCEE FYGHT.

How King Edward and hys menye
Met with the Spaniardes in the sea.

I wuld not spare for to speak, wist I to spede,
Of wight men with weapons and worthy in wede,
That now are driven to dale [2] and dead all their deed;
They sail in the sea, grounde-fishes to feed,—
Fell fishes they feed, for all their grete fare; [3]
It was in the waning that they came thare.

They sailed forth in the Swin [4] in a somer's tyde,
With tromps and tabors and mekil other pryde;
The wordes of those war-men walked full wide;
The goods that they robbed from holds 'gan they to
hide;
In holds they have hidden grete wealths, as I wene,
Of gold and of silver, of skarlet and green.

When they sailed westward, those wight men in war,
Their hurdis, [5] their ankers hanged they on here; [6]
Wight men of the west nighed them nare [7]
And gert them stumble in the snare; might they no
fare [8]
Far might they not flit, but thare must they fine, [9]
And what they before reived that must they tyne. [10]

---

[1] Put an end to the matter.   [2] Driven to death and their deeds
ended.   [3] In spite of their boasting, which is again referred to—
stanza 2, line 3.   [4] At the mouth of the Thames.   [5] Made of
"hurds"—*i.e.* the hard parts of flax and hemp; it was a broad band of
canvas, secured to supports around a galley, to protect rowers from the
enemy's arrows.   [6] Anchored at Winchelsea.   [7], [8] and [9] Brave men
from the west came near and bade the Spaniards to go no further, but
stop and fight.   [10] What they had taken they would have to lose.

Boy with thy black beard [1] I rede that thou blin,
And sune set these to strive with sorrow of thy syn ;
If thou wert in England nought shouldst thou win ;
Come thou more on that coast, thy bale [2] sall bigin ;
 Thare kindles thy care, kene men sall thee kepe,
 And do thy death in a day and dump in the depe.
Ye broght out of Bretayne [3] yowre custom with care ;
Ye met with the merchants and stripped them ful bare :
It is good reason and right that you will misfare,
When ye wuld in England lerne of a new lare—
 New lare sall ye lerne, Sir Edward to lout ; [4]
 For when ye stoode in your strength ye war all too
  stout. [5]

LAURENCE MINOT.

THE SPANISH ARMADA.

FROM merciless invaders,
 From wicked men's advice,—
O God ! arise and helpe us
 To quele owre enemies.

Sinke deepe theyr potent navies,
 Theyr strength and corage breake :
O God ! arise and arm us,
 For Jesus Christ his sake.

Though cruell Spain and Parma
 With heathene legions come,
O God ! arise and arme us—
 Wee'll dye for owre home.

We will not change our Credo
 For Pope nor booke nor bell ;
And yf the devil come hymselfe,
 Wee'll hounde hym backe to hell.

JOHN STILL. [6]

[1] Said to have been a noted pirate. It is worthy of notice that throughout the annals of piracy there has, off and on, been a " Black-beard," who was usually the worst during his time. [2] Downfall, which seems to suggest that Minot did not read the pirate's end in the present fight. [3] These Spanish pirates had lately raided the coast of Brittany. [4] Salute. [5] Here Minot seems to have merely flung satire at the vanquished enemy.

[6] Still (1543-1607) graduated at Christ's College, Cambridge, and

R

THE SPANISH ARMADA.[1]

It was about the lovely close of a warm summer day,
There came a gallant merchantman full sail to Plymouth
Bay;
Her crew had seen Castile's black fleet, beyond
Auvigney's isle,
At earliest twilight, on the waves lie heaving many a
mile.
At sunrise she escaped their van, by God's especial
grace;
And the tall *Pinta* till the moon had held her close in
chase.
Forthwith a guard at every gun was placed along the
wall;
The beacon blazed along the roof of Edgcumbe's lofty
hall;
Many a light fishing bark put out to ply along the coast,
And with loose rein and bloody spur rode inland many a
post.

MACAULAY.

THE DEFEAT OF THE ARMADA.[2]

The Spaniards' long time care and cost, invincible
surnam'd,
Was now afloat, whilst Parma,[3] too, from Flanders
hither aim'd;

---

became Bishop of Bath and Wells. In a literary sense his chief claim
to notice is that he is said—on rather slight evidence—to have written
Gammer Gurton's Needle, which was the second, if not the first (their
dates being so very close together) real comedy in the language.

[1] It may seem to be—so far as wording and time of production are
concerned—out of place to put this extract from Macaulay's ballad in
here; but the purpose is, with these Armada pieces, to give a consecutive impression of the coming of the great fleet, its destroyal, and the
feeling that followed.

[2] From Warner's *Albion's England*. Warner was born in the year
of the Armada; and, as his figures are all wrong, he probably wrote
from hearsay. [3] Duke of Parma (Pier Luigi, natural son of Pope
Paul III), who waited in the neighbourhood of Dunkirk with 30,000
soldiers to invade England.

Like fleet, of eight score ships and odd, the ocean never
    bore,—
So huge, so strong, and so complete in every strength
    · and store :
Carracks, galleons, argosies and galliasses such
They seem'd so many castles, and their tops the clouds
    to touch.
These off the Lizards shew themselves and threaten
    England's fall;
But there were fifty ships of ours that fleet was fought
    withal.
Howbeit of a greater sort our navy did contest;
But part kept diet in the port, that might of health have
    miss'd—
Had Spain's Armada of our wante in Plymouth's haven
    wist !
The rest [1] had eye on Parma, that from Flanders armour
    threets.
Meanwhile Lord Charles, our Admiral, and Drake did
    worthy feats;
Whose fearless fifty molehills how'd their tripl'd
    mountains' base,
And even at first (so pleas'd it God) pursued as if in
    chase.
By this (for over-idle seem'd, to English hearts, the
    shore)
Our gallants did embark each where and made our
    forces more.
But in such warlike order then their ships at anchor
    lay,
That we—unless we them disperse—on bootless labour
    stay :
Nor lackèd policy that to that purpose made us way.
Ours fired [2] divers ships that, down the current sent, so
    scar'd,
That cables cut and anchors lost, the Spaniards badly
    far'd.
Dispersèd thus, we spare not shot, and part of them we
    sink,
And part we board; the rest of them did fly—not fast
    enough they think.

[1] A few vessels, under the command of Lord Seymour, lay off
Dunkirk to prevent Parma and his Flemings from putting to sea.
[2] This was the first use of fire-ships by the English.

R 2

Well-guided little axes so force tallest oaks to fall,
So numbrous herds of stately harts fly beagles few and
   small.
Nine[1] days together chased we them, not actions, save
   in flight;
About eight[2] thousands perished in famine, sea, and
   fight
For treasure, ships and carriages, lost honour, pris'ners
   ta'en,
The Spaniards hardly 'scaping hence, 'scaped not
   rebukes in Spain.
Well might thus much (as much it did) cheer England;
   but much more
Concurrency from one to all to stop that common sore.
Even Catholics (that err'd name doth please the Papists)
   were
As forward in this quarrel as the foremost arms to
   bear,
Recusants and suspects of note—of others was no care:
And had not our God-guided fight on seas prevailed,
   yet
The Spaniards, land whereso they could, had with our
   armies met;
Our common courage wished no less, so lightly feared
   we foes,
Such hope in God, such hate of them, such hearts to
   barter blows.
Here flamed the Cyclops' forges; Mars his armoury
   was here,
Himself he sheds in us, and with our cause ourselves
   we cheer.
But (which had scarrified our wounds, if wounded, with
   the balm
Of her sweet presence, so applaus'd as in sea-storms a
   calm)
Her royal self, Elizabeth, our sovereign gracious
   Queen,
In magnanimous majesty amidst her troops was seen,

[1] The Armada entered the Channel on July 19, 1588; Howard and
Drake attacked it on the 20th; on the 21st the chase began, and ended
on the 27th, with the loss of one English vessel. [2] During the engage-
ment Spain lost fifteen capital ships and 5000 men, while the chase and
the gale on the Irish coast accounted for another 5000 men and seven-
teen vessels.

Which made us weep for joy—nor was her kindess less
    to us.
Think nothing letting, then, that might the common
    cause discuss,
Where prince and people have in love a sympathy as
    thus.
Howbeit force, nor policy, but God's sole providence
Did clear fore-boasted conquest and benighted thraldom
    hence.
He in Sennacherib his nose did put his hook, and
    brought
Him back again the way he came without performing
    aught;
He fought for us, alonely we did shout and trumpets
    sound,
When as the walls of Jericho fell flat upon the ground.
Yea lest (for erst did never hear like strong supplies
    befal,
Like loyal hearts in every one, like warlike minds in all,
Less spare of purses, more foresight, and valiant guides
    to act,
As shew'd our hardy little fleet that battle never slack'd,)
Lest these, I say, might have been said the cause that
    we subdu'd,
Even God to glorify Himself, our gainèd cause pursu'd,
Without our loss of man, or mast, or foe once touching
    shore,
Save such as, wreck'd, were prisoners; or but landing
    lived no more.
And as in public prayers we did His defence implore;
So, being victors, publicly we yielded thanks therefor.
Her Highness' self (good cause she had), in view of
    every eye,
On humbled knees did give Him thanks that gave her
    victory.
Remaineth what she won, what Spain and Rome did
    lose in fame:
Remaineth—Popes use potentates but to retrieve their
    game.

WILLIAM WARNER.

SIR FRANCIS DRAKE; OR, EIGHTY-EIGHT.

SOME yeares of late, in Eighty-eight,
  As I do wel remember, ah!
It was, som say, on the Ninth of May,
  And som say in September, ah!

The Spanish Traine launch'd forth amaine,   .
  With many a fine bravado;
Whereas they thought, but it prov'd nought,
  The Invincible Armado.

There was a lytle manne that dwelte in Spain,
  That shot wel in a gun, ah!
Don Pedro [1] hight, as black a wight
  As the Knight of the Sun, ah!

King Philip made hym admirall,
  And bad hym not to stay, ah!
But to destroy both Man and Boy,
  And then to come away, ah!

The Queen was then at Tilburee [2]—
  What culd wee more desire, ah!
Sir Francis Drake, for Her sweet sake,
  Did sett 'em all on fire, ah!

Away they ranne by Sea and Land,
  Soe that one manne slew three score, ah!
And had not they runne all away—
  O my Soul, wee had killed more, ah!

Then lett them neyther bragg nor boast;
  For if they come againe, ah!
Lett them take care they doe not speede
  As they did—they know when, ah!

                                    ANONYMOUS.

---

[1] The Duke of Medina Sidonia.   [2] I have read that she stood on the shore at Purfleet, watching the vessels go down the river, and was heard to say, "Oh, my poor fleet!" whence the place afterwards took its name; this was also told to me by an old boatswain the first time I sailed up the Thames.

THE LAST FIGHT OF THE *REVENGE*.[1]

(The morning of the second day, September 14, 1591.)

. . . ALL that did encircle him was his foe.

His masts were broken, and his tackle torn,
His upper workes hew'd downe into the sea,
Naughte of his shipp above the surge was borne,
But even levell'd with the ocean lay.

Powder for shott was spent and wasted clean,
Scarce seen a corn[2] to charge a piece withal;
All her pikes broken, halfe his beste men slaine;
The reste, sore wounded, on Death's agents call:
On the other side her foe in rankes remaine,
Displaying multitudes, and store of all
Whatever might avail for victory,
Had they not wanted heart's true valiancie.

When Grenville saw his desperate, dreary case,
He call'd before him all within the place—
The Master, Master-Gunner—and them taughte
Rules of true hardiment to purchas grace,
Show'd them the ende their travail's toil had boughte,—
How sweete it is swift Fame to overgo,
How vile to dive in captive overthrow.[3]

---

[1] It would be idle to repeat here, however briefly, the story of Grenville's Homeric battle with the Spaniards off the Azores—"every schoolboy knows it." In this extract, taken from a very long description of the fight, Gervase Markham shows how it ended. Markham—who was born towards the end of the sixteenth century, and lived into the beginning of the Protectorate—was captain of a royalist troop in the Civil War. He wrote learnèdly on husbandry, hawking, cattle diseases, etc., and was the author of a tragedy named "Herod and Antipater." He was also the importer of the first Arabian horse that was seen in England.   [2] A grain of powder, which at that day was rather larger than a grain of corn.   [3] At this point the little *Revenge* was well-nigh a sinking wreck. She had sunk two galleons out of hand, holed two others so badly that they had drawn off and gone down

"Gallants," he saith, "since three o'clock last noone
　　Until this morning, fifteene houres by course,
We have maintain'd stout war, and still undone
　　Our foes' assaults, and driven them to the worse:
Fifteene Armado's boardings [4] have not won
　　Contente or ease, but beene repell'd by force;
Eight hundrede cannon-shott against her side
Have not our heartes in coward-colours dye'd.

.　　　.　　　.　　　.　　　.

"But as we live by wills victorious,
Soe lett us die victors of them and us.

.　　　.　　　.　　　.　　　.

"And thus resolv'd, since other meane is reft,
　　Sweete Master-Gunner, split our keel in twaine:
We cannot live, whome hope of life hath left;
　　Dying, our deathes more glorious lives retaine:
Lett not our shipp, of shame and foil bereft,
　　Unto our foemen for a prize remaine;
Sink her, and, sinking, with the Greeks we'll cry—
' Best not to be, or being soone to die ! ' "

Scarce had the wordes tooke wing from his dear tongue,
　　When the stout Master-Gunner, over-riche
In heavenly valor and repulsing wrong,
　　Proud that his handes by action might cnriche
His name and nation with a 'worthie song,
　　Tower'd his hearte higher than an eagle's pitch,
And instantly endeavour'd to effect
Grenville's desire, by ending Deathe's defect.

But the other Master and the other Mates
　　Dissented from the honour of their mindes,
And humbly pray'd the Knight to rue their states,
　　Whome misery to noe suche mischief bindes.

.　　　.　　　.　　　.　　　.

They show'd him divers gallante men of might,
　　Whose woundes, not mortal, gave hope of recure;
For their sakes sue'd they to divorce this nighte
　　Of desperate chance, call'd into Deathe's black lure.

.　　　.　　　.　　　.　　　.

---

later on, had put an end to the lives of 2000 Spaniards, and (4) had
driven off fifteen attempts to board her; yet she was still surrounded by
enemies, whom dread and respect now kept silent and at some distance.

"And where thou say'st the Spaniardes shall not brave
  T' have tooke our shipp due to our virgin Queen,
O know that they, nor all the worlde, can save
  This wounded bark, whose like no age hath seen :
Six foote she leakes in hold—three shott beneath the
      wave,
  All whose repaire soe insufficient beene
That when the sea shall angry worke begin,
She cannot choose but sinke and die therein."

O when Sir Richard sawe them start aside,
  More chain'd to life than to a glorious grave;
And those, whome he soe oft in dangers tried,
  Now trembling seeke their hateful lives to save;
Sorrowe and rage, shame and his honour's pride
  Choking his soul, madly compell'd him rave,
Until his rage with vigour did confound
His heavy heart and left him in a swound.

The Master-Gunner, likewise seeing Fate
  Bridle his fortune and his will to die,
With his sharp sworde soughte to set ope the gate
  By which his soul mighte from his body fly,—
Had not his friends perforce preserved his state,
  And lock'd him in his cabin, safe to lie;
While others swarm'd where hapless Grenville lay,
Their cries recalling life, late run away.

In this too restless turmoil of unrest,
  The poor *Revenge's* Master stole away,
And to the Spanish Admiral addrest
  The doleful tidings of this mournful day.

Alonzo, willing to give ende to armes—
  For well he knew Grenville would never yield—
Able his power stoode like unnumber'd swarms,
  Yet daring not on stricter terms to build,
He offer'd all that could allay their harms—
  Safety of lives, nor any thrall to wield,
Free from the gallies, 'prisonment and paine,
And safe returne to their owne soil againe.

To this he yields, as well for his owne sake,
  Whome desperate hazard mighte endamage sore,
As for desire the famous Knighte to take,
  Whome in his hearte he seemèd to deplore;
And for his valour half a god did make,
  Extolling him all other men before,
Admiring with an honourable hearte
His valour, wisdom and his soldier's art.

.   .   .   .   .

No sooner boarded they the crazèd bark,
  But they behelde where speechless Grenville lay,
All smear'd in bloode and clouded in the dark—
  Contagious curtain of Deathe's tragic day:
They weep for pity, and eke silent mark
  Whether his lunges sende living breath away;
Which, when they see in airy blasts to fly,
They strive who first shall staunch his miserie.

.   .   .   .   .

They tooke him up and to the General broughte
  His mangl'd carcass, but unmaimèd mind;
Three days he breath'd, yet never spake he oughte,[1]
  Albeit his foes were humble, sad and kinde:
Then forthe came downe the Lamb that all souls boughte,
  And his pure hearte, from worser parts refin'd,
Bearing his spirit to the lofty skies,
Leaving his body[2]—wonder to wonder's eyes.

GERVASE MARKHAM.

[1] Linschoten's *Diary* (1598) gives it that just before he died he said: "Here die I, Richard Grenville, with a joyful and quiet mind; for that I have ended my life as a true soldier ought to do that hath fought for his country, queen, religion, and honour: wherebye my soul most ioyfully departeth out of this body, and shall always leave behind it an everlasting fame of a valiant and true soldier that hath done his duty as he was bound to do."

[2] Strange enough, as in the finishing of the Armada, hardly was Sir Richard dead when a nor'-west gale broke on the Spanish fleet and drove about thirty sail ashore on St. Michaels and the other islands. The *Revenge* was amongst them. Whether or not the hero was buried, either on sea or land, no one knows.

THE WINNYNG OF CALES BYE THE ENGLISH.

(Air : *Dub-a-dub;* or, *The Seaman's Tantàra-rare.*)

LONG the proude Spaniardes had boasted to conquer us,
  Threatened our countrie with fyer and sworde,
E'en to preparyng their navy so monstrous,
  All with greate plentie as Spaine could afforde.
"Dub-a-dub ! Dub-a-dub ! " thus strike their guns,—
"Tantàra, tantàra, the Englishman comes ! "

To the seas presentlie went our lord Admyral,[1]
  With Knyghtes couragious and captayns full goode ;
The brave Earl of Essex, a prosperous general,
  With him prepar'd to passe the salt floode.
                    Dub-a-dub ! Dub-a-dub !

At Plymouth speedilie took they shippe valiantlie,—
  Braver shippes ne'er have beene seen under sayle ;
With their faire colours spreade, and streamers over
      heade—
  Now braggyng Spaniardes take heede of your tayle.
                    Dub-a-dub ! Dub-a-dub !

Unto Cales cunnynglie came we most speedilie,
  Where the Kynges navy securlie did ryde ;
Then upon their backs, piercyng their butts of sacks,
  Before any Spanish eyes our comynge descryde.
                    Dub-a-dub ! Dub-a-dub !

Greate was the cryng, the runnyng and ridyng,
  Whych was made on that day in all the place ;
The beacones were fyred, as neede then required—
  To hyde their vaste treasure they had little grace.
                    Dub-a-dub ! Dub-a-dub !

[1] The same Lord Howard of Effingham who commanded at the defeat of the Armada. On this occasion he and Essex stormed and took Cadiz, June 21, 1596, after destroying the Spanish fleet in the harbour. For his share in the matter Howard was made Earl of Nottingham ; but soon after their return home Elizabeth smacked Essex's face in the midst of a Privy Council discussion as to a suitable governor for Ireland, and from that day his decline began. Five years later, while Howard—a much less brilliant man, but a " safe " one—was still going steadily up the tricky height of honour, Essex lost his head on the block.

There you myght see their shippes fyred soe furiouslie,
And how their men drownèd themselves in the sea;
There you myght heare them cry, wayle and weep
piteouslie,
When they saw no shift to escape theme away.
Dub-a-dub! Dub-a-dub!

The greate shippe *St. Philip,* the Spaniards pryde,
Was burnte to the water, and sunke in the sea;
But their *St. Andrew,* and *St. Mathew* besyde,
We tooke in fyght manfullie and got away free.
Dub-a-dub! Dub-a-dub!

The Earle of Essex, moste valyant and hardie,
With horsemen and footemen marcht upp to the
towne;
The Spaniardes whych saw them were greatlie afraide,
And did seeke for safeguard, and durste not come
downe.
Dub-a-dub! Dub-a-dub!

"Now," sayde the noble Earle, "courage, my soldiers
all;
Eyght and be valyant, and spoyle you shall have;
And be well-rewarded all, from the greate to the small—
But looke that the children and women you save."
Dub-a-dub! Dub-a-dub!

The Spaniardes, at that syght, thinkying it vaine to
fyght,
Hunge upp flags of truce and yielded the towne;
We marched in presentlie, deckyng the walls on hygh
With Englishe colours that broughte us renowne.
Dub-a-dub! Dub-a-dub!

We entere'd the houses then of their richest men;
For golde and treasure we surch'd eche daie;
In some kitchens we did fynd pyes bakying left behynd,
Meate rostyng at fyre, and folkes run away.
Dub-a-dub! Dub-a-dub!

Of rych merchandize full eche shoppe did we see—
Sattens and damaskes and velvets soe fayre,
Whych soulders did measure by the length of their
swords,—
Of all the commodities eche had hys share.
Dub-a-dub! Dub-a-dub!

Soe Cales was taken, and our brave Generàl
  Did march to the market-place, where he took his
    grounde;
And where manye prisoners fell to our severall shares,
  Manye cravyng mercye, and mercye they founde.
                      Dub-a-dub !   Dub-a-dub !

When our brave Generàl saw they delayèd all,
  And would not ransome the towne, as they sayd,—
With their fayre wainscotts, their presses and bed-
    steads,
  Their joynt-stools and tables a fyre we made.   ˑ
And when the fyne towne was burnyng with flame,
With a Tàra-tan-tàra ! away we all came.
                            ANONYMOUS.

THE SAYLOR'S ONELY DELIGHTE: [1]

(Showing the Brave Fight betweene the *George Aloe*,[2]
the *Sweepstake* and certaine *Frenchmen* on the Sea.)

THE *George Aloe* and the *Sweepstake, too*—
  With hey, with hoe, for and a nony no !
O, they were marchantmen and bound for Safee,[3]
  All alongst the coast of Barbarie !

The *George Aloe* to anchor came—
  With hey, with hoe, for and a nony no !
And the jolly *Sweepstake* kept on her way,
  All alongst the coast of Barbarie !

They had not saylèd leagues two or three—
  With hey, with hoe, for and a nony no !
But they met with a French man-of-war upon the sea,
  All alongst the coast of Barbarie !

---

[1] There is nothing in this song (for as a song it must have been written and used) to say that it did not come into existence in the eighteenth century; but it occurs in Act iii., scene 5, of Shakespeare and Fletcher's *Two Noble Kinsmen;* and was played "att ye Blacke Friars bye ye Kinge's Majestiss servants wyth greate applaws." [2] This name tempts one to the query: Was it originally *George, Hallo*, or, as we should say to-day, " Hallo, George "?   [3] Apparently Saffi, or Asfi, a Moroccan port on the Mediterranean ; in the sixteenth century the Sultans of Morocco had a grand castle on a hill that commanded the town and harbour, which was then and long afterwards the Moroccan gateway of trade with Europe.

"All hayle, all hayle, you lusty gallànts ! "—
  With hey, with hoe, for and a nony no !
" Of whence is your shyp and whither are you bound ? "—
  All alongst the coast of Barbarie !

" We are Englishmen and bound for Safee "—
  With hey, with hoe, for and a nony no !
" Of whence is your shyp and whither are you bound ? "—
  All alongst the coast of Barbarie !

"Amaine, amaine,[1] you gallant English men " —
  With hey, with hoe, for and a nony no !
"Come, you French swads,[2] and strike downe your
    sayles "—
  All alongst the coast of Barbarie !

They laid us aboord on the starboard side—
  With hey, with hoe, for and a nony no !
And they threw us into the sea soe wide—
  All alongst the coast of Barbarie !

When tidyngs to the *George Aloe* came—
  With hey, with hoe, for and a nony no !
That the *Sweepstake* was by a French man ta'en—
  All alongst the coast of Barbarie !

"To top, to top, thou little shyp-boy "—
  With hey, with hoe, for and a nony no !
"And see if this French man thou canst descry "—
  All alongst the coast of Barbarie !

"A sayle, a sayle, under our lee ! "—
  With hey, with hoe, for and a nony no !
"Yea, and another under her obey ! "—
  All alongst the coast of Barbarie !

"Weigh anchor, weigh anchor, O jollie boteswaine ! "—
  With hey, with hoe, for and a nony no !
"We will take this French man-of-war, if we can "—
  All alongst the coast of Barbarie !

---

[1] Give in, strike your colours. [2] Although this may have then
meant a shoit, fat person, and have therefore been meant contemp-
tuously ; it is more probably a misprint for "swabs," the derisive name
of deck-menials since before the date of this song.

We had not saylèd leagues two or three—
  With hey, with hoe, for and a nony no!
When we met this French man-of-war upon the sea—
  All alongst the coast of Barbarie!

"All hayle, all hayle, you lusty gallànts!"—
  With hey, with hoe, for and a nony no!
"Of whence is your shyp and whither are you bound?"—
  All alongst the coast of Barbarie!

"O, wee are marchant men and bound for Safee"—
  With hey, with hoe, for and a nony no!
"O, wee are French men and warre upon the sea"—
  All alongst the coast of Barbarie!

"Amaine, amaine, you English dogs!"—
  With hey, with hoe, for and a nony no!
"Come aboord, you French rogues, and strike down
    your sayles!"—
  All alongst the coast of Barbarie!

The first good shot that the *George Aloe* made—
  With hey, with hoe, for and a nony no!
He shook the French men's hearts sore afraid—
  All alongst the coast of Barbarie!

The second shot the *George Aloe* did affoord—
  With hey, with hoe, for and a nony no!
He strook their main mast over the boord—
  All alongst the coast of Barbarie!

"Have mercy, have mercy, you brave English men!"—
  With hey, with hoe, for and a nony no!
"O, what have you donne with our dear bretherene,
  As they sayled into Barbarie?"

"We laid them aboord on the starboord side"—
  With hey, with hoe, for and a nony no!
"And we threw them into the sea soe wide"—
  All alongst the coast of Barbarie!

"Such mercy as you have shewèd unto them"—
  With hey, with hoe, for and a nony no!
"Then the same sort of mercy shall you have againe"—
  All alongst the coast of Barbarie!

Wee laid them aboord on the larboord side—
　With hey, with hoe, for and a nony no!
And we threw them into the sea soe wide—
　All alongst the coast of Barbarie!

Lord, how it grieves our hearts full sore—
　With hey, with hoe, for and a nony no!
To see the drown'd French men swim along the shore—
　All alongst the coast of Barbarie!

Now gallant seamen all, adieu—
　With hey, with hoe, for and a nony no!
This is the last newes I can write to you,—
　To England's coast from Barbarie.

ANONYMOUS.

SONG: [1]

(From the opera "Sir Francis Drake.")

STEERSMAN.

ALOOF, and aloof!—and steady I steer!
　'Tis a boat to my wish;
　And she slides like a fish
When cheerily stem'd,[2] and when you row clear.
　She now has her trimme,[3]—
　Away let her swim!

[1] This song is too much of a burlesque for it to claim any serious consideration. But as the subject is Drake, and as there is some reflection of the truth behind the thing, its inclusion here may be excused. Besides, it claims some interest as being a part of one of the first operas, if not of the very first, that was written in English, or performed in this country, when the first actress—Mrs. Coleman—appeared on an English stage, 1656. D'Avenant was the son of the landlord of the Crown Tavern, Oxford; he knew Shakespeare, and was not too backward in speaking of the great dramatist as his father. He followed Ben Jonson in the laureateship, saw the inside of the Tower as a result of his share in the Civil War intrigues, escaped to France, had various other ups and downs in life, and should have known enough not to have perpetrated this song as a serious effort. While on his way out to Virginia with colonists he was taken prisoner and brought to London, where he would undoubtedly have lost his head but for Milton's intercessions on his behalf. After Inigo Jones, he and Betterton—who was one of his company—were the first and most important improvers of stage scenery as it was then known in England. [2] "Steer'd," no doubt, which alone would make sense here. [3] A vessel's proper trim is that condition in which she sails best; in small craft it is often obtained by moving anchors, boats, etc., about the deck until the trim is got.

Mackrels are swift in the shine of the moon,
And herrings in gales, when they wind us;
But, timeing our oars, so smoothly we runne,
That we leave them in shoals behind us.

Chorus.

Then cry one and all—
Amain,[1] for Whitehall!
The Diegos wee'll board to rummidge their hold;
And, drawing our steel, they must draw out their gold!

STEERSMAN.

Our master and 's mate, with bacon and peese,
In cabins keep aboard,
Each as warm as a lord—
No queen, lying-in, lies more at her ease:
Whilst we lie in wait
For reals of eight,
And for some gold quoits, which fortune must send.
But, alas! how their ears tingle
When finding, though still like Hectors we spend,
Yet still all our pockets shall jingle.
Then cry one and all, etc.

Oh, how the purser shortly will wonder,
When he sums in his booke
All the wealth we have took,
And finds that wee'l give him none o' the plunder!
He means to abate
The tythe for the State;
Then for our owners some part he'll discount:
But his fingers are pitcht together,
Where so much will stick that little will mount,
When he reckons the shares of either.
Then cry one and all, etc.

At sight of our gold the boteswain will bristle;
But, not finding his part,
He will break his proud heart,
And hang himself straight i' the chain of his whistle.

[1] Not "surrender"; since the previous century the word had lost that meaning, especially in the hands of literary swashbucklers. It then meant merely what it means to-day.

S

Abaft and afore
Make way to the shore,
Softly as fishes which slip through the stream,
    That we may catch their senteries napping.—
Poor little Diegos, they now little dream
    Of us brave warriors of Wapping.
                Then cry one and all, etc.
                            SIR WM. D'AVENANT.

THE HONOUR OF BRISTOL.[1]

ATTEND you, and give ear awhile,
    And you shall understand,
Of a battle fought upon the seas
    By a ship of brave command.
The fight it was so famous
    Men's hearts it did fulfil,
And it made them cry, "To sea,
    With the *Angel Gabriel!* "

This lusty ship of Bristol
    Sailed out adventurously
Against the foes of England,
    Her strength with them to try;
Well victuall'd, rigg'd, and mann'd she was
    With good provision still,
Which made men cry, "To sea
    With the *Angel Gabriel!* "

The Captain, famous Netheway,
    So he was called by name;
The Master's name it was John Mines,—
    A man of noted fame;
The gunner, Thomas Watson,
    A man of perfect skill;
With many another valiant heart
    In the *Angel Gabriel.*

---

[1] From internal evidence this ballad appears to have been written
during the second quarter of the seventeenth century; but there is
no satisfactory proof of its authorship.

They waving up and down the seas,
  Upon the ocean main,—
"It is not long ago," quoth they,
  "That England fought with Spain:
Would we with them might meet,
  Our minds for to fulfil!
We would play a noble bout
  With our *Angel Gabriel!*"

They had no sooner spoken,
  But straight appeared in sight
Three lusty Spanish vessels
  Of warlike force and might.
With bloody resolution,
  They thought our men to spill;
And vowed to make a prize
  Of our *Angel Gabriel.*

Then first came up their admiral,
  Themselves for to advance;
In her she bore full forty-eight
  Piecès of ordinance:
The next that then came near us
  Was the vice-admiral,
Which shot most furiously
  At the *Angel Gabriel.*

Our gallant ship had in her
  Full forty fighting men;
With twenty piece of ordinance
  We played about them then;
With powder, shot, and bullets
  We did employ them still,
And thus began the fight
  With our *Angel Gabriel.*

Our Captain to our Master said,
  "Take courage, Master bold!"
Our Master to the seamen said,
  "Stand fast, my hearts of gold!"
Our gunner unto all the rest,
  "Brave hearts, be valiant still!
Let us fight on in the defence
  Of our *Angel Gabriel!*"

Then we gave to them a broadside,
    Which shot their mast asunder,
And tore the bowsprit off their ship,
    Which made the Spaniards wonder,
And causèd them to cry,
    With voices loud and shrill,
"Help, help, or else we sink
    By the *Angel Gabriel!*"

So desperately they boarded us,
    For all our valiant shot,
Three score of their best fighting men
    Upon our decks were got;
And lo! at their first entrance
    Full thirty did we kill,
And thus we cleared the decks
    Of our *Angel Gabriel.*

With that their three ships boarded us
    Again with might and main;
But still our noble Englishmen
    Cried out, "A fig for Spain!"
Though seven times they boarded us,
    At last we showed our skill,
And made them feel the force
    Of our *Angel Gabriel.*

Seven hours this fight continued:
    So many men lay dead,
With purple gore and Spanish blood
    The sea was coloured red:
Five hundred of their fighting men
    We there outright did kill,
And many more were maimèd
    By our *Angel Gabriel.*

Then, seeing of these bloody spoils,
    The rest made haste away:
For why, they saw it was no boot
    Any longer for to stay.
So they fled into Calès,[1]
    And there they must lie still;
For they never more will dare to meet
    With our *Angel Gabriel.*

---

[1] Cadiz, pronounced Cales by our seamen till long after the date of this ballad.

We had within our English ship
  But only three men slain;
And five men hurt, the which, I hope,
  Will soon be well again.
At Bristol we were landed;
  And let us praise God still,
Who thus hath blest our men
  And our *Angel Gabriel.*

Now let me not forget to speak
  Of the gift given by the owner
Of the *Angel Gabriel*,
  That many years had known her: [1]
Two hundred pounds in coin and plate
  He gave, with free goodwill,
Unto them that bravely fought
  In the *Angel Gabriel.*   Anonymous.

THE FAMOUS FIGHT AT MALAGO; OR, THE ENGLISH MEN'S VICTORY OVER THE SPANIARDS.

Come all you brave saylors
  That sayle on the maine,
I'll tell you of a fyght
  That was lately in Spain;
And of five sayle of frigats
  Bound to Malago,
For to fyght the proud Spaniards—
  Our orders was soe.

There was the *Henry* and *Ruby*
  And the *Antelope* also,
The *Greyhound* and the *Bryan*
  For fyreshipps must goe;
But soe bravely we weighed
  And play'd oure parts,
That we made the proud Spaniards
  To quake in theyr hearts.

[1] I have a strong suspicion that the whole of this stanza is an addition made by a later hand.   These double rhymes, the anti-climax nature of this pat on the back for the owner, and the fact that the older balladists were prone to wind up after the manner of the preceding stanza are, to my mind, convincing evidence for this idea.

Then we came to an ancher,
  Soe nigh to the mould—
"Methinks you proud English
  Doe grow very bold."
But we came to an ancher
  Soe neare to the towne,
That some of theyr churches
  We soon batter'd downe.

They hung out theyr flag of truce
  For to knowe oure intent,
And they sent out theyr long boat
  To knowe what we meant;
But oure Captain he answer'd
  Them bravely—it was soe—
"For to burn all your shippyng
  Before we do goe."

"For to burn all our shippyng?—
  You must us excuse:
'Tis not five sail of frigats
  Shall make us to muse."
But we burnt all theyr shippyng
  And theyr gallies also;
And we left in the city
  Full many a widowe.

"Come, then," said oure Captain,
  "Let's fyre at the church":
And downe came theyr belfry,
  Which grievèd them much;
And downe came theyr steeple,
  Which standeth soe high,
Which made the proud Spaniards
  To the nunnery fly.

Soe great a confusion
  We made in the towne,
That theyr lofty buildings
  Came tumbling downe.
Theyr wives and theyr children
  For helpe they did cry;
But none could relieve them,
  Though danger was nigh.

The flames and the smoak
  Soe increasèd theyr woe,
That they knewe not whither
  To run nor to goe:
Some to shun the fyre
  Lept into the flood,
And there they did perish
  In water and mud.

Oure guns we kept firyng,
  Still shoutyng amaine;
Whilst many a proud Spaniard
  Was on the place slaine:
The rest, being amazèd,
  For succour did cry;
But all was in vaine—
  They had noe where to fly.

At length, being forcèd,
  They thought it most fitt
Unto the brave English men
  For to submit:
And soe a conclusion
  At last we did make,
Upon such conditions
  As was fitt to take.

The Spanish Armado
  Did England no harm—
'Twas but a bravado
  To give us alarm;
But with oure five frigats
  We did them bumbaste,[1]
And made them of English men's
  Valour to taste.

When this noble victory
  We did obtaine,
Then home we returnèd
  To England again;
Where we were receivèd
  With wellcomes of joy
Because with five frigats
  We did them destroy.

ANONYMOUS.

[1] Bombard.

THE ROYAL VICTORY.[1]

LET England and Irelande and Scotlande rejoyce,
And render thanksgivyng with hearte and with voice :
He's surely fanatick that nowe will not sing,
Is false to the kingdom and foe to the King;
    For he that will grutch
    Oure fortune, is suche
      As deals with the Devil
    And eke with the Dutch.
For why should my nature or conscience repine
At takyng his life that would faine take mine?

Soe high a victory wee could not commande,
Had it not been gain'd bye an Almighty hand :
The great Lord of Battels did perfect this work
For God and the King and the good Duke of York,
    Whose courage was suche
    Against the Low Dutch,
      Who vapour'd and swagger'd,
    Like lords in a hutch :
But let the bold Hollander burn, sinke or swimme—
They have honour enough to be beaten bye him.

Fyre, aire, earth and water, it seems, were employ'd
In striving for conquest, which we have enjoyed;
No honour, or profit, or safety can spring
To those who doe fyght against God and the King.

---

[1] This, as a broadside has it, was "obtain'd—with the Providence of Almighty God—on June 3, 1665," by the Duke of York (afterwards James II). The Duke fell in with the Dutch fleet, off Harwich, blew up the Dutch admiral's ship, took eighteen first-raters, and sank fourteen other vessels of different ratings. The duke—so excellent an admiral, yet, alas, so poor a king !—was also in command of the English fleet when it and the French allies fell foul of the Dutch in Southwold Bay, May 28, 1672 ; an action that was bloody and obstinate yet so indecisive that, although the duke chased the Hollanders down to their own coasts, it was not really finished till Prince Rupert defeated Ruyter in the following year, when they agreed thereafter to strike to the British flag on its own seas.

The battel was hot
And bloodilie fought;
   The fyre was like rain,
And like hayle was the shott;
For in this ingagement ten thousand did bleed
Of Flemmings, who now are the Low Dutch indeed!

In this cruell conflict stout Opdam was slaine
By ye great Duke of York, and lies sunke in the maine;
'Twas from the Duke's frigat that he had his doome,
And by the Duke's valour he was overcome:
   It was his goode fate
   To fall at that rate—
     Who sinke under princes
   Are buried in state:
Suche courage fortune in one grave must lye;
It is a greate honour bye greate hands to dye.

The gallant younge fellow, the son of Van Trump [1]—
Whose braines were beat out bye the head of the
   "Rump"—
Engaging with Holmes, a brave captain of ours,
Retreated to Neptune's salte-waterie bowers;
   His fate it grew grimme,
   He noe longer could swimme;
     But he that caught fishes,
   Now fishes catch him.
They eat upp our fishe, without reasone or lawes; [2]
But now they must pay for the cooking and sauze.

---

[1] These references to the Van Tromps, father and son, are all wrong. Marten the elder (who had sailed up and down the Channel with a broom at his masthead, on the supposition that he had swept the English from the seas) lost thirty sail and was killed in an engagement with Monk, off the Dutch coast, July 31, 1653; while Monk—whom Charles II made Duke of Albemarle for his chief share in the Restoration—was certainly a long way from ever being the head of the "Rump" Parliament, which dissolved itself in March 1660, three months after Monk returned from his five years' governance of Scotland. Cornelius, the son of Marten, died peacefully in Amsterdam in 1691.

[2] This was just the old, old complaint against Dutch and French fishermen poaching in English waters, which was done very largely at that time, and often caused fights when the English fishermen caught them; it has continued ever since, but to a far less extent during the past thirty years.

To mocke at men's miserie is not mine aime,—
It never can add to an Englishman's fame;
But I may rejoyce that the battel is wonne,
Because in the victory God's will is done.
>> When Justice appears
>> In suche greate affaire,
>>> Who will for Amboyna [1]
>> Plague them and theirs?
For he that did comber his conscience with guilt,
In shedding of bloode, his own shall be spilt.

In this cruell contest (our fortune was suche)
We tooke eighteen men-o'-war from the Dutch;
And likewise (as then the occasion requir'd,
And as God would have it) fourteen more we fir'd
>> At Amboyna, when
>> They tortur'd our men,
>>> They look'd not to have
>> The same dealt out agen :
With fyre and with water their sinews were crackt—
In fyre and in water these dy'd for the fact.

According as our God of Battel commanded,
The best of their vessels we fyr'd and stranded,—
All shippes, men-o'-war.   (For what pow'r hath man,
To fyght with that army, when God leads the van?)
>> They steere and they stemme;
>> But 'twas soe extream,
>>> Our men were neare dying
>> With killing of them :
They lost, when the muskets and cannons soe thunder'd,
Twice soe manye thousand as we have lost hundred.

'Twould make a brave Englishman's heart leap to see 't,
But forty shippes made an escape from their fleet,

[1] On Feb. 7, 1623, the Dutch settlers on the island of Amboina
(Moluccas) massacred the British factors for a supposed conspiracy to
turn the Dutch off the island.   It appears that nothing was done in
direct retaliation ; it is also curious that the balladist should have in
mind this historical incident, forty-two years after it happened, yet make
such a muddle about Admiral Van Tromp and his son—unless, as
regards the latter, the ballad was written on hearing the first news of
the battle with the misstatement that Cornelius had been killed there.

Whych our men pursue with muche courage and
    strengthe,—
'Tis doubtless but we shall surprise them at lengthe.
    If God be our guide
    And stande bye our side,
      We shall be befriended
    With fayre winde and tide :
If Providence prosper us with a goode gale,
The Dutch nor the Devil shall ever prevail.

Prince Rupert like lightning flew through their fleete ;
Like flame mix't with powder their army did meete ;
Ten thousand slaine bodies the ocean o'erspread,
That in few houres' distance were living then dead :
    Their admirals all,
    Save one, there did falle,
      For Death did commande
    Like a Chief-Generàl :
Bold Smith in the " Mary " did sheare out his way,
As reapers doe wheat, or mowers doe hay.

Brave Lawson and Minn there did play both their parts,
And did empty their guns in their enemies' hearts ;
The burly fat Dutchmen being cut out in slipps,
Their vessels did looke more like shambles than shippes.
    God prosper the Fleete,
    And sende they may meete
    De Ruiter,[1] to make up
    The conquest compleate :
God blesse all the Princes, and every thing
That fyghtes for ye kingdom and prayes for ye King.
                         ANONYMOUS.

[1] This prayer was not answered—perhaps to the chagrin of the
balladist, unless he also put this down to " God's will "—for De Ruiter
died, in the harbour of Syracuse eleven years after this battle, from
the effects of a wound he had received during an engagement with a
French fleet in the Straits of Messina.

THE SEA FIGHT (May 19, 1692).[1]

THURSDAY in the morn, the Ides of May,
  Recorded for ever "the famous ninety-two,"
Brave Russell did discern, by dawn of day,
  The lofty sails of France advancing : Now
All hands aloft, aloft !   Let English valour shine ;
Let fly a culverine,[2] the signal of the line !
Let every hand supply his gun :
    Follow me,
    And you'll see
That the battle will be soon begun.

Tourville[3] on the main triumphant roll'd,
  To meet the gallant Russell in combat on the deep ;
He led a noble train of heroes bold,
  To sink the English seamen to their sleep.
Now every valiant mind to victory doth aspire ;
The bloody fight's begun—the sea itself 's on fire !
And mighty Fate stands looking on,
    Whilst a flood,
    All of blood,
Fills the scuppers of the *Royal Sun!* [4]

Sulphur, smoke and fire, disturbing the air,
  With thunder and wonder affright the Gallic shore,
Their regulated bands stand trembling near,
  To see the lofty streamers now no more.

[1] The battle of La Hogue.   It was here that Russell and Rooke, aided by the Dutch, put an end to Louis XIV's effort to invade England on behalf of James II.   For his victory Russell was created Earl of Orford.   [2] An eighteen-pounder.   [3] Count de Tourville, who overcame the English and Dutch allies, under the Earl of Torrington, off Beachy Head, June 30, 1690.   He was an admiral of whom Louis, and France generally, thought so highly as to believe that he would wipe the English and the Dutch from the seas.   Besides, on this occasion Louis had an understanding with Russell that the latter would not use his fleet to prevent an invasion of England ; this was because Russell was a Jacobite.   (*See* the second stanza of "A Song on Russell's Triumph," next page.)   But Louis, thinking that the part must be as well played as it was dressed, ordered Tourville to attack Russell ; and the first shot from under French colours carried Russell's Jacobitism by the board, he being an Englishman first and an adherent of James II afterwards.   [4] Tourville's flagship ; she was named after Louis's beloved emblem, the rising sun, and bore the reputation of being the super-Dreadnought of her day.

At six o'clock the Red the smiling victors led,
To give a second blow, the fatal overthrow :
  Now death and horror equal reign !
     Now they cry,
      "Run or die—
British colours ride the azure main ! "

See, they fly, amazed, o'er rocks and sands !
  One danger they grasp at to shun the greater fate :
In vain they cry for aid to weeping lands,—
  The nymphs and sea-gods mourn their lost estate.
For ever more adieu, thou dazzling *Royal Sun;*
From thine untimely end thy master's fate begun :
  Enough, thou mighty god of war !
     Now we sing—
      "Bless the King !
Let us drink to every English tar ! " [1]

ANONYMOUS.

A SONG ON RUSSELL'S TRIUMPH. [2]

(Air : "*The King's going to Bulloign," with variations.*)

    COME, brave Protestant boys,
    Here 's a million of joys,
And triumph now brought from the ocean !
    For the mighty French fleet
    Now is shattered and beat,—
And destruction, destruction, boys, will be their portion !

    Here's the Jacobite crew [3]—
    Now believe me, 'tis true—
Invited Monsieurs to this nation ;
    Who was crossing the seas,
    With the Teague Rapparees,—
True cut-throats, true cut-throats, upon my salvation !

---

[1] Kitchener and Ashton have other versions of this song with two additional stanzas, both of which are so obviously by a later hand and are such an anti-climax to the song that they are not included here. [2] As the foregone piece seems to have been intended for a somewhat more developed class of mind, this song, and some inferior ones on the same subject, were no doubt designed for tavern and street-side entertainment.   [3] See notes to "The Sea Fight," p. 268.

But, ho-ho ! they did find
A true Protestant wind,
Which five weeks or longer did last 'em ;
    Then our most royal fleet,
    With the Dutchmen compleat,
Did with thunder, with thunder, go blast 'em !

On the nineteenth of May
The French fleet got under weigh,
To make of our courage some trial ;
    They s'poss'd we shouldn't fight ; [1]
    But they reckon'd out of right,—
For we show'd 'em, we show'd 'em our metal was loyal !

Our admirals bold,
With their brave hearts of gold,
They fell on like great sons of thunder ;
    As the French they drew nigh,
    Their chain-shot they let fly,
Which did tear 'em, and rend 'em, and tear 'em
    asunder !

Our squadron, true blue,
Fought their way thro' and thro' ;
Till fast in Lob's pound,[2] boys, we got 'em,
    Where we gave the proud French
    Such a fiery drench,
That we sent 'em, we sent 'em, pell mell to the bottom !

Such a slaughter we made,
While the loud cannons play'd,
Which laid the poor Monsieurs a-bleeding,—
    And their high admiràl
    We did terribly maul,
And did teach him, did teach him, I hope, better
    breeding !

Our brave admiràl,
Being stout Delavall,[3]
Whose actions all men may admire,

[1] Russell's undertaking to Louis to allow England to be invaded. *See* note 3, " The Sea Fight."   [2] A prison, stocks, or any particularly tight corner ; in Ireland it is called Pook's (Puck's) poundfold.   [3] Sir Ralph, of the Delavalls of Northumberland. He was vice-admiral of the Red on this occasion.

For the French *Rising Sun*[1]
Was not able to run,
Which with seven, with seven more ships he did fire!

Valiant Rook[2] sail'd straightway,
Where a French squadron lay
Close in by the rocks there for shelter;
But we fell on gillore[3]
And we fired twelve more,—
Thus we fired and burn'd the French fleet helter-skelter!

Being sunk, took, and burn'd,
There's not many return'd:
Was this not a mighty disaster?
How they far'd on our coast
Let 'em sail home and boast
To old Lewis,[4] old Lewis, their fistula-master!

When he hears how they sped
It will strike him nigh dead—
Losing what he so long has been gettin';
But we'll have him to know
That we'll still keep him low:
He shall never, no never, boys, conquer Great Britain!

ANONYMOUS.

TO THE DUKE OF ORMOND'S HEALTH.

FROWN, old Neptune; Boreas, roar;
Let your thunder bellow!
Noble Ormond's[5] now come o'er
With each gallant English fellow.

---

[1] There is much conflict of opinion as to whether the name was *Royal Sun*, or *Rising Sun*.   [2] Sir George Rooke, Rear-Admiral of the Red. He held the same rank under Torrington. *See* note 3, "The Sea Fight." For his share in this victory he was made a Vice-Admiral, and was given a knighthood and a pension of £1000 a year.   [3] Galore —with much force.   [4] Louis, by far the most powerful monarch in Europe at the time, was supposed to have paid the piper by wholesale bribery and other expenditure in the cause of James II.

[5] This was James, second Duke of Ormonde, who, although a Jacobite, acted as lord high constable at the coronation of William and Mary. He commanded the troops in Sir George Rooke's abortive

Then to welcome him ashore
And his health, a brimmer pour,
  Till every one be mellow !
Remembering Rodondello,
Remembering Rodondello ;
Remembering, remembering Rodondello—
Rodondello, Rodondello, Rodondello !

Tho' at Cales they 'scap'd our guns
  By strong wall'd umbrello,
Civil jars and plundering Dons—
  Curse upon the metal yellow ! [1]
Had the valiant Duke more men
He had been victor then,
  As late at Rodondello.

                              Chorus.

Monsieur and petite Anjou,[2]
  Plot your State intrigo,
Take new Marshall Château-Regnault,[3]
  Then consult with Spanish Diego ;
And, new glory to advance,
Sing Te Deum all thro' France,
  Pour la victoire at Vigo !

                              Chorus.

We meanwhile, to crown our joy,
  Laughing at such folly,
To their health full bowls employ,
  Who have cur'd our melancholy,

---

expedition to Cadiz (Cales) in 1702, soon after which they fell on the French in Vigo Bay and gained a victory. This was the same Rooke who led the Red division, May 19, 1692. In 1711 Ormonde was commander-in-chief of the British forces against France and Spain, and this song appears to relate to his victories on that occasion, Rodondello being one of them.
  [1] It would seem that bribery was one of the causes of failure in the Cadiz affair.   [2] An honorary title of princes of the French royal family. Louis XIV's grandson was Prince of Anjou, afterwards Philip V of Spain.   [3] The Marshal was convoying a richly laden Plate fleet to Spain when Rooke fell on him and captured it in Vigo Bay. (*See* note on Ormonde.) Queen Anne had been nine years on the throne when Ormonde was sent against the French and Spanish.

And done more to furnish tales
Now from Vigo, next from Cales,
   Than Essex did, or Raleigh.

                  Chorus.

Greet Eliz'beth on the main
   Quell'd the Dons' bostado;
In Queen Ann's auspicious reign
   Valour conquers, not bravado.
Come but such another year,
All the spacious seas we'll clear
   Of France and Spain's Armado.

                  Chorus.

Once more, then, tho' Boreas roar,
   And thunders loud do bellow,
Since great Ormond is come o'er,
   With each gallant English fellow,
Let us welcome them on shore,
To each health a brimmer pour,
   Till every man is mellow!

                  Chorus.
                Anonymous.

THE DEATH OF ADMIRAL BENBOW.[1]

   Come all you sailors bold,
      Lend an ear, lend an ear,—
   Come all you sailors bold,
      Lend an ear—
   'Tis of our admiral's fame,
   Brave Benbow was his name,
   How he fought upon the main,
      You shall hear, you shall hear.

Brave Benbow, he set sail,
   For to fight, for to fight,—
Brave Benbow he set sail,
   For to fight—

[1] *See* Appendix, p. 377.

Brave Benbow he set sail,
With a fine and pleasant gale;
But his captains they turn'd tail
    In a fight, in a fight.

Says Kirby unto Wade,
    " I will run,—I will run ! "
Says Kirby unto Wade,
    " I will run !
I value not disgrace
Nor the losing of my place;
No enemies I'll face
    With a gun, with a gun ! "

'Twas the *Ruby* and *Noah's Ark*
    Fought the French, fought the French,—
'Twas the *Ruby* and *Noah's Ark*
    Fought the French :
And there was ten in all,—
Poor souls they fought them all,
Nor valu'd them at all,
    Nor their noise, nor their noise.

It was our admiral's lot,
    With chain-shot, with chain-shot,—
It was our admiral's lot,
    With chain-shot :
Our admiral lost his legs,
And to his men he begs—
" Fight on, brave boys," he says—
    " 'Tis my lot."

While the surgeon dress'd his wounds,
    Thus said he, thus said he,—
While the surgeon dress'd his wounds,
    Thus said he—
" Let my cradle now in haste
On the quarter-deck be plac'd,
That my enemies be fac'd
    Till I'm dead, till I'm dead."

And there brave Benbow lay,
    Crying out, crying out,—
And there brave Benbow lay,
    Crying out—

"Come, boys, we'll tack once more;
And we'll drive them all ashore,—
I value not a score,
  Nor their noise, nor their noise!"

ANONYMOUS.

ADMIRAL HOSIER'S GHOST.[1]

As near Porto-Bello lying
  On the gently-swelling flood,
At midnight with streamers flying,
  Our triumphant navy rode;
There, while Vernon sate all-glorious
  From the Spaniards' late defeat,
And his crews, with shouts victorious,
  Drank success to England's fleet:

On a sudden, shrilly sounding,
  Hideous yells and shrieks were heard;
Then, each heart with fear confounding,
  A sad troupe of ghosts appeared;
All in dreary hammocks shrouded,
  Which for winding-sheets they wore,
And, with looks by sorrow clouded,
  Frowning on that hostile shore.

On them gleamed the moon's wan lustre;
  When the shade of Hosier brave
His pale bands were seen to muster,
  Rising from their wat'ry grave:
O'er the glimmering wave he hied him,
  Where the *Burford* rear'd her sail,
With three thousand ghosts beside him,
  And in groans did Vernon hail.

"Heed, oh, heed our fatal story!
  I am Hosier's injured ghost;
You, who now have purchased glory
  At this place where I was lost:

[1] *See* Appendix, p. 377.

Though in Porto-Bello's ruin
  You now triumph free from fears;
When you think of my undoing,
  You will mix your joys with tears.

"See these mournful spectres sweeping
  Ghastly o'er this hated wave,
Whose wan cheeks are stained with weeping—
  These were English captains brave.
Mark those numbers, pale and horrid,
  Who were once my sailors bold:
Lo! each hangs his drooping forehead,
  While his dismal tale is told.

"I, by twenty sail attended,
  Did the Spanish town affright;
Nothing then its wealth defended,—
  But my orders: ' Not to fight.'
Oh, that on this rolling ocean
  I had cast them with disdain!
And obeyed my heart's warm motion
  To have quell'd the pride of Spain!

"For resistance I could fear none;
  But with twenty ships had done
What thou, brave and happy Vernon,
  Hast achieved with six alone.
Then the Bastimentos never
  Had our foul dishonour seen,
Nor the sea the sad receiver
  Of this gallant train had been.

"Thus like thee, proud Spain dismaying,
  And her galleons leading home,
Though, condemned for disobeying,
  I had met a traitor's doom;
To have fallen, my country crying—
  ' He has played an English part!'
Had been better far than dying
  Of a grieved and broken heart.

"Unrepining at thy glory,
  Thy successful arms we hail;
But remember our sad story,
  And let Hosier's wrongs prevail:

Sent to this foul clime to languish,
  Think what thousands fell in vain,
Wasted with disease and anguish,—
  Not in glorious battle slain.

"Hence, with all my train attending
  From their oozy tombs below,
Through the hoary foam ascending,
  Here I feel my constant woe:
Here, the Bastimentos viewing,
  We recall our shameful doom;
And, our plaintive cries renewing,
  Wander through the midnight gloom.

"O'er the waves, for ever mourning,
  Shall we roam, depriv'd of rest,
If, to Britain's shores returning,
  You neglect my just request.
After this proud foe subduing,
  When your patriot friends you see,
Think on vengeance for my ruin,
  And for England—shamed in me."

RICHARD GLOVER.

BOLD SAWYER.[1]

COME all ye jolly sailors, with courage stout and bold;
Come enter with Bold Sawyer, he'll clothe you all in
    gold;[2]
Repair on board the old *Nassau*,—
We'll make the French to stand in awe—
She's mann'd with British boys.

[1] Captain James Sawyer, Commander of the *Nassau*.   [2] In "Captain Ivory; or, The Bold English Pirate," the phrase occurs, "I'll clothe you in gold"; and it seems to have been fairly common, when the purpose was to get together a crew of daring spirits by the prospect of unusually good fortune. The facts of the occasion were: On October 26, 1758, Keppel left Portsmouth with a squadron of four ships of the line, the fifty-gun ship *Lichfield*, six vessels of smaller tonnage, and some troops under Colonel Worge. Foul weather drove him back, but he started again on November 11. The *Lichfield* went ashore on the Moroccan coast in a gale of wind that prevented help being given,

Commodore Keppel, with his good design,
Commanded the squadron, five sail of the line—-
   The *Prince Edward* of forty guns;
   The *Firedrake and Furnace,* bombs,
   To take Goree—it must be done
      By true British boys,

The 29th of October, from Spithead we set sail;
Kind Neptune did convey us, with a sweet and pleasant
      gale:
   So, steering on the Barbary shore,
   Distance about ten leagues or more,
   The wind at west aloud did roar—
      "Stand by, ye British boys."

So, steering on the lee-shore until the break of day,
We spy'd a lofty sail on the Barbary shore to lay;
   In great distress she seem'd to be;
   Her guns all overboard threw she,
   Which prov'd the *Lichfield* for to be,
      With all her British boys.

The wind blowing hard we could give them no relief;
A stretching on the lee-shore, we touched at Teneriff;
   Then watering the ships at Santa Cruz,
   Taking good wine for our ship's use,
   We sold our cloaths for good wine to booze,[1]
      Like brave British boys.

---

as stanzas four and five have it.   Apparently there was no loss of life ;
but to save the crew from slavery our Government had to ransom them
from the Emperor of Morocco.   Keppel arrived off Goree—a fortified
French town on a small island, one mile south of Cape de Verd—
on the afternoon of December 28, began operations on the follow-
ing day, and at once compelled the garrison to surrender.   After
comparing this ballad with historical facts and looking closely into
it generally, I am inclined to think that, in spite of certain discrep-
ancies, it was either put together originally by one of the men in the
expedition—not an officer—or such a one afterwards told the story to a
fellow seaman, who made the ballad; and this, added to the illiteracy of
the times, would account for all the errors.

   [1] In the crude essentials of his calling and of himself as a seaman the
sailor has changed but little during the past seven hundred years.   Doubt-
less he sold (bartered, that is) his clothes—when he could not sell the
ship's stores—for strong drink to wash down "salt tack" and pease-soup
in the days of Sir Patrick Spens ; he did so in the eighteenth century, as
this shows, and he does so to-day, though happily not so much as of
old.

Our ship being watered, and plenty of good wine,
We hoisted our topsails and crost the tropic line;
    The wind at west, the leading gale,
    Our gallant ship did sweetly sail,
    Steady along—she ne'er will fail,
        With all her British boys.

Steady a-port!—Don't bring her by the lee![1]
Yonder is the flagstaff of Goree, I do see:
    We brought the city within our sight,
    Clear'd our ships ready to fight,
        Like brave British boys.

Early the next morning the *Prince Edward*, of forty
        guns,
Was stationed off the island to cover our two bombs;
    The old *Nassau* she led the van,
    With all her jovial fighting men;
    The drums did beat: "To quarters stand,"
        Like brave British boys.

We sail'd up to their batteries as close as we could
        lay;
Our guns from the tops and poop did lively play,
    Which made the French cry "Morbleu!
    Diable! what shall we do?
    Here comes Bold Sawyer, and all his crew,
        They're all British boys!"

Then followed the *Dunkirk* and *Torbay*;
The guns aloud did rattle, the shells aloud did play,
    Which made the French their batteries shun,
    And from their trenches for to run;
    The flag was struck, the fight was done:
        Oh, huzza, my British boys!

Boast not of Frenchmen, nor yet of Maclome;
Sawyer's as big a hero as ever you did hear;
    Whilst the shot around him did flee,
    In engaging twice the Isle of Goree,
    He was the bravest man at sea,
        With all his British boys.

[1] Wind on the lee-side—*i.e.* sails aback.

Here's a health to King George, our sovereign majesty,
Likewise to Bold Sawyer that fought the French so
    free;
  Our officers, and all our crew,
  Are valiant men as ever you knew;
  So here's a health to all true blue,[1]
    My brave British boys!

ANONYMOUS.

NEPTUNE'S RESIGNATION.[2]

THE watery god, great Neptune, lay,
In dalliance soft and amorous play,
  On Amphitrite's breast;
When Uproar reared its horrid head;
The Tritons shrunk; the Nereids fled.
  And all their fear confessed.

Loud thunder shook the vast domain;
The liquid world was wrapped in flame:
  The god, amazed, spoke—
"Ye Winds, go forth and make it known
Who dares to shake my coral throne
  And fill my realms with smoke."

The Winds, obsequious at his word,
Sprung strongly up t'obey their lord,
  And saw two fleets a-weigh:
One—victorious Hawke—was thine;
The other, Conflans' wretched line
  In terror and dismay.

[1] This is the earliest use I have found of this phrase as applied to
seamen in the same sense as "stout hearts," "gallant fellows," etc.
  [2] This flamboyant piece was written to commemorate the signal
victory of Sir Edward Hawke over Admiral de Conflans, November 20,
1759. Conflans, with a fleet of twenty ships, was making for Roche-
fort, there to join another French fleet, when Hawke headed him off to
Quiberon in a gale of wind and late in the day. In spite of these
facts, and of his being close in to a very dangerous lee-shore, Hawke
went into Quiberon Bay, forced an engagement and triumphed splendidly
This action broke up Louis XV's plan of invading England, and Hawke
was made Baron of Towton as a consequence. The ballad was
printed on broadsheets down to sixty or seventy years ago, so was "The
fight off Camperdown."

Appalled, they viewed Britannia's sons
Deal death and slaughter from their guns,
   And strike the dreadful blow,
Which caused ill-fated Gallic slaves
To find a tomb in briny waves
   And sink to shades below.

With speed they flew and told their chief
That France was ruined past relief,
   And Hawke triumphant rode.
"Hawke!" cried the Fair. "Pray, who is he
That dare usurp this power at sea,
   And thus insult a god?"

The Winds replied—"In distant lands
There reigns a king who Hawke commands:
   He scorns all foreign force.
And when his floating castles roll
From sea to sea, from pole to pole,
   Great Hawke directs their course.

Or when his wingèd bullets fly
To punish fraud and perfidy,
   Or scourge a guilty land,
Then gallant Hawke—serenely great,
Tho' death and horror round him wait—
   Performs his dread command."

Neptune, with wonder, heard the story
Of George's sway and Britain's glory,
   (Which Time shall ne'er subdue),
Boscawen's deeds and Saunder's fame,
Joined with brave Wolfe's immortal name,
   Then cried—"Can this be true?

"A king?—He sure must be a god,
Who has such heroes at his nod
   To govern earth and sea!
I yield my trident and my crown,
A tribute due to such renown:
   Great George shall rule for me!"

J. WIGNELL.

CAPTAIN DEATH.[1]

THE muse and the hero together are fired,—
The same noble views have their bosoms inspired;
As freedom they love, and for glory contend,
The muse o'er the hero still mourns as a friend.
And here let the muse her poor tribute bequeath
To one British hero.—'Tis brave Captain Death!

His ship was the *Terrible*—dreadful to see!
His crew was as brave and as gallant as he:
Two hundred or more was their good compliment,
And sure braver fellows to sea never went;
Each man was determined to spend his last breath
In fighting for Britain and brave Captain Death.

A prize, they had taken, diminished their force,
And soon the good prize-ship was lost in her course.
Then the French privateer [2] and the *Terrible* met;
The battle begun, all with horror beset!
No heart was dismayed, each as bold as Macbeth;
They fought for old England and brave Captain Death.

Fire, thunder, balls, bullets were seen, heard and felt,—
A sight that the heart of Bellona would melt!
The shrouds were all torn, and the decks filled with
    blood,
And scores of dead bodies were thrown in the flood:
The flood, from the days of old Noah and Seth,
Ne'er saw such a man as our brave Captain Death!

At last the dread bullet came winged with his fate;
Our brave captain dropped, and soon after his mate;
As each officer fell a carnage was seen,
That soon dyed the waves to a crimson from green;
And Neptune rose up and took off his wreathe,
And gave it a Triton to crown Captain Death.

[1] I have read that this account was written by one of the survivors
of the *Terrible*, but have failed to follow it to any definite conclusion.
[2] Said to have been the *Vengeance*, under the notorious Seveillé,
who preyed severely on British shipping from 1795 to 1799.

Thus fell the strong *Terrible*, bravely and bold,—
But sixteen survivors the tale can unfold !
The French were the victors, though much to their cost,
For many brave French were with Englishmen lost :
And so says old Time—"From good Queen Elizabeth,
I ne'er saw the fellow of brave Captain Death."

ANONYMOUS.

THE *ARETHUSA*.

COME all ye jolly sailors bold,
Whose hearts are cast in honour's mould,
While England's glory I unfold—
    Huzza to the *Arethusa* !
She is a frigate tight and brave
As ever stemm'd the dashing wave ;
    Her men are staunch
    To their favourite launch ;
And when the foe shall meet our fire,
Sooner than strike we'll all expire
    On board of the *Arethusa* !

'Twas with the spring-fleet she went out
The English Channel to cruise about,
When four [1] French sail, in show so stout,
    Bore down on the *Arethusa*.
The famed *Belle Poule* straight ahead did lie,—
The *Arethusa* scorned to fly ;

---

[1] It is sometimes a pity to have to knock romance on the head with a fact. In June 1778, the *Arethusa*, with thirty-two guns and under the command of Captain Samuel Marshall, met *La Belle Poule*—a larger vessel—but not four of them, off Ushant ; she was worsted in the engagement, and had to draw off. Eighteen years later, and two years after Howe's signal victory over the French fleet off Ushant, or on the "glorious first of June," the song made its first appearance in an opera called *Lock and Key*, the composer of which was William Shield (1754-1829), "Master of his Majesty's musicians in ordinary," and formerly a boat-builder's apprentice at Scarborough. He was the composer of other successful operas and songs. Hoare (1755-1834), his librettist on this occasion, was the son of William Hoare, R.A.

Not a sheet or a tack
Or a brace did she slack
Though the Frenchmen laughed and thought it stuff;
But they knew not the handful of men—how tough !—
On board of the *Arethusa*.

On deck five hundred men did dance,
The stoutest they could find in France;
We, with two hundred, did advance
On board of the *Arethusa*.
Our captain hail'd the Frenchman—"Ho ! "
The Frenchman he cried out—"Hallo ! "
"Bear down, d'ye see,
To our admiral's lee ! "
"No, no," says the Frenchman, "that can't be ! "
"Then I must lug you along with me ! "
Says the saucy *Arethusa*.

The fight was off the Frenchman's land;
We forced them back upon the strand,
For we fought till not a stick would stand
Of the gallant *Arethusa*.
And now we've driven the foe ashore,
Never to fight us Briton's more,
Let each fill his glass
To his favourite lass;
A health to our captains and officers true,
And all that belong to the jovial crew
On board of the *Arethusa* !

PRINCE HOARE.

THE BOLD BRITISH TARS.[1]

O LONG of the sea was old England the queen,
When republican France thought she'd alter the scene,
So she worked and she worked to make up a marine
To wipe out the tars of old England—
To wipe out the bold British tars.

[1] Seeing that the battle in Aboukir Bay (August 1, 1797) is mentioned in this piece, and no word said of the Copenhagen engagement (April 2, 1801), it would appear that the lines were written during that interval.

But the day they met Howe on the seas they do rue,—
How to show them the difference he very well knew
'Twixt tricoloured cockades and true British blue.
    So huzza for the bold British tars!

They were carried from sea to the land high and dry,
Till they ventured their luck in a fog [1] once to try;
But a gale sent them scurrying in harbour to lie,
    Secure from the bold British tars.

Yet unwilling with Britain's domain to agree
They made up some rods of their Liberty tree,
And with them they lashed other men out to sea,
    To cope with our bold British tars.

Spanish dons in great force of big vessels were seen;
But Nelson and Jervis to fight them were keen;
So they tackl'd and beat twenty-seven, with fifteen
    Mann'd by the bold British tars.

Then France crammed her principles down the Dutch
    throats,
And forced the Mynheers for to alter their notes,
And to don the red cap and become "Sans Cullotes,"
    And to fight with our bold British tars.

To recover their Cape [2] soon a squadron was found:
They slipt us and got there all safely and sound;
But Elphinstone show'd they were fast in Lob's Pound,[3]
    Nabb'd smartly by bold British tars.

Then says Mounseer: "Mynheer, as your trade is all lost,
Rig a fleet and come out!—We'll invade England's
    coast."
But this reck'ning they made without minding their host
    Of brave British, bold British tars.

[1] This might have been either the French fleet slipping out of Brest, May 17, 1794, when they passed, unseen, within sound of the patrolling British fleet's bells; the defeat of the French by Lord Bridport, June 25, 1795, or Jervis's whipping of the Spanish fleet off Cape St. Vincent, Feb. 14, 1797; but there was no succeeding gale in either case.   [2] Cape Town. The engagement took place in Saldanha Bay, Aug. 17, 1796, when Ducas, the Dutch Admiral, lost nine frigates and five other sail, then surrendered. For his success in this expedition Elphinstone was made Baron Keith, and Viscount Keith for landing Abercrombie's army in Aboukir Bay, 1801.   [3] *See* note 2, page 270.

For to block up Brest harbour Lord Bridport set sail;
At the mouth of the Texel our fleet did not fail,[1]
To shut up and keep the Dutch rogues in their jail,
    Lock'd up by the bold British tars.

Our fleet to refit had just sailed away,
When, the cat having gone, the mouse came out to play;
But the game it was bloody and earnest that day,
    At the hands of our bold British tars.

For the news of their sailing had scarce reached our
    ears,
When our anchors were tripp'd to the ring of three
    cheers;
And away to the Texel to fight the Mynheers
    Went the walloping bold British tars.

With their liberty hulks to sheer off was in vain;
For as we got between 'em, no port could they
    gain;
So they weigh'd themselves in a hard fight to maintain
    With the mastering bold British tars.

'Twas twelve o' the clock when the signal was given;
Our guns opened fire, like black thunder from heaven;
By three the Dutch fleet off the water was driven—
    Smashed up by our bold British tars.

Their hulks all riddl'd, their canvas a rag;
Ten struck with their Vice and their Admiral's flag:
Their friends safe ashore had no reason to brag
    Of success 'gainst the bold British tars.

Then Gaul, slinking off by her farthest back door,[2]
Sent a fleet out a-skulking by Africa's shore,
To plunder and waste all the Egyptian store,
    And to bilk all our bold British tars.

---

[1] This was not always true—witness the runaways from the Texel, while the mutiny at the Nore was going on. But this particular occasion was, apparently, Duncan's defeat of the Dutch off Camperdown, Oct. 11, 1797; when, after being called hurriedly from taking in stores and refitting some of his aged craft in Yarmouth Roads, he captured fifteen of the enemy's ships and took Admiral de Winter prisoner.   [2] Toulon.

But Nelson, that brave British Boy, set his sail,
And in their concealment the French fleet did nail:
He upset their fine plan, pull'd the sting from their
tail,
    To the tune of the bold British tars.

On their ships and their batteries so fièrce did he
fall,
That he took, burnt and sunk till he ended them
all—
A piping hot supper of powder and ball,
    Piping hot from the bold British tars!

Britannia's bright trident, still pointing on high,
Bids her tars all be true, and their foes all defy:
To avenge all her wrongs they will conquer or die—
    The jolly, brave, bold British tars.

Now fill up your glasses, and bumpers we'll have
To Howe, Jervis, Duncan and Nelson the brave,
And to our bold hearts that now rule on the wave:
    Huzza for the ships of old England,
    And a health to each bold British tar!

                                  ANONYMOUS.

THE BATTLE OF THE BALTIC.[1]

OF Nelson and the North,
  Sing the glorious day's renown,
When to battle fierce came forth
  All the might of Denmark's crown,
And her arms along the deep, proudly shone;
  By each gun the lighted brand,
  In a bold determined hand,
  And the Prince of all the land
Led them on.—

---

[1] April 2, 1801. On this engagement there are songs and other
pieces, some of which were written in the same year; but they would
not bear publication along with Campbell's lines.

Like Leviathans afloat,
   Lay their bulwarks on the brine;
While the sign of battle flew
   On the lofty British line;
It was ten of April morn, by the chime,
   As they drifted on their path;
   There was silence deep as death,
   And the boldest held their breath
For a time.—

But the might of England flushed
   To anticipate the scene;
And her van the fleeter rushed
   O'er the deadly space between.
"Hearts of Oak!" our captains cried, when each
    gun,
   From its adamantine lips,
   Spread a death—shade the ships,
   Like hurricane eclipse
Of the sun.

Again! again! again!
   And the havoc did not slack,
Till a feeble cheer the Dane,
   To our cheering, sent us back.
Their shots along the deep slowly boom :—
   Then cease—and all is wail,
   As they strike the shattered sail;
   Or in conflagration pale
Light the gloom.

Out spoke the victor then,
   As he hailed them o'er the wave :
"Ye are brothers! Ye are men!
   And we conquer but to save;
So peace instead of death let us bring;
   But yield, proud foe, thy fleet,
   With the crews, at England's feet,
   And make submission meet
To our king."

Then Denmark bless'd our chief,
   That he gave her wounds repose;
And the sounds of joy and grief
   From her people wildly rose,

As death withdrew his shades from the day;
  While the sun look'd smiling bright
  O'er a wide and woeful sight,
  Where the fires of funeral light
Died away.

Now joy, Old England, raise
  For the tidings of thy might,
By the festal cities' blaze,
  Whilst the wine-cup shines in light!
And yet amidst that joy and uproar,
  Let us think of them that sleep,
  Full many a fathom deep,
  By thy wild and stormy steep,
Elsinore!

Brave hearts! to Britain's pride
  Once so faithful and so true,
On the deck of fame that died—
  With the gallant good Riou:
Soft sigh the winds of Heaven o'er their grave!
  While the billow mournful rolls,
  And the mermaid's song condoles,
  Singing glory to the souls
Of the brave!——

CAMPBELL.

TRAFALGAR.

'Twas at the close of that dark morn
  On which our hero, conquering, died,
That every seaman's heart was torn
  By stripe of sorrow and of pride:

Of pride that one short day should show
  Deeds of eternal splendour done—
Full twenty hostile ensigns low,
  And twenty glorious victories won:

Of grief, the deepest tenderest grief
  That he on every sea and shore—
Their brave, belov'd, unconquer'd chief—
  Should fly his master-flag no more.

U

Sad was the eve of that great day;
  But sadder and more dire the night,
When human passion clos'd the fray,
  And elements maintain'd the fight.

All shaken in the conflict past,
  The navies fear'd the tempest loud—
The gale that shook the groaning mast,
  The wave that struck the straining shroud.

By passing gleams of sullen light
  The worn and weary seamen view'd
Their blood-gain'd prizes of the fight
  Go foundering from the awful feud.

And oft, as drown'd men's screams were heard,
  And oft, as sank the ships around,
Some British vessel lost they fear'd,
  And mourn'd some British seamen drown'd.

And oft they cried—as memory told
  Of him, so late their darling pride,
But now a bloody corse and cold—
  "Was it for this our Nelson died?"

Through three short days and three long nights,
  They struggl'd 'gainst the gale's stern force,
And sank the trophies of their fights,
  And thought of that dear hero's corse.

But when the fairer morn arose,
  Bright o'er the still tumultuous main;
They saw no wrecks 'cept those of foes,
  No ruin but of France and Spain.

And, victors now of winds and seas,
  Behold thy British vessels brave
Breasting the ocean at their ease,
  Like sea-birds on their native wave.

And now they cried—because they found
  Their conquering fleet in all its pride,
With Spain's and France's hopes aground—
  "It was for this our Nelson died!"

He died with many a hundred bold
  And sterling hearts as ever beat:
But where's the British heart so cold
  That would not die for such a feat?

Yes, by their memories!—by all
  The honours which their tomb surround,
Theirs was the greatest, noblest fall
  That ever mortal courage crown'd!

Then give them each a hero's grave,
  With no weak tears, no woman's sighs;
Theirs was the death-bed of the brave,
  And heroic be their obsequies.

Haul not your colours from on high,
  Still let your flags of victory soar;
Give every pennant to the sky,
  And let your conquering cannon roar—

That every kindling soul may learn
  How to resign its patriot-breath,
And from an honouring country earn
  The triumphs of a hero's death.

ANONYMOUS.

THE *SHANNON* AND THE *CHESAPEAKE*.

ON board the *Shannon* frigate,[1]
  In the merry month of May,
To watch those bold Americans,
  Off Boston lights we lay.
The *Chesapeake* was in harbour,
  A frigate stout and fine—
Four hundred and forty men had she,
  Her guns were forty-nine.

[1] Of thirty-eight guns.

U 2

'Twas Captain Broke [1] commanded us,—
  A challenge he did write
To the captain [2] of the *Chesapeake*,
  To bring her out to fight :
Our captain says—"Brave Lawrence,
  'Tis not from enmity ;
But 'tis to prove to all the world
  That we do rule the sea.

"Don't think, my noble captain,
  Because you have had success,
That British tars are humbled—
  Not even in distress.
No ! we will fight like heroes,
  Our glory to maintain,
In defiance of your greater size
  And the number of your men."

That challenge was accepted ;
  The Americans came down,—
A finer frigate ne'er belonged
  Unto the British crown.
They brought her into action, [3]
  On our true English plan ;
Nor fired a shot till within hail—
  And then the hell began.

Broadside for broadside quick
  Set up a murderous roar ;
Like thunder it resounded
  From echoing shore to shore.
This dreadful duel lasted
  Near a quarter-of-an-hour ;
Then the *Chesapeake* drove right aboard,
  And put her in our power.

Our captain went to their ship's side
  To see how she did lie,
When he beheld the enemy's men,
  Who from their guns did fly.

[1] Sir Philip Bowes Vere Broke ; he came of an old Suffolk family, was made a baronet, then a Rear-Admiral and a K.C.B. for this action.
[2] James Lawrence, who had previously commanded the *Hornet*, with which he had sunk the *Peacock* and done other damage to British ships.
[3] June 1, 1813.

"All hands for boarding!"[1] now he cried.
   "The victory is sure!
Come, bear a hand, my gallant boys,—
   Our prize we'll now secure!"

Like lions then we rush'd aboard,
   And fought them hand to hand;
And tho' they did outnumber us,
   They could not us withstand.
They fought in desperation,
   Disorder and dismay,
And in about three minutes' time
   Were forc'd to give us way.

Their captain and lieutenant,
   With seventy of the crew,
Were killed in this sharp action,
   And a hundred wounded too;[2]
The ship we took to Halifax,
   And the captain buried there,
And the living of his crew
   As his chief mourners were.

Have courage, all brave British tars,
   And never be dismay'd;
But put the can of grog about,
   And drink success to trade;
Likewise to gallant Captain Broke
   And all his valiant crew,
Who beat the bold Americans
   And brought their courage to.

ANONYMOUS.

THE YANKEE MAN-O'-WAR.[3]

(Air: *The Ranger.*)

'Tis of a gallant Yankee ship
   That flew the stars and stripes,
And the breeze o' wind due nor'-nor'-west,
   That still in winter pipes;

[1] "Follow me who can," were his words.   [2] The *Chesapeake* had sixty-one men killed, including most of her officers, and eighty-five wounded; the British loss was thirty-three killed and fifty wounded.
[3] A traditional ballad.

With her starboard tacks aboard, my boys,
  She hugg'd up to the gale,
As one autumn night we raised the light
  On the Head of old Kinsale.

It was a fine and cloudless night,
  And the breeze held steady and strong,
As gaily over the heaving deep
  Our good ship bowl'd along;
With the foaming crash beneath her bows
  The mounting waves she spread,
And stooping low her breast of snow,
  She buried her lee-cathead.

There was no talk of short'ning sail
  By the Cap'n on the poop;
Then under the tug of her flying jib,
  The boom bent like a hoop;
And the creak of tackle told the strain
  As it held her stout maintack;
But he only laughed as he glanced astern
  At her seething, silvery track.

The flood-tide met in the channel waves,
  As they rolled from shore to shore;
The mist grew thickish on the land
  From Featherstone to Dunmore;
Yet gleamed the light on Tusker Rock,
  Where the old bell tolled the hour;
But the beacon-light, foretime so bright,
  Was quench'd on Waterford Tower.

The spreading robes our good ship wore
  Were her topsails fore and aft,
Her spanker and her standing jib,
  For she was a stiffish craft.
Then "Lay aloft!" the Cap'n cried;
  "Loose out your light sails fast!"
And royals and topgallant-sails
  Were quickly on each mast.

What loom'd upon our starboard bow?
  What hung there in the breeze?
'Twas time our packet haul'd her wind
  Abreast the old Saltee's.

For by her mighty press of sail,
  And by our consorts four,
We saw our morning visitor
  Was a British man-o'-war.

Up spake our noble Cap'n then,
  As a shot went whistling past,
"Haul flat your courses' sheets!
  Lay your topsails to the mast!"
Those Englishmen sent three loud cheers
  From out their three-decked ark;
We answered with a broadside deep
  From the decks of our patriot-bark.

"Drop helm! Out booms!" our skipper cried,—
  "Out booms and slack each sheet!"
And the smartest keel that e'er was launched
  Shot away from the British fleet.
And amidst a murderous hail of shot,
  With stun-sails hoisting away,
Down the North Channel Paul Jones tore on
  In the dawn and the flying spray.

ANONYMOUS.

PIRATES, SLAVE-CARRYING AND SMUGGLING

"Thou salt-water thief!"

SHAKESPEARE.

There was a laughing devil in his sneer;

. . . .

And where his frown of hatred darkly fell,
Hope withering fled, and Mercy sigh'd farewell!

. . . . . .

He left a Corsair's name to other times,
Link'd with one virtue and a thousand crimes.

BYRON.

In pestilential barks they cross'd the flood;
Then were the wretched ones asunder torn
To distant isles, to separate bondage borne.

MONTGOMERY.

We'll run a cargo of silk, yo-ho!
And the Customs men we'll bilk just so!
Just so, just so, yo-ho!

OLD SONG.

"THAT FACE OF HIS."

THAT face of his I do remember well;
Yet, when I saw it last, it was besmear'd
As black as Vulcan in the smoke of war:
A bawbling vessel was he captain of,
For shallow draught and bulk unprizable;
With which such scathful grapple did he make,
With that most noble bottom of our fleet,
That very envy and the tongue of loss
Cried fame and honour on him!

SHAKESPEARE.

SIR ANDREWE BARTON.[1]

WHEN Flora with her fragrant flowers
  Bedeckt the earth so trim and gaye,
And Neptune, with his daintye showers,
  Came to present the monthe of Maye
King Henrye [2] rode to take the ayre,—
  Over the river of Thames past hee,
When eighty merchants of London came,
  And doune they knelt upon their knee.

"O yee are welcome, rich merchànts!—
  Good saylors, welcome unto mee."
They swore bye the Rood they were saylors good,
  But rich merchànts they could not bee.
"To France' nor Flanders dare we pass;
  Nor Bordeaux voyage dare we fare;
And all for a rover who lyes on the seas,
  And robbs us of our merchant ware."

King Henrye frownd and turned him rounde,
  And swore bye the Lord—that was muckle of might—
"I thought hee had not beene in the world,
[Who] durst have wrought England such unright!"

[1] *See* Appendix, p. 378.   [2] Henry VIII.

The merchànts sighed and sayd—' Alas ! "
  And thus they did their answer frame:
" He is a proud Scott, that robbs on the seas,
  And Sir Andrewe Barton is his name."

The King lookt over his left shouldèr,
  And an angrye look then lookèd hee :
" Have I never a lorde in all my realme
  Will feitch yon' traytor unto mee? "
" Yea, that dare I ! " Lord [1] Howard crys,—
  " Yea, that dare I with heart and hand.
If itt please your grace to give mee leave,
  Myselfe wil bee the onely man."

" Thou art but young," the King reply'd,—
  " Yon' Scott hath numbered many a yeàre."
" Trust mee, my liege,—Ile make him quail;
  Or before my prince I wil never appeare."
" Then bowemen and gunners thou shalt have,
  And chuse them over my realme so free—
Besides good mariners and shipp-boyes,
  To guide the great shipp on the sea."

The first man that Lord Howard chose
  Was the ablest gunner in all the realme,
Thoughe hee was threescore yeares and ten—
  Good Peter Simon was his name.
" Peter," sais hee, " I must to sea,
  To bring home a traytor, live or dead;
And, 'fore all others, I have chusen thee
  Of a hundred gunners to bee the head."

" If you, my lord, have chosen mee
  Of a hundred gunners to bee the head,—
Then hang mee upp on your maine-mast tree,
  If I misse my marke one shilling-bread." [2]
My lord then chose a boweman rare,
  Whose active hands had gainèd fame;
In Yorkshire was this gentleman borne,
  And William Horsley was his name.

---

[1] This " Lord "—probably, those times considered, a piece of servile courtesy to the Howards of his day—appears to have been Sir Edmund, son of the then Earl of Surrey, who had already, in council with the King, delivered his say about Barton. (*See* Appendix.)
[2] The breadth of a shilling.

"Horsley," sayd hee, "I must with speede
    Goe seeke a traytor on the sea;
And nowe of a hundred bowemen brave
    To bee the head I have chusen thee."

"If you," quoth hee, "have chusen mee
    Of a hundred bowemen to bee the head,
On your main-màst Ile hangèd bee,
    If I misse twelve-score one penny-bread."

With pikes and gunnes and bowemen bold,
    This noble Howard hee is gone to sea,—
With a valyant heart and a pleasant cheere,
    Out at Thames' mouth hath saylèd hee.
And days hee scant had saylèd three
    Upon the voyage hee tooke in hand,
When there he mett with a noble shipp
    And stoutly made itt staie and stand.

"Thou must tell mee," Lord Howard sayd,
    "Nowe who thou art and what's thy name;
And shewe mee where thy dwelling is,
    And whither bounde, and whence thou came."
"My name is Henrye Hunt," quoth hee,
    With a heavye heart and a carefull mind:
"I and my shipp doe both belong
    Unto New Castle that stands upon Tyne."

"Hast thou not heard, nowe, Henrye Hunt,
    As thou hast saylèd bye day and bye night,
Of a Scottish rover here on the seas?—
    Men call him Sir Andrewe Barton, knight."
Then ever hee sighed and sayd—"Alas,"
    With a grievèd mind and wellaway,
"But over-well I know that wight!—
    I was his prisoner yesterday.

"As I was sayling upon the sea,
    A Bordeaux voyage for to fare,
To his hachborde [1] he claspèd mee,
    And robb'd mee of my merchant ware.

[1] Bulwarks.

And muckle debts, God wot, I owe,—
   And every man will have his owne;
And I am nowe to London bounde,
   Of our good King to beg a boone."

"Thou shalt not need," Lord Howard sais:
   "Let mee but once that robber see,
And for one penny from thee taen
   Itt shall bee doubled shillings three."
"Nowe God forbid, my Lord," quoth hee,
   "That you shold seeke soe far amisse!
God keepe you from that traytor's hands!
   For little you knowe what man hee is.

"Hee is brasse within and steele without,—
   With beames [1] on his topcastle stronge,
And eighteen pieces of ordinance
   He carries on each side along:
And hee hath pinnace deerlye dight,[2]—
   St. Andrewe's crosse, that is his guide;
His pinnace beareth ninescore men,
   And fifteen canons on each side.

"Were ye full twentye shipps and hee but one,
   I sware bye kirke and book and all,
Hee wold o'ercome them everye one,
   If once his beames they doe downe fall."
"This is cold comfort," sais my Lord,
   "To wellcome a stranger thus to sea;
Yett Ile bring him and his shippe to shore,
   Or to Scotland hee shall carrye mee!"

"Then a noble gunner you must have;
   And hee must aim well with his ee,
And sink his pinnace into the sea—
   Or else hee ne'er o'ercome wil bee:
And if you chance his shippe to borde,
   This counsell I must give withall,
Lett noe man to his topcastle goe
   To strive to lett his beames downe fall.

---

[1] It appears from different authorities that these beams were spars, worked from the maintop in such wise as to drop dolphins of iron or other heavy metal on to the decks and men of an opponent, in order to sink the former or kill the latter, much as the ancient seamen of the Mediterranean did with huge stones.   [2] Well-furnished; fine, splendid.

"And seven pieces of ordinance
  I pray your honour lend to mee,
On each side of my shippe along,
  And I will lead you on the sea.
A glasse[1] Ile sett that maye bee seene,
  Whether you sayle bye day or night;
And to-morrowe, I sweare, bye nine of the clocke,
  You shall see Sir Andrewe Barton, knight."

   .   .   .   .   .   .

The merchant sett my Lord a glasse,
  Soe well apparent in his sight;
And on the morrowe, bye nine of the clocke,
  Hee shewed him Sir Andrewe Barton, knight.
His hachborde it was gilt[2] with gold,
  Soe deerlye dight itt dazzled the ee.
"Nowe, by my faith," Lord Howard cris,
  "This is a gallant sighte to see!

"Take in your ancyents[3] standards eke,
  Soe close that no man maye them see;
And put mee forth a white willowe wand,[4]
  As merchants used to sayle the sea."
But they stirred neither top nor mast,[5]
  Stoutly they past Sir Andrewe bye.
"What English churles are yon'," hee sayd,
  "That can soe little curtesye?

"Nowe, bye the Rood, three yeares and more
  I have beene admirall ore this sea!
And never an English nor Portingall
  Without my leave can passe this way."
Then called hee upp his stout pinnàce:

[1] An hour-glass, by the means ot which time was kept aboard most European vessels even up to sixty or seventy years ago. A minute-glass is still used in connection with the old-fashioned log-line. In this case, apparently, the merchant merely wished to show his zeal by his accuracy. [2] Gilded over; covered with. [3] Ensigns—*i. e.* furl the colours, so that they cannot tell what we are. [4] This is explained by the greater clearness of another version, thus:

      "Set upp withal a willowe wand
         That, merchantlike, I shall passe bye."

What Sir Edmund evidently wished to do was to get near enough to force an engagement before the pirate could make him out and sheer off. [5] They kept their fighting-stations manned and made no salute.

"Fetch back yond pedlars nowe to mee !
I sweare bye the masse, yon' English churles
    Shall all hang att my maine-mast tree ! "

With that the pinnace itt shott off,—
    Full well Lord Howard might it ken ;
For itt stroke downe my Lord's fore mast
    And killèd fourteen of his men.
"Come hither, Simon," sais my Lord ;
"Looke that thy worde bee true : Thou sayd
That att my maine-mast thou shold hang,
    If thou misse thy marke one shilling-bread."

Simon was old ; but his heart itt was bold ;
    His ordinance hee layd right lowe ;
He put a chaine [1] full nine yardes long,
    With other great shott lesse and moe :
And he lett goe his great gunnes shott ;
    Soe well he settled it with his ee,
That the first sight Sir Andrewe saw,
    Itt was his pinnace sunke in the sea.

And when hee saw his pinnace sunke,
    Lord, howe his heart with rage did swell !
"Nowe cutt my ropes, itt is time to bee gon,—
    Ile fetch yond pedlars backe mysell ! "
When my Lord sawe Sir Andrewe loose,[2]
    Within his heart hee was full faine : [3]
"Nowe spread your ancyents ; strike upp drummes ;
    Sounde all your trumpetts out amaine ! "

"Fight on, my men ! " Sir Andrewe sais :
    "Weale howe soe'er this geare wil sway,[4]
Itt is my lord admirall of Englànd
    Is come to seeke mee on the sea."
Simon had a sonne who shott right well,
    That did Sir Andrewe muckle scare ;
In att his decke hee gave a shott—
    Killed three score of his men of warre.

[1] Made chain-shot by securing two balls together—a favourite in later times, when navy ships were regularly supplied with chain-shot, for carrying away an opponent's rigging, sails and spars in order to save the hull for a prize.   [2] Made sail apparently to overtake Sir Edmund.
[3] Glad.   [4] No matter how the battle went, they were fighting an authorised English force.

Then Henrye Hunt, with rigour hott,
    Came bravely on the other side;
Soone hee drove downe the foremast tree,
    And killèd four score men beside.
"Nowe out, alas!" Sir Andrewe cryed,
    "What maye a man nowe thinke or say?
Yond merchant theefe that pierceth mee,
    Hee was my prisoner yesterday!

"Come hither to mee, thou Gordon good,
    That aye wast readye att my call;
I wil give thee three hundred markes,
    If thou wilt lett my beames downe fall."
Lord Howard hee then called in haste—
    "Horsley, see thou be true in stead;
For thou shalt at the maine-mast hang,
    If thou miss twelvescore one penny-bread."

Then Gordon swarved the maine-mast tree,—
    Hee swarvèd itt with might and maine;
But Horsley with a brave arròwe
    Stroke downe the Gordon through the braine:
And hee fell into the haches again,
    And sore his deadlye wounde did bleede:
Then word went through Sir Andrewe's men
    Howe that the Gordon hee was dead.

"Come hither to mee, James Hambilton—
    Thou art my onely sister's sonne;
If thou wilt let my beames downe fall,
    Six hundred nobles thou hast wonne."
With that hee swarved the maine-mast tree—
    Hee swarvèd itt with nimble art;
But Horsley with a broad arròwe
    Pierced the Hambilton through the heart:

And downe hee fell upon the deck,
    That with his blood did streame amaine,—
That every Scott cryed, "Well away!
    Alas, a comelye youth is slaine!"
All woe-begon was Sir Andrewe then;
    With griefe and rage his heart did swell:
Goe fetch mee forth my armour of proofe;
    For I wil to the topcastle mysell.[1]

---

[1] Although the balladist fails to show that Sir Andrew had cannon,
it is not to be supposed that he relied on his "beames" to take the

X

"Goe fetch mee forth my armour of proofe,
   That gilded is with gold soe cleare :
God bless my brother John of Bartòn,—
   Against the Portingalls hee itt ware.
And when hee had on this armour of proofe,
   Hee was a gallant sight to see.
Ah, nere didst thou meet with living wight,
   My deere brothèr, could cope with thee ! "

"Come hither, Horsley," sais my Lord,
   "And loke your shaft that itt goe right;
Shoot a good shoote in time of need,
   And for itt thou shalt bee made knight."
"Ile shoot my best," quoth Horsley then,
   "My Lord shall see, with might and maine;
But if I were hanged at your maine-màst,
   I have now left but arrows twaine."

Sir Andrewe hee did swarve the tree—
   With right good wil hee swarvèd then :
Upon his breast did Horsley hitt;
   But the arrowe itt bounded back agen.
Then Horsley spyed a privye place
   With a perfect eye in a secrette part,—
Under the spole of his right arme
   Hee smote Sir Andrewe to the heart.

"Fight on, my men ! " Sir Andrewe sais.
   "A little Ime hurt, but yette not slaine;
Ile but lye downe and bleede a while,
   And then Ile upp and fight againe.[1]
Fight on, fight on, my merry men all !
   And never flinche before the foe;
And stand fast bye St. Andrewe's crosse
   While you doe heare my whistle blowe."[2]

---

place of ordnance ; no doubt fighting with shot was going on up to the last, otherwise how can we account for the incentive to "fight on"? seeing that the Scots did not carry archers as the English did.

[1] It is worthy of note that in none of the different versions of this ballad have any of the various transcribers changed these four lines more than a word or so here and there, which proves that the spirit, the grit and the admirable expression of those traits have appealed alike to all. The second, third and fourth lines deserve to be recorded in brass. [2] They were to fight so long as they heard his whistle intermittently.

They never heard his whistle blowe,
  Which made their hearts waxe sore adread.
Then Horsley sayd—"Aborde, my Lord;
  For well I wott Sir Andrewe's dead."
They boarded then his noble shippe—
  They boarded itt with might and maine:
Eighteen score Scotts alive they found;
  The rest were either maimed or slaine.

Lord Howard tooke a sword in hand,
  And off hee smote Sir Andrewe's head:
"I must have left England many a daye,
  If thou wert alive as thou art dead."
He caused his body to be cast
  Over the hachborde into sea,
And about his middle three hundred crownes:
  "Where'er thou land this will bury thee."

Thus from the fight Lord Howard came;
  And backe hee saylèd ore the maine:
With muckle joy and triumphing
  Into Thames' mouth hee came againe.
Lord Howard then a letter wrote,
  And sealed itt with a seal and ring:
"Such a noble prize have I brought to your grace,
  As never did subject to a king."

"Sir Andrewe's shippe I bring with mee—
  A braver shippe was never none:
Nowe hath your grace two shippes of warre,
  Where 'fore in England was but one."
King Henrye's grace, with royall cheere,
  Welcomed the noble Howard home:
"And where," sayd hee, "is the rover stout?—
  That I, myselfe, may give the doome."

"The rover hee is safe, my liege,
  Full many a fadom in the sea—
If he were alive as he is dead,
  I had left England many a day.
And your grace may thanke four men i' the shippe
  For the victory wee hath wonne;
These are William Horsley, Henrye Hunt,
  And Peter Simon and his sonne."

X 2

To Henrye Hunt the King then sayd,
   "In lieu of what was from thee taen
A noble a daye nowe thou shalt have,
   Sir Andrewe's jewels and his chayne :
And Horsley thou shalt bee a knight,
   And lands and livings shalt have store ;
Howard shall bee Erle Surrye hight,
   As Howards erst have beene before.

"Now Peter Simon, thou art old—
   I will maintain thee and thy sonne ;
And the men shall have five hundred markes
   For the good service they have done."
Then in came the queene with ladyes faire
   To see Sir Andrewe Barton, knight ;
They weend that hee was brought on shore,
   And thought to see a gallant sight.

But when they sawe his deadlye face,
   And eyes soe hollow in his head,
"I wold give," quoth the king, "a thousand markes
   If hee were alive as hee is dead.
Yett for the manfull part hee playd,
   Which fought soe well with heart and hand,
His men shall have twelve pence a daye
   Till they come to my brother-king's high land."
                                    ANONYMOUS.

A FAMOUS SEA-FIGHT BETWEEN CAPTAIN
      WARD [1] AND THE *RAINBOW*.

      STRIKE up, you lusty gallants,
         With musick and sound of drum ; ·
      For we have descryed a Rover
         Upon the Sea is come :
      His name is Captain Ward ;
         Right well it doth appear
      There has not been such Rover
         Found out these thousand year.

[1] Appears to have been a native of Kent, and was rather a scourge
to shipping in home waters from about 1604 to 1608.   In 1609 he and
Dansekar, with whom he joined partnership towards the end of his
depredations, were written of as "the late famous pirates."   It seems

For he hath sent unto our King,[2]
    The sixth of January,
Desiring that he might come in
    With all his company.
"And if your King will let me come,
    Till I my tale have told,
I will bestow for my ransòme
    Full thirty tons of gold." ·

"Oh, nay ! oh, nay ! " then said our King ;
    "Oh, nay, this must not be !
To yield to such a Rover
    Myself will not agree.
He hath deceivèd the French man,
    Likewise the King of Spain :
And how can he be true to me,
    That hath been false to twain?"

With that our King provided
    A ship of worthy fame ;
Rainbow she was callèd,
    If you would know her name.
Now that gallant *Rainbow*
    She roves upon the Sea ;
Five hundred gallant Seamen
    Do bear her company.

The Dutch man and the Spaniard,
    She made them for to flee ;
Alsò the bonny French man,
    As she met him on the Sea.
When as this gallant *Rainbow*
    Did come where Ward did lye,
"Where is the Captain of this Ship? "
    Her master he did cry.

---

that they were not caught, and where they cleared off to is unknown ; but it was said in latter years that Ward was living at Algiers, in the style of a petty prince, in which condition he was kept by a fleet of pirate craft that infested the Mediterranean and the Barbary shore, and enabled him to pay the heavy tax put on him by the native ruler for allowing him to carry on his piracy from there. It will be seen that this is borne out by the next ballad.   [2] James I, Sully's "wisest fool in Christendom." He created the title of baronet, and degraded the crown of England by selling titles of nobility ; a timid man who was scarcely a coward, and should never have been more than a fox-hunting squire.

"Oh, that am I ! " says Captain Ward :
  "There's no man bids me lye ;
And if thou art the King's fair Ship,
  Thou'rt welcome unto me ! "
"I tell thee what," says *Rainbow,*
  "Our King is in great grief,
That thou shouldst lyé here on the Sea
  And play the arrant Thief ;

"And will not let our merchants' Ships
  Pass as they did before :
Such tydings to our King is come
  As grieves his heart full sore."
With that this gallant *Rainbow*
  She shot, out of her pride,
Full fifty gallant brass piecès,
  Chargèd on every side.

And yet those gallant shooters
  Prevailèd not a pin ;
Though they were brass on *the* outside,
  Brave Ward was steel within.
"Shoot on, shoot on ! " cries Captain Ward—
  "Your sport well pleaseth me ;
And he that first gives over
  Shall yield unto the Sea.

"I never wrong'd an English Ship,—
  But Turk and King of Spain,
And the jovial Dutch man,
  As I met him on the Main.
If I had known your King
  But one, two years before,
I would have sav'd brave Essex' life—
  Whose death did grieve me sore.

"Go, tell the King of England—
  Go, tell him this from me,
If he reign King o' all the Land,
  I will reign King at Sea ! "
With that the gallant *Rainbow* shot,
  And shot, and shot in vain ;
Then left the Rover's company
  And *re*-turned home again.

"Our Royal King of England,
  Your Ship's return'd again;
For Ward his ship it is so strong,
  It never will be ta'en."
"O, Everlasting," cries our King,
  "I have lost jewels three,
Who would have gone unto the Seas,
  And brought proud Ward to me!

"The first he was Lord Clifford,
  Earl of Cumberland;
The second was Lord Mountjoy,
  As you may understand;
The third he was brave Essex,
  From field would never flee—
And these had gone unto the Seas
  And brought proud Ward to me!"

ANONYMOUS.

THE SEAMAN'S SONG OF CAPTAIN WARD AND DANSEKAR THE DUTCHMAN.

(Air : *The King's going to Bulloign.*)

GALLANTS, you must understand,
  Captain Ward of Englànd,
A pirate and a rover on the sea—
  Of late a simple fisherman,
  In the little town of Faversham—
Grows famous in the world now merrily.

From the bay of Plymouth
  Sail'd he toward the south,
With many more of courage and of might:
  Christian princes have but few
  Seamen such—were he but true,
And would but for his king and country fight.

Lusty Ward adventurously,
In the Straits of Barbary,
Did make the Turkish gallies sorely shake;
Bouncing cannon, fiery hot,
Spared not the Turks one jot,
But of their lives great slaughter he did make.

The islanders of Malta,
With argosies at sea,
Most proudly braved Ward to his face;
But soon their pride was overthrown,
And all their treasures made his own,
And all their men brought to a woful case.

The wealthy ships of Venice
Afforded him great riches—
Both gold and silver won he with his sword.
Stately Spain and Portugal
Against him dare not send a sail,
But gave him all the title of a lord.

Golden-seated Candie,
Famous France and Italy,
With all the countries of the eastern parts,—
If once their ships his pride withstood,
They surely all were cloth'd in blood—
Such cruelty was recking in their hearts.

The riches he hath gainèd
And by bloodshed obtainèd
May well suffice for to maintain a king :
His fellows all are valiant wights,
Fit to make good princes' knights,—
But that their lives do base dishonour bring.

This wicked-gotten treasure
Doth him but scanty pleasure—
The land takes all what they do get by sea :
In drunkenness and lechery,
Filthy sins of sodomy,
Their evil-gotten goods do haste away.

Such as live by thieving
Do seldom have good ending,
As by the deeds of Captain Ward is shown;

Being drunk among his drabs,
His best friends he sometimes stabs—
Such wickedness within his heart is grown.

When stormy tempest riseth
The Causer he despiseth,
And still denies to pray to the good Lord:
He feareth neither God nor Divil;
His deeds are bad; his thoughts are evil;
His only trust is still upon his sword.

Men of his own country
He still abuseth vilely;
Some back-to-back are cast into the waves;
Some are hewn to pieces small;
Some are shot against a wall,—
A slender number of their lives he saves.

Of truth it is reported
That he is strongly guarded
By Turks who are not of a good Belief;
Wit and reason tell them
He dare not trust his countrymen,
But shews the true condition of a thief.

At Tunis in Barbary
Now he buildeth stately
A gallant palace and a royal place,
Deck'd with delights so trim,
Fitter for a prince than him,
The which at last will prove to his disgrace.

To set the world a-wonder
This captain is commander
Of four-and-twenty ships of spanking sail,
To bring him booty from the sea,
Into the markets ev'ry day,
The which the Turks do buy up without fail.

His name and state so mounteth,
These Turkish-men accounteth
Him equal to the nobles of their land;
But these his honours we shall find
Shortly blown up with the wind,
Or prove like letters written in the sand.

PART TWO.

Sing we sailors now and then
Of Dansekar the Dutchman,
Whose warlike mind hath won him much renown;
To live on shore he counts it base,
But seeks to purchase greater grace
By roving all the ocean up and down.

His heart is so aspiring,
That now his chief desiring
Is for to win himself a worthy name:
The land hath far too little ground;
The sea is of a larger bound,
And of a greater dignity and fame.

Now many a fighting gallant,
Of bravery most valiant,
With him have put their fortunes to the sea:
All the world around hath heard
Of Dansekar and English Ward
And of their proud adventures every day.

There is not any kingdom,
In Turkey nor in Christendom,
But these pirates have done them bloody loss:
Merchant men of ev'ry land
Do daily in great danger stand,
And much do fear the ocean main to cross.

They make children fatherless,
Put widows into woful stresse:
In shedding blood they do take much delight.
Fathers they bereave of sons,
Regarding neither cries nor guns,
So much they joy to see some bloody fight.

They count it gallant faring
To hear the cannons blaring,
And musket-shot a-rattling in the sky:
Their glories would be at the high'st
To fight against the foes of Christ,
And such as do our Christian faith deny.

But their cursèd villainies
And their bloody piracies
Are chiefly bent against our Christian friends:
　Some Christians in evil so delight
　That they become dark devils in the night,
And for the same have divers shameful ends.

　England suffers danger,
　Just like any stranger—
Nations are alike to thieving company:
　Many English merchant men,
　And of London now and then,
Have tasted this in vile extremity.

　London's *Elizabeth*
　Of late these rovers taken have—
A ship well laden with rich merchandise;
　The sprightly *Pearl* and *Charity*,
　All ships of greatest gallantry,
Are by these pirates made unlawful prize.

　Of Hull the *Bonaventure*,
　Which was a great frequenter
And passer of the Straits to Barbary:
　Both ship and men late taken were
　By pirates Ward and Dansekar,
And brought by them into captivity.

PART THREE.

　English Ward and Dansekar
　Greatly now begin to jar
About the dividing of their goods:
　Both ships and soldiers gather head,—
　Dansekar from Ward is fled,
So full of prideful malice are their bloods.

　Ward doth only promise
　To keep about rich Tunis,
And be commander of those Turkish seas;
　But valiant Dutch-land Dansekar
　Doth hover near by Angier,
And there his threat'ning flag he now displays.

These pirates, thus divided,
By God are sure provided,
In secret sort to work each other's woe:
Such wicked courses cannot stand—
The Devil thus puts in his hand,
And God will give them soon an overthrow.[1]

ANONYMOUS.

THE DOWNFALL OF PIRACY;[2]
OR, TEACH THE ROVER.

WILL you hear of a bloody battle lately fought upon the
    seas?
It will make your ears to tingle and your admiration
    please.
You have heard of Teach, the rover, and his knavery on
    the main;
How of gold he was a lover, how he lov'd ill-gotten
    gain.
When the Act of Grace was granted, Captain Teach,
    with all his men,
Unto Carolina steer'd away, and kindly us'd was then:

[1] In spite of this and similar sentiments in some of these pirate
ballads we know that, just as the smugglers of a later time had the
bulk of the people's sympathy, the rover—providing that he was satis-
fied with taking merchandise only—was thought but little the worse of
by those who had no wealth to lose ; it was that fundamental idea of
democracy, old and inherent as wealth and poverty: "If you have
nothing, take something from those who have plenty." As some fur-
ther proof that there was at least a foundation of truth in the stories of
Ward and the *Rainbow*, there are other ballads and songs which were
evidently written to commemorate some of his exploits.
[2] The broadside gives it : "The full and true account of a most
desperate and bloody sea-fight between Lieutenant Maynard and the
noted pirate, Captain Teach, more commonly called by the name of
'Blackbeard.' Maynard had fifty men ; thirty-five were killed or
wounded in the action. Teach had twenty men, the most of whom
were killed ; the others were carried to Virginia, tried and executed."
Teach was a native of Bristol. He went to Jamaica and served in a
privateer before he took to piracy proper.

There he marrièd a lady, worth quite five hundred
  pound;
But to her he prov'd unsteady, and he soon march'd off
  the ground.

He returnèd, as I tell you, to his robberies, as before,—
Burning, sinking ships of value, filling them with purple
  gore.
When he was at Carolina, the Governor [1] did him send
To the Governor of Virginia, that he might assistance
  lend:

Then the man-o'-war's Commander,[2] two small sloops
  he fitted out;
Fifty men he put on board, sirs, who said they'd stand
  it out:
The Lieutenant, he commanded both the sloops; and
  you shall hear
How, before he landed, he suppress'd them, without
  fear.

Valiant Maynard, as he sail'd,[3] soon the pirate did espy;
With his trumpet then he hail'd them, and to him they
  did reply:
"Captain Teach is our commander." Maynard call'd,
  "He is the man
Whom I'm resolv'd to hang, sir; let him do the best he
  can!"

Teach reply'd to Maynard: "Sir, no quarter [4] you shall
  see;
But be hanged on my mainyard, you and all your
  companie!"
Maynard said: "I none desire of such knaves as thee
  and thine;
And none I'll give." Teach reply'd: "My boys, give me
  a glass of wine."

[1] This is the one real error in the ballad; the Governor of Carolina
worked with Teach. It was the Governor of Virginia who was the
prime mover in the matter—at the instance of despoiled merchants.
[2] Two frigates were lying in James River, Chesapeake Bay, but they
were too big to pursue Teach into his holes along the coast; so, at the
governor's request, they fitted out the sloops. [3] November 17, 1717;
and on the evening of the 21st Maynard found Teach in an inlet along
the Maryland shore. [4] It was here that Teach drank success to him-
self and the reverse to his opponent.

He took and drank damnation unto Maynard and his
crew,
To himself and generation luck, then the glass away he
threw.
Brave Maynard said he'd have him, tho' he'd cannons
nine or ten :
Teach a broadside [1] quickly gave him, killing sixteen
valiant men.

Maynard boarded him, and to it they fell with sword
and pistols too ;
They had courage and did show it, killing of the pirate
crew :
Teach and Maynard on the quarter fought it out most
manfully ;
Maynard's sword [2] did cut him shorter—by his head he
there did die.

Every sailor fought as long as he had power to wield
his sword ;
Not a coward was there there, sirs—fear was driven
overboard.
Wounded men fell all about, sirs ; 'twas a doleful sight
to see :
Nothing could their courage hinder—oh, they fought
couragiously !

When the bloody fight was over—we're told by a letter
writ—
Teach's head was by a lanyard hung to Maynard's
sloop's bowsprit : [3]
Thus they sail'd back to Virginia ; and when the tale
was told,
How they kill'd the pirates many, they'd applause from
young and old.

                                                    ANONYMOUS.

[1] The fight was maintained so close inshore that every now and
then one or other of the combatants was aground.   This was on the
following day.   [2] The truth is that Maynard's sword broke, and Teach
was in the act of cutting him down when a bluejacket half-severed his
head with a cutlass.   [3] One version has it " made a cover to the Jack
staff of the ship," which was not true ; such a vessel, if she had a Jack-
staff (upright on the stern, to fly the Union Jack on, in harbour), would
have one so small that a man's head would almost break it down.
Except for the errors pointed out this account is practically true.

THE PRIVATEERSMAN'S LOVE-LETTER.[1]

Susan, I this letter send thee,—
Let not sighs and tears attend thee.
   We are off the coast of France,
      Taking prizes from these nizeys,
   My sweet jewel to advance.

Since old London we forsook
Five rich prizes have we took;
   Two of them Nantz brandy-wine,[2]
      Chests of money, my sweet honey,
   And rich silks and satins fine.

The first merchant-ship we boarded—
Which great store of wealth afforded—
   We fell on most eagerly;
      Search'd and plunder'd, then it sunder'd,
   Making chests and cabins fly.

Where the treasure was enclos'd
We were not the least oppos'd;
   Rich embroider'd silks we found,—
      And more treasure, out of measure,
   Worth nigh seven thousand pound.

Fortune she did still attend us,
And soon another booty send us,
   Twice the worth of that one before;
      Tho' we gain'd it and detain'd it,
   Yet our guns were forced to roar.

While we did so charge and fire,
They endeavour'd to retire;

[1] It would appear that this piece was written about the end oi the seventeenth or the beginning of the eighteenth century. It is one of a number that touch on privateering, though it is very doubtful if any one of them was written by a seaman, or by any person with inside knowledge. As a general thing this is one of the best, which, to judge by its versification and language, did not come, as so many of the ballads of those days did, from an illiterate hand.   [2] From this it seems that Nantes was then famous for its "brandy-wine," which, according to the rhymester, was of exceptional value.

But the contest was not long;
  Then we enter'd,[1] bravely ventur'd,
Yet receiv'd but little wrong.[2]

Love, we'll plunder French and Tory,[3]
For to raise Great Britain's glory,
  And to pull proud Louis down;
    Each great spirit then will merit
Double honour and renown.

Dearest, when I first did leave thee,
Parting with thy love so griev'd thee
  That I vow'd I'd missives write
    To improve thee, for I love thee
All the day and all the night.

Love, this promise is not broken:
Here I send to thee this token—
  A rich chain and a diamond ring;
    And ten times more I have in store,
Which I to thee in time will bring.

Like a lady thou shalt flourish;
Thy poor drooping heart I'll nourish,
  And thy former joys restore,
    Gold and treasure, love and pleasure,
If I live to come on shore.

Love, the world shall thee admire,
When it sees thy grand attire,
  Like a blooming Lady Gay;
    I declare if, thou shalt wear it,
And for it proud France shall pay.

Dearest, though we now are parted,
Still I am thine own true-hearted,
  And prefer no one beside;
    E'er before thee, I adore thee—
None but death shall us divide.

ANONYMOUS.

[1] Boarded.   [2] Damage.   [3] Tories were then mostly Jacobites, therefore, to the common mind, in league with Louis and Catholicism.

THE SALCOMBE SEAMAN AND THE PROUD
PIRATE.[1]

A LOFTY ship from Salcombe came—
   Blow high, blow low, and so sail'd we :
She had golden trucks that shone like flame—
   On the bonnie, bonnie coast of Barbary.

"Masthead, masthead ! " is the captain's hail—
   Blow high, blow low.
"Look out and about !   D'ye see a sail? "—
   On the coast of Barbary.

"There's a ship a-looming straight ahead "—
   Blow high, blow low.
"Her colour's aloft and it blows out red "—
   On the coast of Barbary.

"O ship ahoy ! and where do you steer? "—
   Blow high, blow low.
"Are you a man-o'-war or a privateer? "—
   On the coast of Barbary.

"I am neither the one nor the other," said she—
   Blow high, blow low.
"But I'm a pirate out looking for my fee "—
   On the coast of Barbary.

"I am a jolly pirate, out for gold "—
   Blow high, blow low.
"I'll send my mate to rummage your hold "—
   On the coast of Barbary.

Then the gruntling guns flash'd out and roar'd—
   Blow high, blow low.
Till that pirate's masts went overboard—
   On the coast of Barbary.

---

[1] This song—for as such it must have been written—and its fore-
runner, "The Saylor's Onely Delight," are particularly interesting on
account of their similar construction to that of the "Chanties," which
followed them.   It appears to have been no more than a song.

They fir'd round-shot till the pirate's deck—
      Blow high, blow low.
Was blood and spars and broken wreck—
      On the coast of Barbary.

"Oh, do not haul the red flag down ! "—
      Blow high, blow low.
"But keep all fast until we drown "—
      On the coast of Barbary.

They call'd for kegs of wine and drank—
      Blow high, blow low.
They sang old songs until she sank—
      On the coast of Barbary.

So let us brew long cans of flip—
      Blow high, blow low ;
And drain them all to that Salcombe ship—
      On the coast of Barbary.

Ay, drain our cans to the lads of fame—
      Blow high, blow low ;
Who sank that pirate, to his shame—
      On the coast of Barbary.

                                ANONYMOUS.

THE   PIRATE.

O'ER the glad waters of the dark-blue sea,
Our thoughts as boundless, and our souls as free,
Far as the breeze can bear, the billows foam,
Survey our empire and behold our home !
These are our realms, no limit to our sway—
Our flag the sceptre all who meet obey.
Ours the wild life, in tumult still to range
From toil to rest, and joy in every change.
Oh ! who can tell?   Not thou, luxurious slave,
Whose soul would sicken o'er the heaving wave !
Not thou, vain lord of wantonness and ease !
Whose slumber soothes not, pleasure cannot please.
Oh ! who can tell?—save he whose heart hath tried,
And danced in triumph o'er the waters wide;

Th' exulting sense, the pulse's maddening play,
That thrills the wanderer of this trackless way;
That for itself can woo th' approaching fight,
And turn what some deem danger to delight;
That seeks what cravens shun with more than zeal,
And where the feebler faint, can only feel—
Feel to the rising bosom's inmost core,
Its hope awaken and its spirits soar!
No dread of death—if with us die our foes—
Save that it seems e'en duller than repose:
Come when it will—we snatch the life of life;
When lost—what recks it, by disease or strife?
Let him who crawls, enamoured of decay,
Cling to his couch, and sicken years away;
Heave his thick breath, and shake his palsièd head;
Ours—the fresh turf, and not the feverish bed.
While gasp by gasp he falters forth his soul;
Ours with one pang, one bound, escapes control.
His corse may boast its urn and narrow cave,
And they who loathed his life may gild his grave.
Ours are the tears, though few, sincerely shed,
When Ocean shrouds and sepulchres our dead.
For us, e'en banquets fond regret supply
In the red cup that drowns our memory;
And the brief epitaph in danger's day,
When those who win at last divide the prey,
And cry, Remembrance saddening o'er each brow:
"How had the brave who fell exulted now!"

BYRON.

THE OLD BUCCANEER.

OH, England is a pleasant place for them that's rich and
high;
But England is a cruel place for such poor folk as I;
And such a port for mariners I shall ne'er see again
As the pleasant Isle of Avès, beside the Spanish Main.

There were forty craft in Avès that were both swift and
stout,
All furnished well with small arms and cannons round
about;
And a thousand men in Avès made laws so fair and free
To choose their valiant captains and obey them loyally.

Y 2

Then we sailed against the Spaniard, with his hoards of
    plate and gold,
Which he wrung with cruel tortures from the Indian folk
    of old;
Likewise the merchant captains, with hearts as hard as
    stone,
Who flog men and keel-haul them, and starve them to
    the bone.

Oh, the palms grew high in Avès, and fruits that shone
    like gold,
And the colibris and parrots they were gorgeous to
    behold;
And the negro maids in Avès from bondage fast did flee,
To welcome gallant sailors, a-sweeping in from sea.

Oh, sweet it was in Avès to hear the landward breeze,
A-swing with good tobacco, in a net between the trees,
With a negro lass to fan you, while you listened to the
    roar
Of the breakers on the reef outside, that never touched
    the shore.

But Scripture saith an ending to all fine things must be;
So the king's ships sailed on Avès, and quite put down
    were we:
All day we fought like bulldogs; but they burst the
    booms at night;
And I fled in a piragua, sore wounded, from the fight.

Nine days I floated, starving, and a negro lass beside;
Till, for all I tried to cheer her, the poor young thing
    she died:
But as I lay a-gasping, a British sail came by,
And brought me home to England here, to beg until I
    die.

And now I'm old and going—I'm sure I can't tell where;
One comfort is, this world's so hard, I can't be worse off
    there:
If I might be a sea-dove, I'd fly across the main,
To the pleasant Isle of Avès, to look at it once again.

KINGSLEY.

THE LAST BUCCANEER.

THE winds were yelling, the waves were swelling,
    The sky was black and drear,
When the crew, with eyes of flame, brought the ship
      without a name
    Alongside the last Buccaneer.

"Whence flies your sloop full-sail before so fierce a
      gale,
    When all others drive bare on the seas?
Say, come ye from the shore of the holy Salvador,
    Or the gulf of the rich Caribbees?"

"From a shore no search hath found, from a gulf no
      line can sound,
    Without rudder or needle we steer;
Above, below our bark dies the sea-fowl and the
      shark,
    As we fly by the last Buccaneer.

"To-night shall be heard on the rocks of Cape de Verde
    A loud crash and a louder roar,
And to-morrow shall the deep, with a heavy moaning,
      sweep
    The corpses and wreck to the shore."

The stately ship of Clyde securely now may ride
    In the breadth of the citron shades;
And Severn's towering mast securely now lies fast,
    Through the seas of the balmy Trades.

From St. Jago's wealthy port, from Savannah's royal
      fort,
    The seaman goes forth without fear;
For since that stormy night not a mortal hath had
      sight
    Of the flag of the last Buccaneer.

MACAULAY.

THE SLAVER.[1]

CRUEL as death, insatiate as the grave,
False as the winds that round his vessel blow,
Remorseless as the gulf that yawns below,
Is he who toils upon the wafting flood—
A Christian broker in the trade of blood!
Boisterous in speech, in action prompt and bold,
He buys, he sells—he steals, he kills for gold!
At noon, when sky and ocean, calm and clear,
Bend round his bark one blue unbroken sphere;
When dancing dolphins sparkle through the brine,
And sunbeam-circles o'er the water shine,
He sees no beauty in the heavens serene,
No soul-enchanting sweetness in the scene;
But darkly scowling at the glorious day,
Curses the winds that loiter on their way.
When swollen hurricanes the billows rise,
To meet the lightning midway from the skies;
When from the unburthen'd hold his shrieking slaves
Are cast, at midnight, to the hungry waves;
Not for his victims strangled in the deeps;
Not for his crimes the hardened slaver weeps;
But grimly smiling, when the storms are o'er,
Counts his sure gains, and hurries back for more!

JAMES MONTGOMERY.

THE SLAVE'S DEATH.

WIDE o'er the tremulous sea
  The moon spread her mantle of light;
And the gale, now lessening away,
  Breathed soft on the bosom of night.

[1] The present tense of these lines may be thought to be out of place to-day; but it is not. Although slaving is not now carried on as it was in the time of Montgomery (who, by-the-bye, was one of our early pioneers and sufferers in the cause of political and general freedom), it is still pursued in certain semi-civilised corners of the world.

On the forecastle Maratan stood,
　And poured forth his sorrowful tale;
His tears fell unseen in the flood;
　His sighs passed unheard in the gale.

"Ah, wretch!" in wild anguish he cried,
　"From country and liberty torn!
Ah, Maratan, wouldst thou had died
　Ere o'er the salt waves thou wert borne!

"Through the groves of Angola I strayed;
　Love and hope made my bosom their home :
There I talked with my favourite maid,
　Nor dreamed of the sorrow to come.

"From the thicket the man-hunter sprung.,
　My cries echoed loud through the air :
There was fury and wrath on his tongue;
　He was deaf to the shrieks of despair.

"Accurs'd be the merciless band
　That his love could from Maratan tear!
And blasted this impotent hand
　That was severed from all I held dear!

"Flow, ye tears, down my cheeks ever flow;
　Still let sleep from my eye-lids depart;
And still may the sorrows of woe
　Drink deep of the stream of my heart!

"But, hark! on the silence of night
　My Adila's accents I hear,
And mournful beneath the wan light
　I see her loved image appear!

"Slow o'er the smooth ocean she glides,
　As the mist that hangs light on the wave;
And fondly her lover she chides,
　Who lingers so long from the grave.

"'O Maratan, haste thee!' she cries,
　'Here the reign of oppression is o'er;
The tyrant is robbed of his prize,
　And Adila sorrows no more.'

"Now, sinking amidst the dim ray,
    Her form seems to fade from my view :
O stay then, my Adila, stay !—
    She beckons, and I must pursue.

"To-morrow the white man in vain
    Will proudly account me his slave :
My shackles I plunge in the main,
    And rush to the realms of the brave ! "

PETER PINDAR.[1]

THE SLAVE SHIP.[2]

"OLD, sightless man, unwont art thou,[3]
    As blind men use, at noon
To sit and sun thy tranquil brow,
    And hear the birds' sweet tune.

"There's something heavy at thy heart,
    Thou dost not join the pray'r ;—
E'en at God's word why writhe and start ? "—
    "Oh, man of God, beware !

"If thou didst hear what I could say,
    'Twould make thee doubt of grace,
And drive me from God's house away,
    Lest I infest the place ! "

[1] This poem is ascribed to John Wolcot (" Peter Pindar," 1738–1819), but whether he wrote it or not I cannot say. Certainly Wolcot, while acting as physician to Sir William Trelawny in Jamaica—where he entered the Church—interested himself in the question of slavery, and wrote "The Lousiad," "Lyric Odes," etc., after his return home to Cornwall. There he found Opie, the painter, in obscurity, took him to town, pushed him into recognition, and made his own self conspicuous by writing satires.

[2] "The case of the *Rodeur*, mentioned by Lord Lansdowne. A dreadful ophthalmia prevailed amongst the slaves on board this ship, which was communicated to the crew, so that there was but a single man who could see to guide the vessel into port."—*Quarterly Review*, vol. 26, p. 71.   [3] Milman's manner of telling this ghastly affair is too reminiscent of "The Ancient Mariner" to pass unnoticed. And as Coleridge's poem was in popular favour when Milman was in his teens, he probably copied something of the manner unconsciously.

"Say on; there's nought of human sin
  Christ's blood may not atone."
"Thou can'st not read what load's within
  This desperate heart."—"Say on."

"The skies were bright; the seas were calm;
  We ran before the wind,
That, bending Afric's groves of palm,
  Came fragrant from behind.

"And merry sang our crew; the cup
  Was gaily drawn and quaff'd;
And when the hollow groan came up
  From the dark hold, we laugh'd.

"For deep below and all secure
  Our living freight was laid;
And long with ample gain, and sure,
  We had driven our awful trade.

"They lay, like bales, in stifling gloom—
  Man, woman, nursling-child,
As in some plague-struck city's tomb
  The loathsome dead are piled.

    .   .   .   .   .

"'Mid howl and yell and shuddering moan,
  The scourge, the clanking chain,
The cards were dealt, the dice were thrown—
  We staked our share of gain.

"Soon in smooth Martinico's coves
  Our welcome bark should moor,
Or underneath the citron-groves
  That wave on Cuba's shore.

"'Twas strange!—ere many days were gone
  How still grew all below;
The wailing babe was heard alone,
  Or some low sob of woe.

"Into the dusky hold we gazed—
  In heaps we saw them lie;
And dim, deep asking looks were raised
  From many a blood-red eye.

"And helpless hands were groping round
    To catch their scanty meal;
Or at some voice's well-known sound,
    Some well-known touch to feel.

"And still it spread, the blinding plague
    That seals the orbs of sight;
Their eyes were rolling, wild and vague—
    Within was black as night.

"They dared not move; they could not weep;
    They could but lie and moan;
Some, not in mercy, to the deep,
    Like damaged wares, were thrown.

"We cursed the dire disease that spread,
    And cross'd our golden dream;
These godless men did quake with dread
    To hear us thus blaspheme.

"And so we drank, and drank the more,
    And each man pledged his mate:
'Here's better luck from Gambia's shore
    When next we load our freight.'

"Another morn, but one—the bark
    Lurch'd heavy on her way:
The steersman shriek'd—'Hell's not so dark
    As this dull, murky day!'

"We look'd—and red, through films of blood,
    Glared forth his angry eye:
Another, as he mann'd the shroud,
    Came toppling from on high.

"Then each alone his hammock made,
    As the wild beast his lair;
No friend his nearest friend would aid,
    In dread his doom to share.

"Yet every eve some eyes did close
    Upon the sunset bright;
And when the glorious morn arose,
    It bare to them no light.

"Till I, the only man, the last
    Of that dark brotherhood,
To guide the helm, the log to cast,
    To tend the daily food.

"I felt it steal—I felt it grow,
    The dim and misty scale;
I could not see the compass now,—
    I could not see the sail.

"The sea was all a wavering fog,
    The sun a hazy lamp,
As on some pestilential bog
    The wandering fire-damp.

"And there we lay,—and on we drove,
    Heaved up, then pitching down.
Oh, cruel grace of Him above,
    That would not let us drown!

"And some began to pray for fear,
    Some 'gan again to swear;
Methought it was most dread to hear
    Upon such lips the prayer.

"And some would fondly speak of home—
    The wife's, the infant's kiss:
Great God, that parents e'er should come
    To such a trade as this!

"And some I heard plunge down beneath
    And drown—that could not I:
Oh, how my spirit yearn'd for death!
    Yet how I fear'd to die!

"We heard the wild and frantic shriek
    Of starv'd, blind men below;
We heard them strive their bonds to break,
    And burst the hatches now.

"We thought we heard them on the stair,
    And trampling on the deck:
I almost felt their blind despair
    Wild grappling at my neck.

"Again I woke, and yet again,
  With throat as dry as dust,
And famine in my heart and brain,
  And—speak it out I must—

"A lawless, execrable thought,
  That scarce could be withstood,
Before my loathing fancy brought
  Unutterable food!

"No more!—my brain can bear no more,—
  No more my tongue can tell:
I know I breathed no air, but bore
  A sick'ning, grave-like smell.

"And all, save I alone, could die—
  They on death's awful brink,
All thoughtless, feelingless, could lie—
  I still must feel and think!

"At length, when ages had pass'd o'er,
  Ages, it seem'd of night,
There came a shock, and then a roar
  Of billows in their might.

"I know not how, when next I woke,
  The numb waves wrapp'd me round;
And in my loaded ears there broke
  A dizzy, bubbling sound.

"Again I woke, and living men
  Stood round—a Christian crew;
The first, the last, of joy was then,
  That since those days I knew.

"I've been, I know, since that black tide,
  Where raving madmen lay,
Above, beneath, on every side,
  And I as mad as they.

"And I shall be where never dies
  The worm, nor slakes the flame,
When those two hundred souls shall rise
  The judge's wrath to claim.

"I'd rather rave in that wild room
  Than see what I have seen;
I'd rather meet my final doom
  Than be—where I have been.

"Priest, I've not seen thy loathing face;
  I've heard thy gasps of fear:
Away—no word of hope or grace.—
  I may not—will not hear!"

DEAN MILMAN.

THE SMUGGLER'S GIRL.

OH, my true love's a smuggler bold,
  And he sails the salt, salt sea;
And I wish I were a sailor too,
  To go along with he—
To go along with he o' nights
  For the satin and the wine,
And run the tubs on Slapton beach
  When the merry stars do shine.

Oh, Hollands is a warming drink,
  When nights are wet and cold;
And brandy is a good man's drink
  For them as getting old.
There's lights on the cliff-top high,
  When boats are homeward bound;
And we run the tubs on Slapton beach,
  When the welcome word goes round.

The King he is a great, proud man,
  All in his purple coat;
But me, I love a smuggler lad
  In his little fishing boat;
For he brings the Mallin laces fine,
  And he spends his money free;
And I wish I were a seaman, oh,
  To sail along with he!

ANONYMOUS.

SMUGGLER'S EPITAPHS[1]

" Here lie the Mortal Remains of
ROBERT MARK
Late of Polperro,[2] who unfortunately
was Shot at Sea the 24th day of Jany.
in Year of our Lord God 1802,
in the 40th Year of his Age.

IN Prime of Life most suddenly,
  Sad Tidings to relate,
Here view My utter Destiny
  And Pity my sad State.
I by a Shot, which rapid flew,
  Was instantly struck Dead;
Lord pardon the Offender who
  My precious Blood did shed;
Grant Him to rest, and forgive Me
  All I have done amiss,
And that I may Rewarded be
  With everlasting Bliss.

Sacred to the Memory[3]
of
WILLIAM LEWIS
Who was Killed by a Shot
from the *Pigmy* Schooner
21st April, 1822, aged 53 years.

---

[1] Such epitaphs as these few examples are to be found in lonely churchyards close to the coast, from the Wash to Land's End in particular, and less frequently on the north-east and the westerly coasts. They are usually accompanied by a rudely-carved Iugger or cutter, or crossed pistols and a keg, or a skull and crossbones; the last being most common along the Essex shore and thereabouts, and used as an emblem of death, not of piracy. [2] Near Fowey, Cornwall.
[3] In the graveyard at Wyke by Weymouth.

Of Life bereft (by fell Design),
I mingle with my fellow clay,
On God's protection I resign
To Save me on the Judgment Day.
There shall each Blood-stain'd Soul appear :
Repent, all, ere it be too late;
Or else a dreadful Doom you'll Hear,
For God will sure Avenge my Fate.

This Stone is erected by his Wife
as the last Mark of Respect to an
Affectionate Husband.

We have not a moment to call our own.[1]

In Memory of THOMAS JAMES, aged 35 years,
Who on the evening of the 7th Dec., 1814,
on His returning to Flushing from St. Mawes
in a Boat was Shot by a Customs House
Officer and Expired a few days after.

Officious Zeal in luckless Hour laid wait,
And wilful sent the murderous Ball of Fate :
James to his Home, which late in Health he left,
Wounded return'd—of Life is soon bereft.

To the Memory of ROBERT TROTMAN,[2]
late of Rowd, in the County of Wilts,
who was barbarously Murdered on the
Shore near Poole, the 24th March, 1765.

A little Tea, one leaf I did but Steal;
For guiltless Bloodshed I to God appeal :
Put Tea in one Scale, human Blood in t'other,
And think what 'tis to Slay a harmless Brother.

[1] In the parish churchyard, Mylor, Falmouth.
[2] At Kinson by Bournemouth.

HUMOROUS PIECES

CABIN PASSENGER.

Tell me, O mariner, dost thou never feel
The grandeur of thine office?—to control
The keel that cuts the ocean like a knife,
And leaves a wake behind it like a seam
In the great shining garment of the world!

HELMSMAN.

Belay y'r jaw, y' swab!—y' horse-marine!
(To the Captain.)
Ay, ay, sir! Stiddy, sir! Sou'-west b' sou'!
                    OLIVER WENDELL HOLMES.

Z

"TO ALL YOU LADIES."

To all you ladies now on land
   We men at sea indite;
But first would have you understand
   How hard it is to write.
The Muses, then, and Neptune too,
We must implore to write to you.
   With a fa la, la, la, la, la!

For though the Muses should prove kind,
   And fill our empty brain;
Yet, if rough Neptune rouse the wind
   To wave the azure main,
Our paper, pen, and ink, and we
Roll up and down our ships at sea.
   With a fa la, la.

Then, if we write not by each post,
   Think not we are unkind;
Nor yet conclude our ships are lost
   By Dutchmen or by wind:
Our tears we'll send a speedier way—
The tide shall bring them twice a day.
   With a fa la, la.

The King, with wonder and surprise,
   Will swear the seas grow bold;
Because the tide will higher rise
   Than e'er it did of old:
But let him know it is our tears
Bring floods of grief to Whitehall stairs.
   With a fa la, la.

Should foggy Opdam chance to know
   Our sad and dismal story,
The Dutch would scorn so weak a foe,
   And quit their fort at Goree:

Nor what resistance can they find
From men who've left their hearts behind?
   With a fa la, la.

Let wind and weather do its worst;
   Be you to us but kind,
Let Dutchmen vapour, Spaniards curse,
   No sorrow shall we find :
'Tis then no matter how things go,
Or who's our friend, or who's our foe.
   With a fa la, la. .

To pass our tedious hours away
   We throw a merry main,
Or else at serious ombre play :
   But why should we in vain
Each other's ruin thus pursue?—
We were undone when we left you.
   With a fa la, la.

But now our fears tempestuous grow
   And cast our hopes away;
While you, regardless of our woe,
   Sit careless at a play—
Perhaps permit some happier man
To kiss your hand, or flirt your fan.
   With a fa la, la.

When any mournful tune you hear—
   That dies in ev'ry note—
As if it sighed with each man's care
   For being so remote,
Then think how often love we've made
To you, when all those times we played.
   With a fa la, la.

In justice you cannot refuse
   To think of our distress,
When we for hopes of honour lose
   Our certain happiness;
All these designs are but to prove
Ourselves more worthy of your love.
   With a fa la, la.

And now we've told you all our loves,
   And likewise all our fears,
In hopes this declaration moves
   Some pity for our tears :
Let's hear of no inconstancy—
We have too much of that at sea.
   With a fa la, la.

EARL OF DORSET.

[As the foregoing "song" was written by Dorset on the night before an engagement during the first Dutch War, 1665, it may appear to be rather inappropriate to put it into this section of the book ; but to my mind there is such a sense of sly humour—or shall we say smiling jollity in which there is no touch of graver things?—running through the whole composition that it would be out of place in any other part of the book.]

PROLOGUE TO THE *MASQUE OF BRITANNIA* (1753).

(Spoken by Garrick, in the Character of a Sailor, Fuddled, and Talking to Himself.)

Enters, singing :

"How pleasant a sailor's life passes ! "
Well, if thou art, my boy, a little mellow;
A sailor, half-seas o'er, 's a pretty fellow !
What cheer, ho?   Do I carry too much sail?
No ! Tight and trim I scud before the gale !
But softly tho'; the vessel seems to heel.—
Steady, my boy !—she must not show her keel.
And now, thus ballasted—what course to steer?
Shall I again to sea, and bang Mounseer?
Or stay on shore, and try with Sall and Sue?
Dost love 'em, boy? By this right hand I do !
A well-rigged girl is surely most inviting :
There's nothing better, faith—save flip and fighting.
I must away—I must—
What, shall we sons of beef and freedom stoop,
Or lower our flag to slavery and soup?
What, shall these *Parly-voos* make such a racket,
And I not lend a hand to lace their jacket?

Still shall old England be your Frenchman's butt?—
Whene'er he shuffles should we always cut?
I'll to 'em, faith!—Avast! Before I go,
Have I not promised Sall to see the show?
(Pulls out a playbill.)
From this same paper we shall understand
What work's to-night—I read your printed hand.
First let's refresh a bit; for, faith, I need it!
I'll take one sugar-plum (takes tobacco), and then I'll
    read it.
    (He reads the bill of "Zara," played that evening.)
    "At the Theatre Royal, Drury Lane—
    Will be presen-ta-ted a tragedy called Sarah."
I'm glad 'tis Sarah; then our Sall may see
Her namesake's tragedy: and as for me,
I'll sleep as sound as if I were at sea.
    "To which will be added a new mask——"
Zounds! why a mask? We sailors hate grimaces:
Above-board all—we scorn to hide our faces!
But what is here, so very large and plain?
    "Brit-an-nia"—Oh, Britannia! Good again!
Huzza, boys! By the Royal George I swear
Tom Coxen and the crew shall straight be there!
All free-born souls must take Brit-an-nia's part,
And give her three round cheers, with hand and heart!
(Going off, he stops.)
I wish you landsmen, though, would leave your tricks,
Your factions, Parties and damned politics;
And, like us honest tars, drink, fight and sing,—
True to yourselves, your country and your King.
GARRICK.

THE MIDSHIPMAN.

AID me, kind Muse, so whimsical a theme,
No poet ever yet pursued for fame:
Boldly I venture on a naval scene,
Nor fear the critic's frown, the pedant's spleen.
Sons of the ocean, we their rules disdain;
Our bosom's honest, and our style is plain.
Let Homer's heroes and his gods delight;
Let Milton with infernal legions fight;

His favourite warrior polish'd Virgil show;
With love and wine luxurious Horace glow:
Be such their subjects,—I another choose,
As yet neglected by the laughing Muse.

Deep in that fabric,[1] where Britannia boasts
O'er seas to waft her thunder and her hosts,
A cavern![2]—unknown to cheering day;
Where one small taper lends a feeble ray;
Where wild disorder holds her wanton reign,
And careless mortals frolic in her train—
Bending beneath a hammock's friendly shade,
See Æsculapius[3] all in arms display'd;
In his right hand th' impending steel he holds,
The other round the trembling victim folds;
His gaping myrmidon the deed attends,
While in the pot the crimson stream descends:
Unawed young Galen bears the hostile brunt,
Pills in his rear, and Cullen in his front;
Whilst, muster'd round the medicinal pile,
Death's grim militia stand in rank and file.

In neighbouring mansions[4]—lo! what clouds arise;
It half-conceals its owner from our eyes.
One penny light with feeble lustre shines,
To prove the MID in high Olympus dines.
Let us approach—the preparation view,—
A Cockpit Bean is surely something new!
To him Japan her varnished joys denies,
Nor bloom for him the sweets of eastern skies;
His rugged limbs no lofty mirror shows,
No tender couch invites him to repose;
A pigmy glass upon his toilet stands,
Cracked o'er and o'er by awkward, clumsy hands;
Chesterfield's page polite, the "Seaman's Guide,"
A half-eat biscuit, Congreve's "Mourning Bride,"
Bestrew'd with powder, in confusion lie,
And form a chaos to th' intruding eye.
At length this meteor of an hour is dressed,
And rises, an Adonis, from his chest:

---

[1] A frigate.   [2] The midshipmen's quarters.   [3] The ship's surgeon, with bare arms, probably bleeding a middy.   [4] A midshipman preparing to dine, on invitation, with his superior officers.

Cautious he treads, lest some unlucky slip
Defile his clothes with burgoo [1] or with flip:
These rocks escaped, arrives *in status quo;*
Bows; dines and bows; then sinks again below.

Not far from hence a joyous group are met,[2]
For social mirth and sportive pastime set;
In cheering grog the rapid course goes round,
And not a care in all the circle's found,—
Promotion, mess-debts, absent friends, and love
Inspired by hope, in turn their topics prove:
To proud superiors then they each look up,
And curse all discipline in ample cup.

Hark! yonder voice in hollow murmur falls:
Hark! yonder voice the MID to duty calls.
Thus summoned by the gods, he deigns to go,
But first makes known his consequence below,—
At slavery rails, scorns lawless sway to hell,
And damns the powers allow'd a white lapel;[3]
Vows that he's free!—to stoop, to cringe disdains,
Ascends the ladder and resumes his chains.[4]
In canvas'd berth,[5] profoundly deep in thought,
His busy mind with sins and tangents fraught,
A MID reclines—in calculation lost,
His efforts still by some intruder cross'd.
Now to the longitude's vast height he soars,
And now formation of lobscouse [6] explores;
Now o'er a field of logarithms bends,
And now to make a pudding he pretends:
At once the sage, the hero and the cook,
He wields the sword, the saucepan and the book.
Opposed to him a sprightly messmate lolls,
Declaims with Garrick, or with Shuter drolls:
Sometimes his breast great Cato's virtue warms,
And then his task the gay Lothario charms;

[1] Which shows that oatmeal porridge has been longer known on board ship than many persons would believe. [2] The middies in their own quarters. [3] A kind of badge on a lieutenant's coat. [4] This Crabbe, or Hogarth-like picture, taking it all in all, is as true to-day, changes in comforts allowed for, as it was in Falconer's time, especially in these eight lines—for I have seen apprentices in a large sailing-ship do exactly the same. [5] Hammock. [6] Ship's hash, into which it were not always wise to inquire too closely.

Cleone's griefs his tragic feelings wake;
With Richard's pangs th' Orlopian caverns shake!
No more the mess for other joys repine,
When pea-soup entering, shows 'tis time to dine.

But think not meanly of this humble seat,
Whence sprung the guardians of the British fleet;
Revere the sacred spot, however low,
Which form'd to martial acts a Hawke, a Howe.

FALCONER.

"HAD NEPTUNE, WHEN FIRST."

HAD Neptune, when first he took charge of the sea,
Been as wise, or at least been as merry, as we,
He'd have thought better on't, and instead of brine
Would have filled the vast ocean with generous wine.

What trafficking then would have been on the main,
For the sake of good liquor as well as for gain!
No fear then of tempests, or danger of sinking—
The fishes ne'er drown that are always a-drinking.

The hot thirsty sun then would drive with more haste,
Secure in the evening of such a repast;
And when he'd got tipsy would have taken his nap
With double the pleasure in Thetis's lap.

By the force of his rays, and thus heated with wine,
Consider how gloriously Phœbus would shine;
What vast exhalations he'd draw up on high,
To relieve the poor earth as it wanted supply.

How happy us mortals when blessed with such rain,
To fill all our vessels, and fill them again!
Nay, even the beggar, that has ne'er a dish,
Might jump in the river, and drink like a fish!

What mirth and contentment on ev'ry one's brow!—
Hob as great as a prince, dancing after the plough!
The birds in the air, as they play on the wing,
Although they but sipped, would eternally sing.

The stars, which, I think, don't to drinking incline,
Would frisk and rejoice at the fumes of the wine;
And, merrily twinkling, would soon let us know
That they were as happy as mortals below.

Had this been the case, then what had we enjoy'd,
Our spirits still rising, our fancies ne'er cloy'd!
A pox then on Neptune, when 'twas in his pow'r,
To slip, like a fool, such a fortunate hour!

ANONYMOUS.

EPITAPH ON AN HONEST SAILOR.[1]

WHETHER sailor or not, for a moment avast!
Poor Tom's [2] mizzen top-sail is laid to the mast;
He'll never turn out, or more heave the lead;
He's now all aback, nor will sails shoot ahead:
He ever was brisk,[3] and, though now gone to wreck,
When he hears the last whistle he'll jump upon deck.

THE SEA-SPELL.

I.

IT was a jolly mariner!
The tallest man of three,—
He loosed his sail against the wind,
And turned his boat to sea:
The ink-black sky told every eye
A storm was soon to be!

II.

But still that jolly mariner
Took in no reef at all,
For, in his pouch, confidingly
He wore a baby's caul;
A thing, as gossip-nurses know,
That always brings a squall! [4]

---

[1] This is said to have been written by the Rev. Francis Blackburne,
Archdeacon of Cleveland.   [2] and [3] "Poor Tom" and "brisk."   Did
this precede "Tom Bowlin(g)?"   If so, this looks like being its father.
[4] A satirical inversion of the old superstition that a baby's caul averted
disaster at sea.

III.

His hat was new, or newly glazed,
Shone brightly in the sun;
His jacket, like a mariner's,
True blue, as e'er was spun;
His ample trousers, like St. Paul,
Bore forty stripes save one.

IV.

And now the fretting foaming tide
He steered away to cross;
The bounding pinnace played a game
Of dreary pitch and toss;
A game that, on the good dry land,
Is apt to bring a loss!

V.

Good Heaven befriend that little boat,
And guide her on her way!
A boat, they say, has canvas wings,
But cannot fly away!
Though like a merry singing bird,
She sits upon the spray!

VI.

Still east-by-south the little boat,
With tawny sail kept beating;
Now out of sight, between two waves,
Now o'er th' horizon fleeting:
Like greedy swine that feed on mast,—
The waves her mast seemed eating!

VII.

The sullen sky grew black above,
The wave as black beneath;
Each roaring billow showed full soon
A white and foamy wreath;
Like angry dogs that snarl at first,
And then display their teeth.

VIII.

The boatman looked against the wind,
The mast began to creak,
The wave, per saltum, came and dried,
In salt upon his cheek !
The pointed wave against him reared,
As if it owned a pique !

IX.

Nor rushing wind, nor gushing wave,
That boatman could alarm,
But still he stood away to sea,
And trusted in his charm;
He thought by purchase he was safe,
And armed against all harm !

X.

Now thick and fast and far aslant,
The stormy rain came pouring,
He heard upon the sandy bank
The distant breakers roaring,—
A groaning intermitting sound,
Like Gog and Magog snoring !

XI.

The seafowl shrieked around the mast,
Ahead the grampus tumbled,
And far off, from a copper cloud,
The hollow thunder rumbled;
It would have quailed another heart,
But his was never humbled.

XII.

For why? he had that infant's caul;
And wherefore should he dread?
Alas ! alas ! he little thought,
Before the ebb-tide sped,
That like that infant he should die,
And with a watery head !

XIII.

The rushing brine flowed in apace;
His boat had ne'er a deck;
Fate seemed to call on him, and he
Attended to her beck;
And so he went still trusting on,
Though reckless—to his wreck!

XIV.

For as he left his helm, to heave
The ballast bags a-weather,
Three monstrous seas came roaring on,
Like lions leagued together.
The two first waves the little boat
Swam over like a feather.

XV.

The two first waves were past and gone,
And sinking in her wake;
The hugest still came leaping on,
And hissing like a snake,
Now helm a-lee! for through the midst
The monster he must take!

XVI.

Ah me! it was a dreary mount!
Its base as black as night,
Its top of pale and livid green,
Its crest of awful white,
Like Neptune with a leprosy,—
And so it reared upright!

XVII.

With quaking sails the little boat
Climbed up the foaming heap;
With quaking sails it paused awhile,
At balance on the steep;
Then rushing down the nether slope,
Plunged with a dizzy sweep!

XVIII.

Look, how a horse, made mad with fear,
Disdains his careful guide;
So now the headlong, headstrong boat,
Unmanaged, turns aside,
And straight presents her reeling flank
Against the swelling tide!

XIX.

The gusty wind assaults the sail;
Her ballast lies a-lee!
The sheets to windward, taunt and stiff!
Oh! the Lively—where is she?
Her capsized keel is in the foam,
Her pennon's in the sea!

XX.

The wild gull, sailing overhead,
Three times beheld emerge
The head of that bold mariner,
And then she screamed his dirge!
For he had sunk within his grave,
Lapped in a shroud of surge!

XXI.

The ensuing wave, with horrid foam,
Rushed o'er and covered all,—
The jolly boatman's drowning scream
Was smothered by the squall;
Heaven never heard his cry, nor did
The ocean heed his caul.

HOOD.

THE DEMON SHIP.

T'was off the Wash—the sun went down—the sea
    looked black and grim,
For stormy clouds, with murky fleece, were mustering
    at the brim;
Titanic shades! enormous gloom! as if the solid night
Of Erebus rose suddenly to seize upon the light!
It was a time for mariners to bear a wary eye,
With such a dark conspiracy between the sea and sky!

Down went my helm—close-reefed—the tack held freely
    in my hand—
With ballast snug—I put about, and scudded for the
    land.
Loud hissed the sea beneath her lee—my little boat flew
    fast,
But faster still the rushing storm came borne upon the
    blast.
Lord! what a roaring hurricane beset the straining sail!
What furious sleet, with level drift, and fierce assaults
    of hail!
What darksome caverns yawned before! What jaggèd
    steeps behind!
Like battle-steeds with foamy manes wild tossing in
    the wind.
Each after each sank down astern, exhausted in the
    chase,
But where it sank another rose and galloped in its place;
As black as night—they turned to white, and cast
    against the cloud,
A snowy sheet, as if each surge upturned a sailor's
    shroud:
Still flew my boat; alas! alas! her course was nearly
    run!
Behold yon fatal billow rise—ten billows heaped in one!
With fearful speed the dreary mass came rolling, rolling,
    fast,
As if the scooping sea contained one only wave at last!
Still on it came, with horrid roar, a swift pursuing
    grave;
It seemed as though some cloud had turned its hugeness
    to a wave!

Its briny sleet began to beat beforehand in my face—
I felt the rearward keel begin to climb its swelling base!
I saw its alpine hoary head impending over mine!
Another pulse—and down it rushed—an avalanche of
    brine!
Brief pause had I, on God to cry, or think of wife at
    home;
The waters closed—and when I shrieked, I shrieked
    below the foam!
Beyond that rush I have no hint of any after deed—
For I was tossing on the waste, as senseless as a weed.

   .   .   .   .   .   .

"Where am I?—in the breathing world, or in the world
    of death?"
With sharp and sudden pang I drew another birth of
    breath;
My eyes drank in a doubtful light, my ears a doubtful
    sound—
And was that ship a *real* ship whose tackle seemed
    around?
A moon, as if the earthly moon, was shining up aloft;
But were those beams the very beams that I had seen
    so oft?
A face, that mocked the human face, before me watched
    alone;
But were those eyes the eyes of man that looked against
    my own?
Oh, never may the moon again disclose me such a sight
As met my gaze when first I looked, on that accursèd
    night!
I've seen a thousand horrid shapes begot of fierce
    extremes
Of fever, and most frightful things have haunted in my
    dreams—
Hyenas—cats—blood-loving bats—and apes with hate-
    ful stare—
Pernicious, and shaggy bulls—the lion and she-bear—
Strong enemies with Judas-looks of treachery and
    spite—
Detested features, hardly dimmed and banished by the
    light!
Pale-sheeted ghosts, with gory locks, up starting from
    their tombs—
All phantasies and images that flit in midnight glooms—

Hags, goblins, demons, lemures, have made me all
  aghast—
But nothing like that *Grimley One* who stood beside
  the mast!

His cheek was black—his brow was black—his eyes and
  hair as dark:
His hand was black, and where it touched, it left a
  sable mark;
His throat was black, his vest the same, and when I
  looked beneath,
His breast was black—all, all was black, except his
  grinning teeth.
His sooty crew were like in hue, as black as Afric
  slaves!
Oh, horror! e'en the ship was black that ploughed the
  inky waves!
"Alas!" I cried, "for love of truth and blessed mercy's
  sake!
Where am I? in what dreadful ship? upon what dread-
  ful lake?
What shape is that, so very grim, and black as any
  coal?
It is Mahound, the Evil One, and he has gained my
  soul!
Oh, mother dear! my tender nurse! dear meadows that
  beguiled
My happy days, when I was yet a little sinless child,—
My mother dear—my native fields, I never more shall
  see:
I'm sailing in the Devil's Ship, upon the Devil's Sea!"

Loud laughed the Sable Mariner, and loudly in return
His sooty crew sent forth a laugh that rang from stem
  to stern—
A dozen pairs of grimly cheeks were crumpled on the
  nonce—
As many sets of grinning teeth came shining out at
  once.
A dozen gloomy shapes at once enjoyed the merry fit,
With shriek and yell, and oaths as well, like Demons
  of the Pit.
They crowed their fill, and then the chief made answer
  for the whole;—

A A

"Our skins," said he, "are black ye see, because we
    carry coal;
You'll find your mother sure enough, and see your
    native fields—
For this here ship has picked you up—the Mary Ann
    of Shields!"

HOOD.

A SAILOR'S APOLOGY FOR BOW-LEGS.

THERE's some is born with their legs straight by natur—
And some is born with bow-legs from the first—
And some that should have growed a good deal
      straighter,
    But they were badly nursed,
And set, you see, like Bacchus, with their pegs
    Astride of casks and kegs.
I've got myself a sort of bow to larboard
    And starboard,
And this is what it was that warped my legs:

'Twas all along of Poll, as I may say,
That fouled my cable when I ought to slip;
    But on the tenth of May,
    When I gets under weigh,
Down there in Hartfordshire, to join by ship.
    I sees the mail
    Get under sail,
The only one there was to make the trip.
    Well, I gives chase
    But as she run
    Two knots to one,
There warn't no use in keeping on the race!

Well, casting round about, what next to try on,
    And how to spin,
I spies an ensign with a Bloody Lion,
And bears away to leeward for the inn,
    Beats round the gable,
And fetches up before the coach-horse stable.

Well, there they stand, four kickers in a row,
    And so
I just makes free to cut a brown 'un's cable.
But riding isn't in a seaman's natur;
So I whips out a toughish end of yarn,
And gets a kind of sort of a land-waiter
    To splice me heel to heel,
    Under the she-mare's keel,
And off I goes, and leaves the inn a-starn!

    My eyes! how she did pitch!
And wouldn't keep her own to go in no line,
Tho' I kept bowsing, bowsing at her bow-line,
But always making leeway to the ditch,
And yawed her head about all sorts of ways.
    The devil sink the craft!
And wasn't she tremendous slack in stays!
We couldn't, no how, keep the inn abaft!
    Well, I suppose
We hadn't run a knot—or much beyond—
(What will you have on it?)—but off she goes,
Up to her bends in a fresh-water pond!
    There I am! all a-back!
So I looks forward for her bridal-gears,
To heave her head round on the t'other tack;
    But when I starts,
    The leather parts,
And goes away right over by the ears!

    What could a fellow do,
Whose legs, like mine, you know, were in the bilboes,
But trim myself upright for bringing-to,
And square his yard-arms and brace up his elbows,
    In rig all snug and clever,
Just while his craft was taking in her water?
I didn't like my berth though, howsomdever,
Because the yarn, you see, kept getting tauter.
    Says I—I wish this job was rayther shorter!
    The chase had gained a mile
A-head, and still the she-mare stood a drinking:
    Now, all the while

Her body didn't take, of course, to shrinking.
Says I, she's letting out her reefs, I'm thinking;

A A 2

And so she swelled and swelled,
   And yet the tackle held,
Till both my legs began to bend like winkin'.
My eyes! but she took in enough to founder!
And there's my timbers straining every bit,
   Ready to split,
And her tarnation hull a-growing rounder!

Well, there—off Hartford Ness,
We lay both lashed and water-logged together,
   And can't contrive a signal of distress.
Thinks I, we must ride out this here foul weather,
Tho' sick of riding out, and nothing less;
When, looking round, I sees a man a-starn
"Hallo!" says I, "come underneath her quarters!"
And hands him out my knife to cut the yarn.
So I gets off, and lands upon the road,
And leaves the she-mare to her own consarn,
   A-standing by the water.
If I get on another, I'll be blowed!
And that's the way, you see, my legs got bowed!
                 HOOD.

THE SUB-MARINE.

IT was a brave and jolly wight,
   His cheek was baked and brown,
For he had been in many climes
   With captains of renown,
And fought with those who fought so well
   At Nile and Camperdown.

His coat it was a soldier coat,
   Of red with yellow faced,
But (merman-like) he looked marine
   All downward from the waist;
His trousers were so wide and blue,
   And quite in sailor taste!

He put the rummer to his lips,
   And drank a jolly draught;

He raised the rummer many times—
  And ever as he quaffed,
The more he drank, the more the ship
  Seemed pitching fore and aft!

The ship seemed pitching fore and aft,
  As in a heavy squall;
It gave a lurch, and down he went,
  Head-foremost in his fall!
Three times he did not rise, alas!
  He never rose at all!

But down he went, right down at once,
  Like any stone he dived,
He could not see, or hear, or feel—
  Of senses all deprived!
At last he gave a look around
  To see where he arrived!

And all that he could see was green,
  Sea-green on every hand!
And then he tried to sound beneath,
  And all he felt was sand!
There he was fain to lie, for he
  Could neither sit nor stand!

And lo! above his head there bent
  A strange and staring lass!
One hand was in her yellow hair,
  The other held a glass;
A mermaid she must surely be
  If ever mermaid was!

Her fish-like mouth was open wide,
  Her eyes were blue and pale,
Her dress was of the ocean green,
  When ruffled by a gale;
Thought he "beneath that petticoat
  She hides a salmon-tail!"

She looked as siren ought to look,
  A sharp and bitter shrew,
To sing deceiving lullabies
  For mariners to rue,—
But when he saw her lips apart,
  It chilled him through and through!

With either hand he stopped his ears
  Against her evil cry;
Alas, alas, for all his care,
  His doom it seemed to die,
Her voice went ringing through his head,
  It was so sharp and high!

He thrust his fingers further in
  At each unwilling ear,
But still, in very spite of all,
  The words were plain and clear;
"I can't stand here the whole day long,
  To hold your glass of beer!"

With opened mouth and opened eyes,
  Up rose the Sub-marine,
And gave a stare to find the sands
  And deeps where he had been:
There was no siren with her glass!
  No waters ocean-green!

The wet deception from his eyes
  Kept fading more and more,
He only saw the barmaid stand
  With pouting lips before—
The small green parlour of The Ship,
  And little sanded floor.

                                        HOOD.

TO A DECAYED SEAMAN.

HAIL! seventy-four cut down! Hail, top and lop,
  Unless I'm much mistaken in my notion,
Thou wast a stirring tar, before that hop
  Became so fatal to thy locomotion;
Now, thrown on shore, like a mere weed of ocean,
  Thou readest still to men a lesson good,
To King and Country showing thy devotion,
  By kneeling thus upon a stump of wood!
Still is thy spirit strong as alcohol;
  Spite of that limb, begot of acorn-egg—
Methinks—thou Naval History in one vol.
  A virtue shines, e'en in that timber leg,
For unlike others that desert their Poll,
  Thou walkest ever with thy "Constant Peg!"
                                        HOOD.

PAIN IN A PLEASURE-BOAT.

BOATMAN.

SHOVE off there! ship the rudder, Bill—cast off! she's
under way!

MRS. F.

She's under what?—I hope she's not! good gracious,
what a spray!

BOATMAN.

Run out the jib, and rig up the boom! Keep clear of
those two brigs!

MRS. F.

I hope they don't intend some joke by running of their
rigs!

BOATMAN.

Bill, shift them bags of ballast aft—she's rather out of
trim!

MRS. F.

Great bags of stones! they're pretty things to help a
boat to swim!

BOATMAN.

The wind is fresh—if she don't scud, it's not the breeze's
fault!

MRS. F.

Wind fresh, indeed!   I never felt the air so full of salt!

BOATMAN.

That schooner, Bill, harn't left the roads with oranges
and nuts!

MRS. F.

If seas have roads, they're very rough—I never felt
such ruts!

BOATMAN.

It's neap, ye see, she's heavy lade, and couldn't pass
the bar.

MRS. F.

The bar! what, roads with turnpikes too? I wonder
where they are!

BOATMAN.

Ho! Brig ahoy! hard up! hard up! that lubber cannot
   steer!

MRS. F.

Yes, yes—hard up upon a rock! I know some danger's
   near!
Lord, there's a .wave! it's coming in! and roaring like
   a bull!

BOATMAN.

Nothing, Ma'am, but a little slop! go large, Bill! keep
   her full!

MRS. F.

What, keep her full! what daring work! when full she
   must go down!

BOATMAN.

Why, Bill, it lulls! ease off a bit—it's coming off the
   town!
Steady your helm! we'll clear the *Pint!* lay right for
   yonder pink!

MRS. F.

Be steady—well, I hope they can! but they've got a
   pint of drink!

BOATMAN.

Bill, give that ship another haul—she'll fetch it up this
   reach.

MRS. F.

I'm getting rather pale, I know, and they see it by that
   speech!
I wonder what it is now, but—I never felt so queer!

BOATMAN.

Bill, mind your luff—why, Bill, I say, she's yawing—
   keep her near!

MRS. F.

Keep near! we're going further off; the land's behind
   our backs.

BOATMAN.

Be easy, Ma'am, it's all correct, that's only 'cause we
    tacks;
We shall have to beat about a bit—Bill, keep her out
    to sea.

MRS. F.

Beat who about? keep who at sea?—how black they
    look at me!

BOATMAN.

It's veering round—I knew it would! off with her head!
    stand by!

MRS. F.

Off with her head! who's? where? what with?—an axe
    I seem to spy!

BOATMAN.

She can't keep her own, you see; we shall have to pull
    her in!

MRS. F.

They'll drown me, and take all I have! my life's not
    worth a pin!

BOATMAN.

Look out, you know, be ready, Bill—just when she takes
    the sand!

MRS. F.

The sand—O Lord! to stop my mouth! how everything
    is planned!

BOATMAN.

The handspike, Bill—quick, bear a hand! now, Ma'am,
    just step ashore!

MRS. F.

What! ain't I going to be killed—and weltered in my
    gore?
Well, Heaven be praised! but I'll not go a-sailing any
    more!

HOOD.

THE WHITE SQUALL.

On deck, beneath the awning,
I dozing lay and yawning;
It was the grey of dawning,
   Ere yet the sun arose;
And above the funnel's roaring,
And fitful wind's deploring,
I heard the cabin snoring
   With universal nose.
I could hear the passengers snorting;
I envied there disporting;
Vainly I was courting
   The pleasure of a dose.

So I lay, and wondered why light
Came not, and watched the twilight,
And the glimmer of the skylight
   That shot across the deck,—
And the binnacle pale and steady,
And the dull glimpse of the dead-eye,
And the sparks in the fiery eddy,
   That whirled from the chimney-neck.
In our jovial floating prison
There was sleep from fore to mizzen,
And never a star had risen
   The hazy sky to speck.

Strange company we harboured:
We'd a hundred Jews to larboard
Unwashed, uncombed, unbarbered,—
   Jews black, and brown, and grey;
With terror it would seize ye,
And make your souls uneasy,
To see those Rabbis greasy,
   Who did nought but scratch and pray:
Their dirty children puking;
Their dirty saucepans cooking;
Their dirty fingers hooking
   Their swarming fleas away!

To starboard Turks and Greeks were;
Whiskered and brown their cheeks were;
Enormous wide their breeks were,—
   Their pipes did puff alway.

Each on his mat allotted
In silence smoked and squatted;
Whilst round their children trotted
   In pretty, pleasant play.
He can't but smile, who traces
The smile on those brown faces,
And the pretty, prattling graces
   Of those small heathen gay.

And so the hours kept tolling;
And through the ocean rolling
Went the brave *Iberia,* bowling
   Before the break of day.

When a squall, upon a sudden,
Came o'er the waters scudding;
And the clouds began to gather;
And the sea was lashed to lather;
And the lowering thunder grumbled;
And the lightning jumped and tumbled;
And the ship and all the ocean
Woke up in wild commotion.
Then the wind set up a-howling,
And the poodle-dog a-yowling;
And the cocks began a-crowing;
And the old cow raised a-lowing,
As she heard the tempest blowing ·
And the fowls and geese did cackle;
And the cordage and the tackle
Began to shriek and crackle;
And the spray dashed o'er the funnels,
And down the deck in runnels.
And the rushing water soaks all,
From the seamen in the fo'ksal,
To the stokers, whose black faces
Peer out of their bed-places.
And the captain he was bawling;
And the sailors pulling, hauling;
And the quarter-deck tarpauling
Was shivered in the squalling;
And the passengers awaken,
Most pitifully shaken;
And the steward jumps up and hastens
For the necessary basins.

Then the Greeks they groaned and quivered,
And they knelt and moaned and shivered;
And the plunging waters met them,
And splashed them and overset them:
And they call, in their emergence,
On countless saints and virgins;
And their marrow-bones are bended,
And they think the world is ended.

And the Turkish women for'ard
Were frightened and behorror'd;
And, shrieking and bewildering,
The mothers clutched their children.
The men sang—"Allah!   Illah!
Marshallah!—Bismillah!"
As the warring waters doused them,
And splashed them and soused them;
And they called upon the Prophet,
And thought but little of it.

Then all the fleas in Jewry
Jumped up and bit like fury;
And the progeny of Jacob
Did on the main-deck wake up.
(I wot those greasy Rabbins
Would never pay for cabins!)
And each man moaned and jabbered in
His filthy Jewish gaberdine,
In woe and lamentation,
And howling consternation.
And the splashing water drenches
Their dirty brats and wenches;
And they crawl from bales and benches,
In a hundred-thousand stenches!

This was the White Squall famous,
Which latterly o'ercame us,
And which we all will well remember—
On the 28th September:
When a Prussian captain of Lancers
(Those tight-laced, whiskered prancers)
Came on the deck astonished,
By that wild squall admonished,
And wondering cried—"Potz tausend,
Wie est der Sturm jetzt brausend?"

And looked at Captain Lewis,
Who calmly stood and blew his
Cigar in all the bustle,
And scorned the tempest's tussle.

And oft we've thought hereafter,
How he beat the storm to laughter;
For well he knew his vessel
With that vain wind could wrestle.
And when a wreck we thought her,
And doomed ourselves to slaughter,
How gaily he fought her,
And through the hubbub brought her;
And, as the tempest caught her,
Cried—"George, some brandy and water!"
And when, its force expended,
The harmless storm was ended,
And as the sunrise splendid
　Came blushing o'er the sea,
I thought, as day was breaking—
My little girls are waking
And smiling, and making
　A prayer at home for me.

THACKERAY.

APPENDIX

FALCONER,
AND "THE ANCHOR'S WEIGH'D."

FALCONER was a Scots merchant seaman, born about 1730, and apparently of humble parentage, like so many bards of "Caledonia girt and wild." He, then sailing as second mate, was wrecked in the Mediterranean, and on that experience he penned his first effort. This was published in 1762 as "The Shipwreck, a poem in three Cantos by a SAILOR"; it was inscribed to Edward, Duke of York—a Rear-Admiral at the time—who, immediately on the success of the poem, had its author entered as a midshipman aboard the *Royal George*. Seven years later he was drafted, as purser, to the frigate *Aurora*. On her way out to India she put in at Cape Town, left there in December of the same year, 1769, and was never heard of again.

But before this sad, untimely end came to Falconer, he had lengthened the poem by one-third, added some smaller pieces, and seen it going well in a second edition. As a partizan of his patron he was also the author of "The Demagogue," a fierce satire on Pitt, Churchhill, Wilkes, etc.; and of *The Marine Dictionary*, a seaman's handbook that went into many editions. In the poem he is "Arion," a youth, hence Campbell's reference in "The Pleasures of Hope":

> "Thy woes,
> Arion, and thy simple tale
> O'er all the earth shall triumph and prevail.'

As Falconer's ship was lost with all hands at the end of 1769 or very early in 1770, and Campbell was born in 1777, this mention could not possibly have come out of a personal acquaintance; but there is a curious coincidence in the fact that in 1745 Falconer was servant to Archibald Campbell, a classical scholar who had formerly been a purser in the Navy. It was this Campbell who gave the young Scot a grounding in education and set his mind wandering after the Muses; as a matter of fact he was the author of "Sexiphanes," a squib discharged at Johnson, and "The Sale of Authors," a general satire on the writers of his day. Thus, although there is no "Life" of Falconer —because there appear to be no materials for one— we see how and where the sailor-to-be got his first lead on the tempestuous sea of authorship.

As to "The Shipwreck" and "The Anchor's Weigh'd": Arnold (1774–1852), the author of the latter, was twenty-two years of age and studying music when the former was attracting the attention of all reading England. His father, Samuel Arnold, composed the music of "All's Well," oratorios, operas, etc., became organist to the King, and wrote songs for his own airs. All there is in "The Anchor's Weigh'd" occurs in the farewell between Palemon and Anna in "The Shipwreck." Not that the wording is altogether the same; in the one case it is descriptive, in the other purely lyrical. But the situation and the suggestions are identical; and similar phrases are: Falconer—"Go then, dear youth, and let——" "Shall never change, my love; this heart, incapable of change, is only thine." Arnold—"Dear youth, she cried." "Doubt not a constant heart like mine." "Dear maid, this last embrace." "Go then, she cried." (Also Campbell, apparently before "The Anchor's Weigh'd" was written: "This last embrace, still cherished in my heart.") Further, Falconer's scene, without being so near the same in actual phrases, is worded and carried through in a manner that so closely suggests Arnold's song as almost to say that the latter came out of the former. In both cases the parting is "on the shore"; tears are "falling gently"; the separation is possibly for ever; the ship is waiting close by, and the same general sentiments dominate both scenes: also, the song·first appeared in "The Shipwreck," at Drury Lane, 1796.

"SIR PATRICK SPENS."

THE literary importance of this ballad as, probably, the first of its kind, together with the historical incident on which it is based, necessitate far more than an ordinary note. First, who was the author? No one knows; but a name has been advanced. In 1859 Dr. Robert Chambers made the statement that Lady Wardlaw (1677–1727) was the authoress of both this, "The Douglas Tragedy" and other traditional pieces; yet he gave *no evidence*. In his "Scottish Ballads" (issued for the Percy Society) James Henry Dixon repeated Chambers, again without proof; and in 1892 Professor Mason added his opinion to the statement; but we are still asking for more than the bare idea. It is true that Lady Wardlaw's authorship of "Hardycanute: A Fragment," was not known till Bishop Percy (1728–82) issued the second edition of his "Reliques"; although that "Fragment" had been first published, as a really ancient piece of work, in 1719, and was drawn out from 216 to 336 lines and twice reprinted before the appearance of Percy's first edition. Yet are we not entitled to ask why the Bishop, who originally put eleven of these stanzas into print, did not discover their authorship along with that of "Hardycanute"? Instead of which he put his shortened form of the ballad forward as "Anonymous" and traditional, gathered orally in the eastern part of the Lowlands—as the other stanzas were secured from time to time by such gleaners as Scott, Robert Hamilton, Motherwell, Finlay, Buchan, Jamieson, etc.—not to include Allan Cunningham's "enriching the old and simple narrative with a number of new verses." Again would not Lady Wardlaw have known better than to have put "hats" and "cork-heeled shoon" (or "coalblack" ones, as some versions have it) on Scots lords in 1282? As a matter of fact these anachronisms have probably crept into the ballad, from some illiterate expander of the original, in the course of its oral descent from one generation to another, as we know has often been the case with other traditionary pieces. Pliny tells us that cork was used in the soles of shoes in his time; and we gather gener-

B B

ally, from other ancient writers, that it was in fairly common use in Europe for that purpose. But it is very doubtful if the Scots aristocracy took to using it till after they were well initiated into the ways of the French Court, which was long subsequent to the eighteenth century. Beyond all this, however, the seamanship of the ballad must be considered in any effort to arrive at its authorship, and here I find the strongest reason for doubting that this belongs to Lady Wardlaw. Examine this portion of the story as I may, the conviction remains—except for "the silken claith," to be dwelt on presently—that it came from the hand of a man who had been to sea more than once. On the other hand it must be admitted that "Hardycanute" is good external evidence that Lady Wardlaw was as capable of writing this ballad, its seamanship alone excepted, as she was of penning the piece attributed to her. Besides, she was a Fifeshire woman, who lived near Dunfermline and not far from Aberdour, and Spens was anciently a Fifeshire name. These points —which are not put forward elsewhere—are the only ones that I can find for the supposition that Lady Wardlaw wrote the ballad. As to the "silken claith": This might be held as good evidence of the hand of a woman who knew nothing of life at sea, especially if we were to accept Scott's opinion that a plank had come out of the vessel. On the contrary, the leak was probably caused by a bolt working out of its place, because in that case a piece of twisted silk would form a better plug than canvas, which could not be pressed into such close folds. At that time ships had no lining, and a plank staved would have sunk a vessel almost immediately. One of Buchan's additional verses makes Sir Patrick say here:

> " There are five-and-fifty feather beds
> Well packèd in ae room,
> And ye'll get as muckle gude canvàss
> As wrap the ship a' roun'."

Which is sheer nonsense, under the circumstances. Canvas for that purpose, which presupposes a big hole in the vessel, would not come from feather beds, but from spare sails; or, as a last resource, from sails in use. Besides, in this stanza—a fair sample of the inter-polated ones—Buchan puts into Sir Patrick's mouth a confusion of remarks such as only a landsman might *think* a sailor would use at the time. With regard to the wisdom of using either silk or canvas, or driving in a wooden plug, or nailing tarred canvas and wood over a leak—all this must always depend on where the leak is, and what the weather conditions are at the time. In Sir Patrick's case the initial trouble was prob-ably caused by the starting of a bolt, which would presently be the means of a plank working, and so eventually of a leak that would fill the ship in a short time.

When we come to the incident on which the story is based we find ourselves on a little firmer ground, that is, there are three actual happenings, on either one of which the student can fasten his opinion. In order of time these are : The marriage of Margaret, daughter of Alexander III of Scotland, to Erik of Norway, 1282 ; the bringing home of Margaret's daughter, the Maid of Norway, 1290; and the marriage of James III to Margaret of Denmark in 1469, when cork-heeled shoon were possibly worn by Scottish courtiers. To begin with the third incident. In spite of Finlay's "great proba-bility," this must be dismissed as being scarcely worthy of consideration. It appears that the connection of James's marriage with the ballad is due mainly, if not solely, to the confusion of Norway with Denmark, it having often been written that he married a Norwegian princess. Then there was his enactment—similar to those of the Venetians and the Genoese—against sailing from Scottish ports during the period between the SS. Simon and Jude's Day and Candlemas, which was due to the disasters that had taken place year after year and generation after generation, till the coastwise dwellers had grown to look on those months as a time of calamity. Very plainly, as the sixth stanza shows, there was no such law when Sir Patrick was bidden "to sail across the sea." As to the second point : In the opinion of Scott and others the errand was to bring home little Margaret, who was then seven years of age. This (1290) was four years after the death of her grandfather, Alexander ; in which case what is the King doing in the ballad? At that time there was no king to order the Maid of Norway to be brought home to become Queen of Scotland. Sir Walter adds: "The introduction of the king into the ballad seems a deviation from history, unless we suppose that the aged monarch was desirous to see his grandchild before he died." But "the aged monarch" was only forty-five years old and seemingly quite healthy when he was accidentally thrown from his horse and killed, one dark night, March 12, 1286, not far from Aberdour. Again, if Sir Patrick was sent on that errand, why is the "queen's fee" (i. e. the elder Margaret's dowry) mentioned in the ballad, and no word given of the little princess?—who could not have a "queen's fee." And if he went for her, why did he sail again without her? Leaving the matter of baby Margaret and Sir Patrick, Leland translates from the *Scala Chronica:* "One Master Weland, a Clerk of Scotland, sent into Norway for Margaret, died with her by tempest on the sea, coming out of Norway to Scotland in the coasts of Boghan." Here, apparently, we have a fact that puts an end completely to the supposition that Sir Patrick went to fetch Alexander's granddaughter, whose untimely death was, so far as can be seen, the indirect cause of so much malgovernance and misery in Scotland. For Boghan we must read Bergen; formerly Björgvin, which was founded by Olaf Kyrre in 1070, and was the scene of considerable trafficking between the native and early Scots and English traders. Thus we come to the marriage of Margaret and Erik, by which means Alexander cemented the peace that followed his victory over Erik's brother Hako, and added the Orkneys and Shetlands to his crown, the last additions that were made to Scotland. Of this sending forth there appears to be no authentic record. But note that Alexander lived at Dunfermline Castle; that Aberdour was a kind of port to it; that the Spenses were resident in the district, and that coming of a sort of waterside family it was only natural that one or more of them—no matter what their Christian names were—should take to the sea in days when it yielded so much of both adventure and profit. Again, lines three in the fourth and seventh stanzas have often been made to read: "The king's daughter o' Noroway"; and this, taken in conjunction with "bring" or "fetch her hame" in the next lines, would appear to point to Margaret's daughter as the object of the voyage. But replace "o'" with "to"; give this use of "fetch" and "bring" in old ballads their modern equivalent of "take"; put to these points Margaret's marriage, "queen's fee," the carousing among the lords, and there being no reference in the ballad to the infant princess, and surely the wedding shoulders the other two incidents out of consideration. So, although Margaret and her ladies might, probably did, go under the personal care of some particular lord of the Court, it was quite as likely that Sir Patrick was the admiral in charge of the expedition. In fact stanza four shows us that the King's letter to him began with the command to take Margaret to Norway; and Sir Patrick—plainly, as shown in "Who . . . told the king of me," so far a stranger to royal favour—laughed with glee at this promotion. But the end of the missive, ordering the errand to begin forthwith, instead of waiting till the following spring, dashed down his cup of joy with a premonition of disaster. And here, as in the quarrel between the Scots and Norwegian lords and in the seamanship, I find quite satisfactory evidence that these parts of the ballad were the work of a survivor of the expedition—one who knew how it all came about, from the "braid letter" to the sinking of the principal vessel "half ower fra Aberdour," where the water is, indeed, "fifty fathoms deep."

"THE BEAUTIFUL LADY OF KENT."

[1] THIS ballad—which I have not found in any collection of recent times—appears to be a genuine piece of English work. Somewhere about the middle of the eighteenth century it was printed on a broadsheet, in four Parts; but in a much older copy, from which the present version is taken, there are no divisions, the first word in each part being printed in capitals.

[2] and [3] It is worthy of notice, however, that here, in the heroine's search for her lover, there is a strong similarity to an important feature in the older ballad of "Lord Beichan," which I, in boyhood, learnt, together

with its air, from my father's mother. There Beichan
—spelt Bateman in a corrupted South of England
version—goes adventuring abroad and becomes the
prisoner of a Turkish Pasha. The Pasha has a hand-
some daughter who falls in love with Lord Beichan;
she contrives his freedom after he has vowed

> " I have got houses ; I have got lands,
>   And half Northumberland it 'longs to me ;
> I'll give them all to the ladye fair,
>   That out of prison shall set me free."

Then, having taken "him to her father's harbour,"
where "a ship of fame to him gave she," a seven years'
compact is made, he to return at the end of that time
and marry her. But the period passes, and there is no
Lord Beichan.

> " So she's set her foot on the good ship board,
>   And turned her back on her own countrie."

After some wandering she reaches Northumberland
and finds a "bonnie shepherd" who says :

> " There is a weddin' in yonder hall,
>   Has lasted thirty days and three ;
> But young Lord Beichan won't bed with his bride,
>   For love of one that's ayond the sea."

The remainder of this half-sea ballad, which is told
with considerable detail and local colouring, can be
gathered from the following lines. The Pasha's
daughter has gone to the castle and sent up her half
of the ring that she broke with Beichan; she has been
let in :

> " Then out and spake the forenoon bride,
>   ' My Lord, your love is changéd soon
> At morning I am made your bride ;
>   But another's chosen, ere 'tis noon.'
>
> ' Oh, sorrow not, thou forenoon bride ;
>   Our hearts could ne'er united be.
> You must return to your own countrie,
>   A double dower I'll send with thee.'
>
> And up and spak' the young bride's mother,
>   Who never before had spoke so free—
> ' And so you treat my only daughter,
>   Because Saphia has crossed the sea ! '

I own I made a bride of your daughter ;
But she's no whit the worse for me :
She came to me on her horse and saddle ;
She may go back in her coach and three.'

.   .   ..

He's ta'en Saphia by the white hand,
And gently led her up and down ;
And aye he's kist her rosy lips,
And aye said, ' Welcome to your own.'

He's ta'en her by the milk-white hand,
And led her to yon' fountain stane ;
Her name he's changed from Saphia,
And called his bonnie love Lady Jane.

Lord Beichan prepared another marriage,
And sang with heart so full of glee ;
' I'll range no more in foreign countries,
Now since my love she has crossed the sea.' "

"A SEA-SONG."

[1] Some years ago it fell to my lot to review an anthology that contained this song, with the word "snoring" here. Thirty-odd years before that I had learnt the song—I know not where, nor how—with the expression "snorting breeze." To me, as a seaman, it was only right to sing "snorting breeze" along with "white waves heaving high," a bending mast, a flying ship, and all the tear-away business of the song generally. Besides, "snorting" was in common use at sea in such a situation, thus: "It's a-snorting!" "Now she snorts!"—i. e. racing before a half-gale. Whereas "snoring," a term that was heard very rarely, did but mean that easy, slumbrous motion which one gets in the trade-winds; while the other carried, as this song does, all the sense of "the roaring forties." So what should I do but point out, in the review, that the word without the "t" made nonsense of the situation. Immediately down came a party of critics—of verse, not of seafaring matters, and in a portion of a journal where I was not allowed to answer them! Their great contention was

that Palgrave, with Tennyson's approval, wrote "snoring." Therefore what should a poor sailor do but take what such men had written, and murmur not? My reply was exactly as given above. Then, wherever possible, I searched the libraries of London for the earliest publication of the song; this was found—to the best of my present knowledge—in the *London Magazine* for August 1822, and the word was "snoring." Coals of fire on my head, thought I, then cogitated thus: Who knows that Cunningham passed the proof with this word in it? Or that the "t" was not dropped out after he passed the proofs? All the context, and the physical facts are against the word. So the hunt was continued, and in "Songs of Scotland, Ancient and Modern," edited by Cunningham himself three years later, I found the expression to be "swelling breeze." Evidently the poet had seen and corrected his error. Enough. Five years after Allan's death in 1842, Peter, the son, replaced "snoring" in a new edition of his father's poems. But he appears generally to have known nothing of the sea, nor of anything appertaining thereto. It was he who changed Allan's "wakening loud" to "piping loud," merely, one can only suppose, because "piping" was more common at the time and had a more nautical swing about it than the other word had. And, to conclude my evidence by preparing for the last chance of attack, if it be pointed out that in the last line of the first stanza Allan wrote "*on* the lee" where a seaman would say "under," it must be borne in mind that the line would not carry a disyllable. True, Falconer would have written "'neath," as: "The wretched victims die beneath the lee," where the pentameter measure requires "beneath," and would not admit the trochee "under." But, then, Falconer's daily life had taught him that all "on's," in this sense, were—and still are—weatherbearings.

"THE DEATH OF ADMIRAL BEN·BOW."

BENBOW—born at Shrewsbury, 1650—was a fine example of the English seaman. Early in his career he worsted a Barbary corsair, of much weightier metal and more heavily manned than he was; this led to a rapid rise for Benbow. In August 1702, he, with two other sail, met a French squadron under Du Casse, off Cartagena, in the West Indies. He at once gave battle, lost a leg by a chain-shot, and was immediately deserted by his two subordinates, Captains Kirby and Wade. In spite of all this he fought on through the night, till the Frenchmen sailed away just before dawn. The admiral then put into Port Royal, Jamaica, where he found the runaways and had them tried by court-martial; they were found guilty of gross coward-ice, brought to Plymouth and shot. Whilst he lay in Port Royal, Du Casse wrote to him, from Cartagena, under date August 22, saying : "On Monday last I had but small hopes of anything other than to have supped in your cabin; but it pleased the Almighty to order it differently, and I am thankful. As for the captains who ran away, the cowards, string them up; for by God they ought to be hung." In the following October Benbow died of his wound, and was buried in Kingston. Port Royal. Another piece on the same subject, "O we sail'd to Virginia and thence to Fyal," appears to be of a later date and is an inferior composition.

ADMIRAL HOSIER'S GHOST.

THIS was written in 1739, when Glover—author of "Leonidas," etc.—was twenty-seven years of age. Hannah More heard him sing it, as he appears to have done on many occasions. He meant it as a sort of commemoration of Vernon's crushing the Spaniards at Porto-Bello on November 22nd of that year. It was done for the purpose of arousing afresh the national hatred of England's then hereditary enemy afloat.

Smollett gives it that in April 1726, Hosier was sent, with a powerful fleet, "to block up the galleons in the ports of the Spanish West Indies, or, should they presume to come out, to seize and carry them into England." He was another victim to red-tape procedure as made at home. He was not to attack the ports. So after long lying about off Porto-Bello and Bastimentos, seeing his officers and men go down by the dozen with fever and dysentery, and being the butt of the Spaniards' derision, he sailed for Cartagena; where he remained, still losing hands, till he died of a broken heart. Glover's ballad became so popular that it was at last parodied by an unknown scribe; and where one was heard, in public, the other was screeched out, till at last the parody was left in possession of "the Town," and presently died for lack of its parent to feed on—as most parodies do when the original is no longer on the popular tongue.

"SIR ANDREWE BARTON."

As this ballad is the record of a piratical fight (much as Scots writers, like Americans concerning Paul Jones, have refused to look on Barton as a rover), it may seem to be out of place amongst stories of naval fights. But behind it there was, so far as one can ascertain at this day, a matter of great national importance. What we know is this: A Scots merchant seaman named Barton had a valuable cargo taken from him by the Portuguese; being unable to gain redress, he secured a letter-of-marque from James IV, which apparently remained in force so long that Barton's sons—some accounts say two, as the ballad has it, others give the number as three—eventually practised common piracy on Portuguese and English craft, mainly in the lower part of the English Channel, under that letter. The depredations of Andrew became notorious in most of the ports of England. Then, in June 1511, the Earl of Surrey said, at the King's Council, that if his Majesty did not move in the matter he himself would "furnish out a ship" to meet

and destroy the pirate. The result was that two vessels
were fitted out under the command of the Earl's two
sons, Sir Edmund—or Edward—and Sir Thomas. After
cruising about for some time they fell in with Barton
(there appears to be some doubt as to whether he was
a knight or not), whose vessel was named *Lion*. Sir
Thomas engaged him, while Sir Edward did the same
with Barton's other craft, the *Union*. The fight was
protracted; but the Howards won, and took the
damaged *Lion* to Deptford on August 2, 1511—or 1512,
as Burton has it in his "History of Scotland." Now it
became the turn of James to seek redress from Henry;
but the English king refused. It has evidently been the
opinion of English writers that James had a material
interest in Barton's piracy; whether so or not, he con-
tinued for some time to trouble Henry for a monetary
payment on the loss of Barton and his vessels, and was
so greatly chagrined at his non-success that the affair
seems to have been almost the beginning of James's
animosity towards Henry. Whilst this went on an
English army joined issue with Spain against France.
James remained friendly to the old ally of his country;
and the Queen of France wrote to him a letter in which
she dubbed herself his mistress and entreated him to
amass an army and advance into England, if only a
few feet, in the hope that such a move would compel
Henry to draw off his allies to the Spaniards. Inflamed
by this letter and embittered by Bluff King Hal's treat-
ment of the Barton matter, James gathered together an
army of 30,000 men, crossed the border and there dallied
about—contrary to the strenuous advice of both his
counsellors and his queen, who was the daughter of
Henry VII—till the Earl of Surrey (the father of Bar-
ton's conquerors) scratched up 32,000 men and hurried
north. The result was Flodden Field, Scotland's most
disastrous battle, in which the Sir Edmund of the ballad,
as leader of the right wing of the English army, was
defeated by the left wing of the Scots under the Earls
of Home and Huntly. Thus, in a way, a piratical
encounter in the English Channel was partially the
cause of Flodden Field.

INDEX TO AUTHORS' NAMES

RICHARD CLAY & SONS, LIMITED,
BRUNSWICK STREET, STAMFORD STREET, S.E.,
AND BUNGAY, SUFFOLK.

Lightning Source UK Ltd.
Milton Keynes UK
UKHW050032021218
333191UK00019BA/767/P